Criminal Justice
Recent Scholarship

Edited by
Marilyn McShane and Frank P. Williams III

A Series from LFB Scholarly

South University Library
Richmond Campus
2151 Old Brick Road
Glen Allen, Va 23060

FEB 15 2012

But is it Racial Profiling? Policing, Pretext Stops, and the Color of Suspicion

Vikas K. Gumbhir

LFB Scholarly Publishing LLC
New York 2007

Copyright © 2007 by LFB Scholarly Publishing LLC

All rights reserved.

Library of Congress Cataloging-in-Publication Data

Gumbhir, Vikas K. (Vikas Kiernan), 1972-
  But is it racial profiling? : policing, pretext stops, and the color of suspicion / Vikas K. Gumbhir.
      p. cm. -- (Criminal justice, recent scholarship)
   Includes bibliographical references and index.
   ISBN-13: 978-1-59332-214-4 (alk. paper)
    1. Racial profiling in law enforcement--Oregon--Eugene--Surveys. 2. Racial profiling in law enforcement--Oregon--Eugene--Statistics. I. Title.
   HV7936.R3G86 2007
   363.2'32--dc22

2007023805

ISBN 9781593322144

Printed on acid-free 250-year-life paper.

Manufactured in the United States of America.

Table of Contents

List of Figures	*vii*
List of Tables	*ix*
Acknowledgements	*xiii*
CHAPTER 1: From National Issue to Local Crisis	1
John Gainer's Story	1
Racial Profiling Across the United States	3
Racial Profiling in Eugene, Oregon	7
CHAPTER 2: What is Racial Profiling?	9
A Brief History of Racial Profiling	10
Current Conceptualizations of Racial Profiling	15
Reconceptualizing Racial Profiling	26
Conclusion	39
CHAPTER 3: From Disparities to Discrimination	41
A Brief History of Vehicle Stop Data Collection	42
A Framework for Interpreting Racial/Ethnic Differences in Vehicle Stop Data	48
Conclusion	70
CHAPTER 4: Case Study: Eugene, Oregon	73
Data	77
Methodology	83

CHAPTER 5: Results of the Eugene Vehicle Stop Study 93
General Characteristics of Vehicle Stops 93
Racial/Ethnic Group Comparisons 103

CHAPTER 6: Making Sense of the Disparities 187
Review of Key Findings 187
Data Quality Issues 210
But is it Racial Profiling? 215
Recommendations for Future Research 223

CHAPTER 7: Epilogue 227

Appendix 1 241

Appendix 2 247

References 253

Index 275

List of Figures

Figure 1. Law Violation in the Driving Population   67
Figure 2. Law Violation in the Driving and Observed
    Populations   68
Figure 3. Law Violation and Suspicion in the Driving
    and Observed Populations   69
Figure 4. Law Violation, Suspicion, and the Selection of
    Drivers for Vehicle Stops   70

List of Tables

Table 1. Summary of Variables	78
Table 2. Variable Coding for Logistic Regression Analysis	90
Table 3. Frequency Distribution of Driver's Race/Ethnicity, Indentifiability of Driver's Race/Ethnicity, and Presence of a Language Barrier	94
Table 4. Frequency Distribution of Driver's Age, Sex, Residency Status, and Number of Passengers in the Vehicle	95
Table 5. Frequency Distribution of Time of Stop and District of Stop	96
Table 6. Frequency Distribution of Reason for Stop and Result of Stop	97
Table 7. Arrest Estimate	98
Table 8. Frequency Distribution of Reason for Arrest and Duration of Stop	99
Table 9. Search Estimate	100
Table 10. Frequency Distribution of Search Success Rate	101
Table 11. Frequency Distribution of Contraband Found in Successful Searches	102
Table 12. Racial/Ethnic Distribution of Eugene (OR) Driving Age Population	104
Table 13. Differences Between Exclusive and Inclusive Census Population Estimates	106

List of Tables

Table 14. Age Distribution of Eugene Driving Age Population by Race/Ethnicity	107
Table 15. Age Distribution of Eugene Driving Age Population by Race/Ethnicity and Sex	108
Table 16. General Demographic Characteristics of Vehicle Stops by Race/Ethnicity	111
Table 17. 2002 Stop Rates	114
Table 18. 2003 Stop Rates	115
Table 19. Stop Rate Changes from 2002 to 2003	116
Table 20. 2002 Population Benchmark Modifications	124
Table 21. 2003 Population Benchmark Modifications	125
Table 22. Modified Stop Rates	126
Table 23. Reason for Stop by Race/Ethnicity	131
Table 24. District of Stop by Race/Ethnicity	134
Table 25. Result of Stop by Race/Ethnicity	137
Table 26. Logistic Predictors of Enforcement Action	139
Table 27. Logistic Predictors of Arrests	141
Table 28. Duration of Stop by Race/Ethnicity	145
Table 29. Logistic Predictors of Stop Duration, 15-Minute Split	146
Table 30. Logistic Predictors of Stop Duration, 30-Minute Split	149
Table 31. General Demographic Characteristics of Any Search Indicator Present (ASIP) Searches by Race/Ethnicity	153
Table 32. General Demographic Characteristics of Minimum Reporting Threshold (MRT) Searches by Race/Ethnicity	154
Table 33. Search Conducted by Race/Ethnicity	157
Table 34. Logistic Predictors of Any Search Indicator Present (ASIP) Searches	158
Table 35. Logistic Predictors of Minimum Reporting Threshold (MRT) Searches	161
Table 36. Search Success Rates for Any Search Indicator Present (ASIP) Searches by Race/Ethnicity	164
Table 37. Search Success Rates for Minimum Reporting Threshold (MRT) Searches by Race/Ethnicity	166
Table 38. Contraband Found in Productive Any Search Indicator Present (ASIP) Searches by Race/Ethnicity	167

List of Tables xi

Table 39. Contraband Found in Productive Minimum Reporting Threshold (MRT) Searches by Race/Ethnicity — 168

Table 40. Discretionary Search Conducted by Race/Ethnicity — 171

Table 41. Logistic Predictors of Any Search Indicator Present (ASIP) Discretionary Searches — 172

Table 42. Partial Reporting by Race/Ethnicity — 175

Table 43. Logistic Predictors of Any Search Indicator Present (ASIP) Discretionary Searches Including Cases Missing Data on Independent Variables — 176

Table 44. Logistic Predictors of Minimum Reporting Threshold (MRT) Discretionary Searches — 179

Table 45. Logistic Predictors of Minimum Reporting Threshold (MRT) Discretionary Searches Including Cases Missing Data on Independent Variables — 182

Table 46. Discretionary Search Success Rates for Any Search Indicator Present (ASIP) Discretionary Searches by Race/Ethnicity — 184

Table 47. Discretionary Search Success Rates for Minimum Reporting Threshold (MRT) Discretionary Searches by Race/Ethnicity — 186

Table 48. Summary of Racial/Ethnic Distribution of EPD Contacts — 188

Table 49. Racial/Ethnic Distribution of Eugene Population by Patrol District — 197

Acknowledgements

I would like to thank the Eugene Police Department, who, as a group, demonstrated a remarkable level of integrity and commitment to community policing in this research effort. Captain Elvia Williams, Captain Becky Hanson, and Linda Phelps did tremendous job of managing the data collection process, and were always available when I needed assistance. Stan Lenhart's management of the data entry process, most notably his quality control work, was invaluable to this research. Terry Smith made numerous practical contributions to this project. The commitment of former chief Jim Hill and former interim chief Thad Buchanan were essential to the success of the data collection effort. Finally, I would like to offer special thanks to the officers of the Eugene Police Department, for without their willingness to participate in this project, this research would never have happened.

I would also like to thank all the members of the Racial Profiling Data Collection Task Group, whose efforts both motivated and shaped the data used in this research. Tammam Adi, Ray G. Brown, Norma Dominguez, Dave Fidanque, Mark W. Flowers, Kathy L. Flynn, Jim Garcia, Carmen J. Gelman, Beebee L. Head, Francisca E. Johnson, Ladaria Johnson, Munir Katul, Pete M. Kerns, Bobby R. McDermed, Carolyn G. McDermed, Marcy H. Middleton, Mark Montes, Polly Nelson, Lynn Reeves, Ron R. Roberts, Adrian Rodriguez, Johann Schneider, Dennis Shine, Angie A. Sifuentes, Maria Thomas, Mark Tracy, Carmen X. Urbina, Tonee M. Webber, and Dee A. Williams are just a few of the individuals who contributed to the group's work, and they all deserve recognition for their labor.

I wish to express sincere appreciation to Dr. Paul Goldman, Dr. Patricia Gwartney, Dr. Jocelyn Hollander, Dr. Ken Hudson, Dr. Robert O'Brien, Dr. Caleb Southworth, Dr. Mia Tuan, and Dr. Daniel Wojcik, all of whom were all instrumental to the development and execution of this research. I would like to extend special recognition to Dr. Marion Goldman for her encouragement, guidance, and unique insight.

Finally, I would like to express my most profound gratitude to two very important people—my partner Christina Turner and my mother Lynn Gumbhir—for their confidence and unwavering support.

CHAPTER 1
From National Issue to Local Crisis

JOHN GAINER'S STORY

John Gainer is an unlikely man to find at the center of a police controversy. An adjunct professor of music at the University of Oregon, an ordained minister, and founder of the Inspirational Sounds gospel choir, Gainer claims to have been targeted by Eugene Police Department (EPD) officers in April 1997 and December 1998 because of his race—Gainer is African-American.

In April 1997, Gainer searched for a rental house in a residential area of Eugene, Oregon. Because of a visual impairment, Gainer looked closely at mailboxes on the street, trying to locate an address he had seen advertised. A neighbor, fearing that Gainer may have been a thief, called 911 and three EPD officers were dispatched. The police flagged down the bus Gainer had boarded (after he waited at the stop for 25 minutes) and asked him to step off so they could investigate the situation (Tallmadge 1998). Even after Gainer informed the officers of the reason for his trip and provided them with his University of Oregon identification, he was ordered to show the officers the contents of his briefcase and empty his pockets. Gainer further charged that the three officers treated him rudely during his detention, noting that the officers provided a "sarcastic apology" (Hartman 1998b:A9) after the episode. In response to a formal complaint filed by Gainer, EPD conducted an official investigation into the incident and found that the officers "had acted in a professional and courteous manner" (Bishop 1998a:A1). Gainer then filed suit against EPD, claiming that the officers' actions violated his civil rights. Almost one year after the incident, Gainer's case was dismissed by Lane County Circuit Court Judge Jack Mattison, who found that the police had reasonable suspicion to question Gainer. Since there was no evidence of "undue harassment" or excessive force, Mattison found there was no violation of Gainer's civil rights. Following the decision, Gainer resolved to leave Eugene:

> This incident, to me, is a sign I need to get out of here...I cannot live in a community where people of color are considered to be criminals or suspicious just walking down the street...It's just not the type of environment I wish to live in. (Bishop 1998a:A1)

When EPD officers pulled Gainer off another bus in December 1998, a front-page article in the Eugene Register-Guard, the local daily newspaper, described the incident a "bad bout of déjà vu" (Hartman 1998a:A1)—a disturbingly casual description of a serious situation. After making several purchases, Gainer walked through a local shopping center towards the bus pavilion, during which time he was identified as a robbery suspect by a security guard. The suspect in question, wanted for robbing a local motel at gunpoint, was a dark-skinned black male, 37 years old, 6 feet tall, 210 pounds, while Gainer was 44 years old, 5 feet 9 inches tall, 180 pounds, and had a light complexion. The guard, working from a photocopied picture of the suspect, called 911 with a description—not of Gainer, but rather of the robbery suspect as described in the newspaper—and two EPD officers were dispatched. When the officers boarded Gainer's bus, Mike Carter (an African-American officer) recognized Gainer and informed his partner, Sean Hughes (a white officer), that Gainer was not the suspect in question. Hughes, however, disregarded Carter's comments and motioned for Gainer to get off the bus. The officers quickly determined Gainer's identity and he was released with numerous apologies from Carter. In response to a formal complaint filed by Gainer regarding this incident, an internal investigation by the EPD determined, once again, that there was nothing inappropriate about the officers' conduct.

EPD claimed that its officers handled both incidents properly and according to departmental policy. The department justified the April 1997 incident by citing an extensive mail theft investigation involving over 3,000 victims (Hartman 1998b). In December 1998, EPD contended that because the officers were able to determine that Gainer was not the suspect within 90 seconds, it did not constitute harassment (Hartman 1998a). Despite the belief that his officers had acted properly, Chief Jim Hill expressed his "empathy" for Gainer as a result of the first incident (Hartman 1998b), and offered a formal apology for the second.

Gainer vehemently disagreed with EPD's conclusions regarding the officers' conduct, maintaining that he was the target of harassment because of his race. He noted that the officers in the April 1997 incident disregarded his university identification and insisted on conducting a search, and that in 1998 officer Hughes discounted the informed opinion of officer Carter and demanded that Gainer step off the bus. Gainer further asserted that the actions of EPD and its officers were not only publicly humiliating; they also caused him considerable emotional pain and suffering (Williams 1999).

As a result of his experiences with EPD and the Eugene community, Gainer decided to leave Eugene, his position at the University of Oregon, his ministry, and the choir he founded. Before he departed, he wrote a guest column in a local independent newspaper where he explained his decision:

> Many people in Eugene, of course, will say that race was not the issue…in either of my situations. Here, people are immediately on the defensive when acts of racism are brought to their attention. Individuals who experience racism either openly or thinly disguised are told over and over they are misinterpreting the situation. Or we are told that the way a situation was handled was "in line with approved policies."…It's time for people to acknowledge that there is a problem, and that the community and police need to do something about it…Myself, and others who've experienced similar situations, are tired of being told race was not a factor. Race is a factor, and it's time for people to face it. (Gainer 1999:4)

RACIAL PROFILING ACROSS THE UNITED STATES

Prior to John Gainer's experiences making headlines in Eugene, similar situations involving the targeting and mistreatment of minority suspects by law enforcement agencies nationwide were coming to light. Several incidents involving the use of excessive force by police garnered significant media attention:

- In March 1991, after a high-speed chase, four Los Angeles Police Department officers were videotaped striking Rodney King with their batons over 50 times before handcuffing the badly beaten black motorist. The acquittal of three officers[1] who assaulted King sparked riots in Los Angeles that left 53 dead. The Department of Justice indicted all four officers on federal charges, claiming that their actions violated King's civil rights. Two of the four officers—Stacey Koon and Laurence Powell—were found guilty and sentenced to 30-month prison terms. There was considerable public outrage at the leniency of the sentences.

- After a fight outside a New York nightclub in 1997, New York Police Department (NYPD) officers arrested Haitian immigrant Abner Louima, and afterwards he became the victim of one of the most extreme cases of police brutality in U.S. history. Louima was handcuffed and taken into a bathroom at the station where officer Justin Volpe sodomized him with a broomstick, causing Louima severe internal trauma including a torn intestine and a ruptured bladder. Volpe negotiated a plea bargain that included a 30-year prison term, and he testified against other officers involved in the incident. The assault convictions of three officers—Thomas Bruder, Charles Schwarz, and Thomas Wiese—were overturned in 2002.

- In February 1999, Liberian immigrant Amadou Diallo was returning home after a trip to a local restaurant when he encountered four NYPD officers. The officers approached Diallo because he matched the description of a rape suspect. After identifying themselves as police, the officers claim that Diallo ran towards his apartment door. When the officers instructed Diallo to show his hands, Diallo reached into his jacket. As he pulled his hand from his coat, one officer mistakenly identified the item in Diallo's hand as a gun, and at that same moment another officer

---

[1] The jury was unable to reach a verdict with regarding the fourth officer, Laurence Powell.

tripped and fell to the ground, possibly leading the others to believe that he had been shot. The incident ended with the officers firing 41 shots, 19 of which hit Diallo. After the gunfire had subsided, the officers learned that the item in Diallo's hand was not a gun, but rather his wallet. In February 2000, the officers were acquitted of second-degree murder and reckless endangerment charges.

While these and similar cases involving accusations of police brutality captured much of the media gaze, the vast majority of complaints involved the routine harassment of minority citizens. In communities across the United States, minority groups charged that law enforcement officers at all levels (federal, state, local, etc.) were targeting minorities for vehicle and pedestrian contacts, stopping minorities for minor/false reasons or because they fit a profile or description, questioning minorities about their involvement in the drug trade, and searching minorities without probable cause or reasonable suspicion. Claiming that these patterns and tactics violated the rights of minority citizens, several victims sued police agencies. Like John Gainer's case against EPD, many were dismissed. However, two cases took the complaints of communities of color more seriously:

- *State of New Jersey v. Pedro Soto*[2]: In November 1994, Pedro Soto and 16 co-defendants sued the New Jersey State Police (NJSP) seeking to suppress drug evidence they claimed was illegally seized. Working from an abundance of anecdotal evidence, Soto's lawyers charged that NJSP engaged in a practice of targeting black drivers for stops and searches. To prove this, the defense called on John Lamberth to ascertain the rate at which black drivers were stopped, cited, and arrested, as well as the racial/ethnic breakdown of the driving population. Relying on NJSP activity logs and structured observations of the driving behavior of New Jersey Turnpike motorists, Lamberth (1994) concluded that "blacks in general are several times more likely to be stopped than non-blacks" (p. 28). On the basis of Lamberth's findings, as well as "evidence that the state police hierarchy, from the superintendent on down, had long known about these practices but at best failed to do anything about them and at worst even condoned them" (Harris

---

[2] 734 A.2d 350 (N.J. Super. Ct. Law Div. 1996).

2002:56), New Jersey Superior Court Judge Robert Francis dismissed the charges against Soto and his co-defendants.

- *Wilkins v. Maryland State Police*[3]: In May 1992, Robert Wilkins, a black Harvard Law School graduate, was a passenger in a vehicle that was stopped and searched without cause by Maryland State Police (MSP) troopers. Wilkins sued MSP, claiming that the stop violated his civil rights. After a memorandum surfaced explicitly instructing MSP officers to target black drivers, Wilkins' suit was settled out of court (Harris 2002). A central feature of the settlement was the requirement that MSP collect data on vehicle stops that resulted in searches, and this data would be evaluated to determine if the racial/ethnic discrimination was continuing. The MSP data collection project became a foundational model for the study of discriminatory practices in vehicle stops.

The systematic harassment of minority motorists, coupled with cases involving police brutality, evoked accusations of racism directed at officers, law enforcement agencies, and the criminal justice system as a whole. Despite the denials of politicians, police officials, and police supporters, empirical and anecdotal evidence painted a picture of rampant racial/ethnic discrimination at all levels. While these allegations covered a wide range of police conduct, they would come to be collectively known by a single name: racial profiling. In June 1999, community and government leaders, civil rights activists, and law enforcement professionals gathered in Washington D.C. for the "Strengthening Police-Community Relationships" conference to discuss this emerging social problem. In his remarks to conference attendees, President Clinton addressed growing concerns surrounding racial profiling:

(Racial profiling is a) morally indefensible, deeply corrosive practice...(R)acial profiling is in fact the opposite of good police work, where actions are based on hard facts, not stereotypes. It is wrong, it is destructive, and it must stop. (Ramirez, McDevitt, and Farrell 2000:1)

---

[3] Civ. No. CCB-93-468 (D. Md.) (1993).

RACIAL PROFILING IN EUGENE, OREGON

This research examines the problem of racial profiling in Eugene, Oregon. As a result of John Gainer's experiences, as well as similar complaints from other minority residents, EPD initiated a data collection program designed to gather information about vehicle stops conducted by its officers. The purpose of this effort was to describe in detail vehicle stops involving EPD officers, with a focus on identifying and exploring differences between racial/ethnic groups in terms of enforcement practices. Following the recommendations set forward by the U.S. Department of Justice (Ramirez et. al. 2000), EPD recruited community members, activists, criminal justice professionals, and department representatives to cooperatively design the project. From February through June of 2001, the Racial Profiling Data Collection Task Group evaluated and discussed numerous research issues, including the specific types of information to be collected, and produced the research design employed by EPD. More specifically, the task group agreed on a 19-item survey to be completed by officers after every officer-initiated vehicle stop.

Overview of Book

Chapter Two defines the problem of racial profiling. Beginning with a review of the complaints associated with racial profiling and a critique of current definitions of this problem, I argue for a more complex and complete understanding of this concept. Moving beyond understandings rooted in officer decision-making, I offer the study of the "symbolic suspect" as a conceptual tool for understanding the how police view both criminality and race/ethnicity. I also provide a new operational approach to interpreting evidence of racial profiling in empirical data.

Chapter Three provides a framework for examining and understanding racial/ethnic disparities in law enforcement practices. Working with dominant and popular explanations used to explain differences, I collapse these considerations into a six-pronged perspective that highlights four causal theories and two contextualizing factors. A conceptual map illustrates how these explanations combine and overlap to produce racial/ethnic differences in enforcement practices.

Chapter Four introduces Eugene, Oregon as a case study. Starting with some history of the community and the police department, I review important aspects the vehicle stop data collection and analysis processes.

Chapter Five discusses the racial/ethnic disparities detailed in EPD's vehicle stop data as well as the influence of race/ethnicity on important dependent variables. Because of limitations associated with vehicle stop data,[4] much of this analysis is restricted to bivariate comparisons and chi-square tests; however, multivariate analysis is employed in the examination of several variables where these techniques could reasonably produce meaningful results.

Chapter Six interprets the results of the EPD vehicle stop study. I present nine findings that address important differences between racial/ethnic groups in terms of law enforcement practices. After addressing three potential problems with the data, I conclude with a discussion of the main question underlying this research—do the observed disparities constitute evidence of racial profiling? In the process of answering this question, I explore the overall racial/ethnic context of law enforcement in Eugene, and I argue the data demonstrate that EPD disproportionately applied pretext stop tactics to black and Latino drivers.

Chapter Seven provides an update on recent happenings in Eugene, as well as the impact of this research on EPD and the Eugene community. While John Gainer's experiences served as a motivating factor for the data collection, several noteworthy incidents involving minority civilians, harassment, and the use of force by EPD had an impact on how this research was received, as well as the future of police-community relations in Eugene.

---

[4] Data limitations are discussed in Chapter Four.

CHAPTER 2
What is Racial Profiling?

In order to effectively study a social phenomenon, it is necessary to have a basic definition of what is being investigated. While the definition need not be comprehensive as the area of study is first developing, some fundamental parameters are needed in order to differentiate things of interest from those of little value. However, insofar as theory construction and the conceptualization process are inexorably linked (at least in ideal terms), definitional issues can only be deferred for so long (Gibbs 1989). An inclusive definition of a social phenomenon, or at the very least an ongoing attempt to develop such a definition, is needed to produce sound theoretical perspectives and robust empirical research.

There is considerable disagreement among researchers, police officials, and community members as to how the concept of racial profiling should be defined. At the core of all racial profiling definitions is the idea of racial discrimination; however, moving beyond this initial imagery has proven quite challenging. Currently, two simplistic conceptualizations of racial profiling permeate the literature. These definitional perspectives have developed in relative isolation, rarely confronting the issues addressed by the competing perspective. To some degree, this is a reflection of the political divide associated with racial profiling, with each perspective encapsulating one side's relevant issues and arguments. Missing from the overall conceptualization process are attempts to synthesize these two schools of thought into an inclusive definition of racial profiling.

What has gone largely unchallenged in the conceptualization of racial profiling is its domain—that is, racial profiling is located in officer decision-making. The importance of officer decision-making is undeniable; however, the exclusive focus on this fact has obscured other relevant and illuminating factors, most notably the law enforcement practices that were central to the emergence of racial profiling accusations. More specifically, current definitions of racial profiling fail to consider the profound impact of the War on Drugs and the institutionalization and transformation of criminal profiling practices, most notably pretext stop tactics (Engel, Calnon, and Bernard 2002; Withrow 2006).

In this chapter I lay the foundation for a historically and tactically grounded understanding of racial profiling. Appropriately, I start with a brief history of the police practices and civilian complaints that comprise to what is widely recognized as the racial profiling debate. Building on this historical base, I analyze current decision-based conceptualizations of racial profiling with attention to workable solutions. Next, drawing on Skolnick's (1966) concept of the "symbolic assailant," I propose an examination of the "symbolic suspect" as a new way of understanding the problem of racial profiling. Finally, I critique the use of decision standards as operational definitions of racial profiling, introducing pretext stop identification as an alternative for empirical research.

A BRIEF HISTORY OF RACIAL PROFILING

In the late 1980's and early 1990's, civilian complaints, legal actions, empirical research, and a number of high-profile incidents brought several law enforcement practices to the forefront of debates on racial/ethnic bias in policing. More specifically, the aforementioned sources charged that law enforcement agencies nationwide participate in the following forms of racial discrimination:

- *Police target minorities for contacts.* Much of the evidence used to support this claim was associated with racial/ethnic disparities in police-civilian contact data. Lamberth's (1994) New Jersey turnpike study found that black drivers comprised 13.5% of the turnpike driving population and 34.9% of all drivers stopped by NJSP officers. New York Attorney General Eliot Spitzer's (1999) examination of the NYPD's "stop and frisk" practices revealed that while blacks comprised 25.6% and Latinos 23.7% of the New York City population, these groups accounted for 50.6% and 33% of NYPD contacts. Whites, who made up 43.4% of the New York City population, accounted for 12.9% of NYPD stops.

- *Police initiate contacts with minorities for minor reasons.* In terms of vehicle stops, minority drivers complained about being pulled over for trivial and obscure equipment and moving violations. Critics further charged that the official violation(s) were little more than legal "excuses" used to justify the questionable investigation of minority drivers. During his ride-alongs with the Los Angeles County Sheriff's Department, Goldberg (1999) noted a typical case where deputies identified a type of car "known to be favored by gangsters" (p. 94). One deputy studied it for a moment and identified the lack of mud flaps as an equipment violation. The vehicle was subsequently stopped and searched, and the occupants were interrogated about where they were going and why.

- *Police initiate contacts with minorities because of suspicious circumstances as opposed to actual violations of the law.* Three common complaints of minority drivers were associated with being stopped for false or nonexistent reasons, being in "the wrong place," and for driving the "wrong type of car." Attorney Curtis Rodriguez, a Latino, was stopped by California Highway Patrol officers for weaving—an accusation that he challenged as wholly unfounded. As a result of observing an alarming number of Latino drivers pulled over earlier that day, Rodriguez claimed that he was meticulously following the rules of the road (Webb 1999). In *State v. Dean*,[5] a Latino male was stopped and questioned while sitting in a car outside an apartment complex for several reasons, including because he was, in the officer's own words, "a Mexican male in a predominantly white neighborhood" (Kennedy 1997:141). Dr. Elmo Randolph, a black dentist who and owner of a gold BMW, reported being stopped by NJSP officers more than 50 times between 1991 and 1999 without receiving a single citation. During these stops, he was consistently questioned about his reasons for being on the road and whether or not he was carrying drugs or weapons (Ramirez et. al. 2000). Such

---

[5] 543 P.2d 425 (Ariz. Sup. Ct. 1975).

questioning has been frequently noted in situations where the reason for the stop lacks substance or significance.

- *Police target minority drivers for searches.* In his analysis of Maryland State Police (MSP) stop-and-search data, Lamberth (1996) found that black drivers made up 16.9% of the I-95 driving population and were the subjects of 72.9% of all searches conducted by MSP officers. Conversely, white drivers made up 75.6% of the driving population and were the subject of 19.7% of searches.

- *Police detain minorities using extraordinary measures.* The 1999 Police-Public Contacts Survey showed that black and Latino drivers were more likely than white drivers to be handcuffed during traffic stops. More specifically, "blacks were 11.6% of drivers stopped by police but 23.4% of drivers who were handcuffed, and Hispanics were 8.4% of stopped drivers but 13.2% of those handcuffed, while whites were 77% of stopped drivers and 61.8% of the ones who were handcuffed" (Langan et. al. 2001:16). Bob Vogel, former Volusia (FL) County Sheriff and drug interdiction pioneer, admitted that it was standard practice during selective drug stops to remove drivers and passengers from their vehicles, detain them in the back of the police cruiser (where they were legally recorded without their knowledge or consent), and call in K-9 units to search for drugs and other contraband (Vogel and Sadler 2001). Insofar as Vogel and his department were the targets of a Pulitzer Prize-winning investigation that found evidence of racial discrimination (Brazil and Berry 1992; Curtis 1992), it is reasonable to infer that these measures were disproportionately applied to minority drivers.

- *Police use force more frequently in contacts involving minorities.* The Police-Public Contacts Survey showed that, of persons who had face-to-face contact with the police in 1999, a larger percentage of blacks (2.1%) and Latinos (1.85%) reported that officers used some form of force during the encounter compared to the percentage of whites (0.7%—Langan et. al. 2001:24). Buerger and Farrell (2002) review a 1998 stop involving one black and three Latino youths driving on the New Jersey Turnpike. After the stop, the vehicle accidentally shifted into reverse, and NJSP officers fired 11 shots into the vehicle. While the officers initially claimed that their reaction was based on the fear of being run down, eyewitness reports and forensic reconstruction established that the officers were in no such danger. Additional investigation revealed that both officers had been involved in illegal and discriminatory conduct, including the falsification of official records used to track the race/ethnicity of officer contacts.

While discrimination against minorities by the law enforcement has been present since the earliest days of the modern police in the United States (Cooper 2001; Dulaney 1996; Walker and Katz 2005; Williams and Murphy [1990] 2000; Wintersmith 1974), a specific link was made between these particular accusations and the integration of criminal profiling tactics into the work of the Drug Enforcement Administration (DEA) and other law enforcement agencies as part of the War on Drugs (Harris 1999, 2002; Heumann and Cassak 2003; Holbert and Rose 2004; Ruiz and Woessner 2006; Webb 1999; Withrow 2006). Criminal profiling refers to formal law enforcement procedures used to recognize individuals who may be engaged in criminal behavior through the identification of salient characteristics associated with specific crimes. Criminal profiles provide officers with a rough sketch of potential offenders, highlighting demographic and behavioral characteristics thought to be related to certain criminal enterprises. The DEA first applied criminal profiling techniques to the problem of drug transportation by commercial airline passengers (Fredrickson and Siljander 2002). The effectiveness of these tactics, increasing media attention and public concern about crack cocaine (Chiricos [1998] 2002), and the success of smaller-scale community-based criminal profiling programs in New York, Los Angeles, Chicago, Atlanta, and Memphis[6] contributed to the development of Operation Pipeline, the DEA's highway drug interdiction program (Holbert and Rose 2004). Starting in 1986, this relatively covert program constructed and circulated drug courier profiles and interdiction tactics designed to help officers identify drivers and vehicles involved in the drug trade to over 27,000 officers in 48 states (Harris 1999).

It remains unclear whether race/ethnicity was part of the profiles disseminated through Operation Pipeline and other drug interdiction

---

[6] All of these programs were confined to impoverished urban areas with primarily minority populations.

programs. Harris (1999) cites guidelines promoted by the Florida Department of Highway Safety and Motor Vehicles that instructed officers to be suspicious of racial/ethnic groups associated with drug trafficking—clearly shorthand for "minorities". He adds that the materials used in Operation Pipeline training implicitly (possibly even explicitly) endorsed the targeting of minority motorists for drug interdiction stops. A MSP memorandum uncovered as part of the *Wilkins v. Maryland State Police* litigation instructed troopers to focus their drug interdiction efforts on black drivers (Harris 2002). Two deputies who served under Bob Vogel admitted that the former Volusia County Sheriff had directed them to focus on black and Latino drivers for drug-related stops, though Vogel denies this accusation (Webb 1999). The DEA contends that its profiles did not advocate the use of race/ethnicity as a factor in drug interdiction, and a 1997 review by the Department of Justice's Civil Rights Division found no evidence to reject the DEA's claim (General Accounting Office 2000).

In addition to the dissemination of drug courier profiles, Operation Pipeline trained officers in the practice of pretextual vehicle stops. When a driver, vehicle, or situation aroused officers' suspicions, they were instructed to follow and observe the vehicle until they identified law violation, which they would then use as probable cause for stopping the vehicle. Given the number of laws governing roadway conduct and vehicle condition, it is likely that all drivers, police officers included, violate some law during every trip (Harris 2002). After stopping the vehicle, the officer would briefly question the driver and any passengers while visually inspecting the automobile for additional indicators that "fit the profile." If officers suspected that the vehicle was being used to transport drugs, funds related to the drug trade, or any other contraband, the officer would then attempt to obtain consent to search the car. In cases where officers could not get consent, they frequently detained the driver, vehicle, and any passengers until a drug-sniffing dog could be deployed to inspect the vehicle (Harris 1999). It is important to note that tactics associated with pretext stops matched many of the complaints made by minority drivers.

As drug courier profiling was integrated into the customs and culture of police departments, as well as the work habits and daily routines of officers, the development of profiles moved away from its scientific roots. Criminal profiling was originally conceived as a rigorous process founded in the analysis of representative and systematically compiled data on crime and victimization. From this empirical base, professionals could make reasonable extrapolations about personality features and other characteristics associated with specific criminals. Harris (2002) and Holbert and Rose (2004) argue that contemporary practices have diverged from the scientific foundation of criminal profiling, abandoning the empirical in favor of a base comprised of personal experience, ideology, and folk wisdom. Without the meticulous analysis and representative samples that were key to the first profiles, contemporary profiles run the very real risk of being inaccurate and discriminatory against groups who have contentious relationships with law enforcement.

Along with these new law enforcement strategies came challenges to the legality of profiling tactics, and, with very few exceptions, the courts supported the police and their actions. *United States v. Mendenhall*,[7] *United States v. Sokolow*,[8] and *United States v. Weaver*[9] all affirmed the general use of profiles by law enforcement. In terms of tactics, *Whren v. United States*[10] endorsed the practice of pretextual traffic stops, ruling that an officer's actual motivations were irrelevant so long as a traffic or vehicle code violation were present to justify the stop. *Ohio v. Robinette*[11] and *United States v. Drayton*[12] both stated that it was unrealistic to expect officers to inform detainees that consent searches were voluntary and that they were free to refuse the search. *Maryland v. Wilson*[13] and *Wyoming v. Houghton*[14] expanded the officer's investigative purview to include passengers and their possessions, irrespective of the fact that they likely played no part in the legal reason for the stop.

CURRENT CONCEPTUALIZATIONS OF RACIAL PROFILING

Directly derived from the concept of criminal profiling, the term racial profiling loosely refers to race based policing (Withrow 2002) or racially biased policing (Fridell et. al. 2001), though there is

---

[7] 446 U.S. 544 (1980).
[8] 490 U.S. 1 (1989).
[9] 996 F.2d 391 (CA 8 1992).
[10] 517 U.S. 806 (1996).
[11] 519 U.S. 33 (1996).
[12] 536 U.S. 194 (2002).
[13] 519 U.S. 408 (1997).
[14] 526 U.S. 195 (1999).

considerable disagreement among police officials, academic researchers, activists, and community leaders with regard to details beyond this. Much of this dissent centers on acceptable uses of information related to race/ethnicity in policing. Despite the debates over definitional specifics, one fundamental principal remains at the core of every racial profiling definition—the idea of racial discrimination, or "using race as a criterion for treating one person or group differently from others" (Kennedy 1997:x).

Current definitions of racial profiling can be roughly categorized into two general schools of thought. One defines racial profiling as the intrusion of racial/ethnic biases into officers' decision-making processes, while the other focuses on improper uses of information on race/ethnicity in criminal profiling procedures. These conceptualizations share two common features. First, both accept as fact that racial/ethnic disparities are present in law enforcement practices. There is little debate about the overall existence of racial/ethnic differences in terms of the frequency of vehicle stops, searches, citations, and arrests, though the magnitude of such disparities is frequently contested at the jurisdictional level. Second, both conceptualizations locate the source of racial profiling in officer decision-making, abandoning the institutional aspects of criminal profiling. The roles and responsibilities of institutions are framed in terms of their potential for monitoring and addressing problems associated with individual officer decision-making. At most, institutional factors are seen as complicit; rarely are they viewed as possible causes of racial/ethnic disparities. This constrained understanding of racial profiling has significantly limited both research and public policy.

Racial Stereotyping as Racial Profiling

Ramirez et. al. (2000) provide the following definition as part of the U.S. Department of Justice's *Resource Guide on Racial Profiling Data Collection Systems*:

> Racial profiling is defined as any police-initiated action that relies on race, ethnicity, or national origin rather than the behavior of an individual or information that leads the police

to a particular individual who has been identified as being, or having been, engaged in criminal activity (P. 3).

This definition is grounded in the theory that it is the use of racial/ethnic stereotypes in officer decision-making that causes differential treatment. Stereotypes may be related to the overt racial prejudices of individual officers; Holbert and Rose (2004) note a study of 650 officers in which 25% reported believing that racial/ethnic biases and prejudices impacted the work of fellow officers and their treatment of minority suspects (p. 104). Ogletree (1995) reviews numerous accusations of prejudice leveled against police nationwide, including one black driver's recollection of a stop where officers spouted numerous racial epithets (p. 10). Kennedy (1997) and others argue that overt prejudice is not a necessary component, contending that the genesis and application of racial/ethnic stereotypes is likely related to the everyday work of law enforcement. For example, a considerable number of law enforcement officials believe that minorities are responsible for the bulk of the drug trade in the United States. Paul Mangleson, Utah State Trooper and Operation Pipeline instructor, reported in a deposition that he believed "a lot of Hispanics are transporting narcotics" (Webb 1999). Former NJSP Chief of Troopers Carl Williams was quoted as saying that the groups who traffic marijuana and cocaine were made up of "mostly minorities" (Harris 1999). While the content of these stereotypes are similar to those borne in explicitly racist ideologies, the difference in etiology is important, especially from a policy standpoint.

The definition proposed by Ramirez et. al. juxtaposes racial profiling (the use of race/ethnicity or racial stereotypes in officer decision-making) with acceptable law enforcement tactics (reliance on a suspect's behavior and known information on crimes and criminal enterprises). This conceptual distinction becomes muddled when considering the everyday work of law enforcement officers. Withrow (2002) describes policing as "a dynamic and reactive process" where "officers make and remake thousands of decisions based on fluid and incomplete fact situations" (p. 50). Furthermore, the practice of criminal profiling instructs officers to consider multiple indicators of suspiciousness (Fredrickson and Siljander 2002), and it is likely that officers who consider race/ethnicity in their decision-making also consider aspects of a suspect's behavior as well as descriptions of suspects-at-large in this process. This definition lacks an explicit mechanism for weighing these multiple influences on officer decision-making. Without a clear set of criteria, the presence of behavioral indicators or information can be (and have been) used to dismiss claims of racial profiling. This approach is embraced by the Supreme Court in their *Whren v. United States* ruling, where they state that as long as officers can provide some legal or valid reason for their action, questions about stereotyping and judgments based on race/ethnicity are rendered moot.

To be fair, the lack of a weighing mechanism could be interpreted in the opposite fashion. In other words, the use of racial/ethnic stereotypes by an officer may cancel the legal reason for the officer's actions. Ramirez et. al. provide an example that condemned the use of race/ethnicity to identify members of known criminal groups, which indicates that this interpretation may have been their intention. The Leadership Conference on Civil Rights Education Fund (2003) concurs with this idea, identifying racial profiling as "any use of race, religion, ethnicity, or national origin by law enforcement officers as a means of deciding who should be investigated" (p. 11). In *State of New Jersey v. Pedro Soto*, Judge Robert Francis found that NJSP troopers had been targeting black drivers, and this finding compelled him to dismiss the charges against Soto and 16 co-defendants despite the presence of probable cause for the stop and overwhelming evidence of guilt. However, the *Soto* decision is one of the few rulings that affirmed this position. In addition to complications with the law, this colorblind standard contradicts much of what officers are being taught in terms of tolerance and diversity. At one moment, officers are expected to be highly sensitive to cultural differences related to race/ethnicity, and at the next they are expected to ignore it. While this expectation is by no means an unreasonable goal, it does carry with it a number of obstacles, especially considering the conservative nature of police culture (Stark 1972).

Ramirez et. al. allow for an exception under this definition, noting that it is acceptable for officers to consider race/ethnicity when they are working from a description of a suspect in a known crime. This exception reveals a critical distinction between reactive and predictive or proactive police action (Black [1971] 2004). In terms of reactive police action, working from descriptions provided by witnesses to crimes is a longstanding investigative tool. Interestingly, criminal profiling began as a means of extrapolating offender characteristics

What is Racial Profiling?

from the evidence found at a crime scene (Alison and Canter 1999), and in this sense its initial use was as a reactive tactic. Harris (2002) points out that criminal profiling techniques were transformed from their descriptive roots into a predictive tool when these tactics were applied to drug couriers. Instead of describing individuals who were believed to be involved in known crimes, predictive criminal profiling relies on demographic and behavioral characteristics as indicators of crimes that are not known to the police.

One of the complications associated with using race/ethnicity in reactive police action is related to the predictive orientation of modern criminal profiling. Given the fact that much of the criminal profiling found in law enforcement today lacks a systematic and scientific foundation and is primarily based on officer experiences and shared, informal "cop knowledge" or "street sense," sanctioning of the use of race/ethnicity in reactive action is likely to spill over into proactive actions. Officers may cross-apply descriptions from known crimes to similar crimes, working under the theory that they may have been committed by the same suspect. Furthermore, common descriptions are likely to build into generalizations and stereotypes about the characteristics of criminals, possibly confined to certain crimes, but more likely applied to criminals as a broad class.

At the very least, officers could use the existence of a description as a justification for actions that would otherwise be deemed inappropriate and abusive. Harris (1999) describes a 1997 vehicle stop involving San Diego Chargers defensive lineman Shawn Lee (an African-American), who was stopped, handcuffed, and detained for 30 minutes. The officers claimed that Lee and his vehicle fit the description of an automobile theft that had been reported earlier. Additional investigation revealed that the stolen vehicle in question was a Honda sedan, which is highly unlikely to be mistaken for a sport utility vehicle like the Jeep Cherokee driven by Lee.

In addition to the misuse of descriptions, there is evidence that descriptions themselves may lack validity. Russell (1998) casts considerable doubt on the reliability of such information, noting a disturbing trend of racial hoaxes, or cases where crimes, real or fabricated, are falsely attributed to minority suspects. Racial hoaxes prey on larger cultural images and beliefs associated with race/ethnicity and crime, drawing on the public's fears and misgivings to intentionally conceal aspects of the overall situation. Russell presents data on 67 racial hoaxes, including the case of Susan Smith, a white mother of two who, in 1994, accused a black male of carjacking and kidnapping her children, when in fact she had murdered her two sons. Under Ramirez et. al.'s exception, these hoaxes would permit officers to use race/ethnicity in the pursuit of phantom suspects. While such hoaxes are likely infrequent occurrences, the existence of race-based ruses casts some doubt what Ramirez et. al. and others consider to be reasonable and reliable information. If the content of crime reporting and witness statements can be influenced by racial/ethnic biases, for whatever reason, then this information should not be embraced with the blind faith embodied in Ramirez et. al.'s exception.

Hard Profiling as Racial Profiling

MacDonald (2001) draws a distinction between "hard profiling," which is equated with racial profiling, and "soft profiling," or criminal profiling:

> What we may call "hard" profiling uses race as the only factor in assessing criminal suspiciousness: an officer sees a black person and, without more to go on, pulls him [sic] over for a pat-down on the chance that he [sic] may be carrying drugs or weapons. "Soft" racial profiling is using race as one factor among others in gauging criminal suspiciousness. (P. 14)

Hard profiling is almost universally condemned as discriminatory and improper police action. However, the practice of hard profiling is undoubtedly rare—in part because criminal profiling trains officers to consider multiple variables, but also because officers cannot help but observe other aspects of the suspect and the situation, all of which will inevitably have an impact on officers' decisions. Fridell et. al. (2001) and Walker (2001) dismiss the notion of hard profiling as absurd and unrealistic. Furthermore, to associate racial profiling exclusively with hard profiling would prematurely exclude from the discussion valid instances of racial discrimination.

MacDonald and others argue that soft profiling, or including race/ethnicity as a variable in criminal profiling, should be considered a legitimate and acceptable law enforcement practice. This position's justification rests on differential offending theory, or the idea that racial/ethnic minorities, more specifically blacks and Latinos, are more likely to commit certain crimes that whites. Two types of differential offending are of particular importance to discussions of racial profiling—differences in drug offending and differences in driving-related violations. In terms of drug crimes, recent Uniform Crime Report data have consistently shown that the percentage of all drug arrests involving black subjects is significantly greater than this group's representation in the U.S. population. According to the 2000 Census, blacks accounted for 12.1% and whites for 75.1% of the U.S. population.[15] Uniform Crime Reports for that same year noted that 64.2% of all arrests for drug abuse violations involved white offenders, while 34.5% involved black offenders.[16]

Even though the presence of racial/ethnic differences in drug offending is generally accepted, the magnitude and causes of these disparities is a topic of considerable debate. From a methodological standpoint, relying on statistics generated by the criminal justice system in general, and law enforcement specifically, is very problematic. Given the influence of social, political, historical, economic, logistical, and legal factors on the character and behavior of law enforcement at the institutional and organizational levels, to assume that enforcement-related data reflect an unbiased estimate of offending would be naïve and ill-advised. Data on arrests are nowhere close to being a representative sample of offending in a given jurisdiction. For example, deployment policies dictate where officers will patrol, influencing the people, places, and types of situations that officers will encounter. Furthermore, characteristics of the situation will influence officers' choices and actions. In terms of arrests, Black ([1971] 2000) notes that the seriousness of the crime, the strength of available evidence, the relationship between the victim and suspect, and the suspect's attitude towards the officer all have an impact on whether or not a suspect is taken into custody. Considering the multitude of factors influencing the occurrence of arrests, and by extension other decisions and processes throughout the criminal justice system, it is

---

[15] The calculation of these percentages used only those respondents who selected a single race on the 2000 Census form. Furthermore, respondents who identified themselves as Hispanic or Latino were not removed from the single race estimates. These data can be found in table P3 of the 2000 Census Summary File 1. Retrieved on April 19, 2007 (http://www.census.gov/Press-Release/www/2001/sumfile1.html).
[16] Retrieved April 19, 2007 (http://www.fbi.gov/filelink.html?file=/ucr/cius_00/00crime4.pdf).

clear that such data measure a number of factors above and beyond the presence of law violations.

Despite methodological flaws, few researchers have actually questioned the existence of some level of drug offending disparity between whites and minorities. Instead, social scientists have focused their attention on identifying those factors that shape both differences in drug use and differences in policing across racial/ethnic groups. Beckett et. al. (2005) review three approaches to explaining apparent differential offending in drug arrest rates. First, insofar as larger percentages of black and Latino populations live in impoverished conditions, socio-economic inequality may exercise a disproportionately strong influence on minority populations, pushing these groups towards the use "hard" drugs—"poverty and unemployment fuel the most destructive forms of drug use" (p. 420). The authors' add that persistent poverty and unemployment are likely to weaken one's attachment to mainstream norms, hence decreasing the power of normative incentives to discontinue drug use. Second, the fact that drug transactions involving blacks and Latinos (dealers and users) are more likely to occur in public spaces makes these populations more vulnerable to policing simply because of their visibility. Third, the authors argue that apparent differential offending may actually be thinly veiled differential enforcement:

> Specifically, many contemporary race scholars highlight the cultural and political processes by which certain categories or behaviors are racialized; that is, they are imbued with racial meanings...From this perspective, drug policies and enforcement practices may be influenced by the cultural construction and racial coding of drugs and those who ingest them; ostensibly race-neutral practices (such as the tendency to treat users of crack cocaine more harshly that users of powder cocaine) may reflect the association of certain substances or modes of ingestion with racially stigmatized groups. (p. 421)

The racialization argument recasts claims of differential offending by emphasizing the racial subtext of the processes that either reveal or produce (depending on your perspective) racial/ethnic disparities. Instead of differential drug offending simply being understood as an "objective fact", this perspective draws attention to the socio-political context in which drug agendas are set and drug policies are implemented. As such, the criminal justice system's preoccupation with crack cocaine is embedded in larger issues of racial/ethnic conflict, and disparities are not exclusively reflections of objective reality, but also the products of a system that must rationalize institutionalized discrimination in order to maintain legitimacy.

Much like the debates over drug offending, there is little agreement on racial/ethnic differences in driving behavior and vehicle code violations. Engel et. al. (2004) provide a comprehensive review of transportation literature, highlighting racial/ethnic differences in the possession of a valid driver's license, vehicle ownership, frequency of driving, seat belt use, frequency of driving under the influence, and fatal accident involvement (p. 9). Using radar-triggered cameras on the New Jersey Turnpike, Lange, Johnson, and Voas (2005) concluded that black drivers were more likely than white drivers to exceed the speed limit. Conversely, Lamberth's research in New Jersey (1994) and Maryland (1996) found minimal differences between white and black drivers in terms of speed limit violations. It is important to note that both Lange et. al. and Lamberth confine their exploration of law violation to speeding, and while survey data indicate that this is the most commonly reported reason for stop (Boyle, Dienstfrey, and Sorothon 1998), it is still a far too limited definition to draw meaningful conclusions about larger racial/ethnic differences across a wide variety of offenses.

When considering complaints associated with racial profiling, however, differential offending in terms of driving behavior and vehicle code violations is of minor importance. Many of the reasons employed by officers during the execution of pretext stops are not addressed in previous research, much of which focuses on more serious offenses. Furthermore, when considering criminal profiling tactics, suspicion often precedes the observation of a law violation, which means that the violation is a secondary factor and not a major contributor to the actual motivation for the stop.

It is also important to distinguish between empirical evidence of differential offending and officers' beliefs and perceptions. Given that scientifically derived profiles have been pushed aside in favor of informal criminal profiling practices that rely on officers' beliefs and experiences, it is likely that officer decisions based on race/ethnicity lack the scientific foundation claimed by those who promote this perspective. Belief in or commitment to the idea of differential offending is likely to produce experiences that reinforce these beliefs, creating a self-fulfilling prophecy. When officers use their beliefs about the involvement of blacks and Latinos in drug trafficking to focus on these minorities in their enforcement practices, the fact that officers will inevitably find drugs and other contraband on a portion of civilians of any race/ethnicity is interpreted as evidence that their beliefs are valid, regardless of the fact that they lack similar, comparable experiences with white drivers (largely because they choose not to approach whites in the same way they approach blacks and Latinos). Considering the character of contemporary criminal profiling, the introduction of race/ethnicity into decision-making processes will almost inevitably produce differences between racial/ethnic groups, as opposed to independently revealing existing differences.

One of the most troublesome aspects of MacDonald's definition of soft profiling is the lack of restraints on the use of race/ethnicity by officers. As it stands, race/ethnicity can be used as the primary reason behind officers' decisions to stop, search, arrest, etc., provided that officers can cite other tertiary reasons that contributed to their choices. When race/ethnicity is the primary reason for officers' decisions and/or actions, even when coupled with other reasons (including law violations), officers are clearly discriminating on the basis of race/ethnicity. The charge of discrimination can reasonably extended to decisions and actions where race/ethnicity is among several key factors considered by officers. Furthermore, this contention can be applied to reactive as well as proactive police action, for racial discrimination cuts across this distinction despite Ramirez et. al.'s exception.

If race/ethnicity is to be included in criminal profiles in a non-discriminatory fashion, then racial/ethnic information must be treated like any other indicator of suspiciousness. This consideration poses a significant challenge to the dynamic process of revising and reconstructing criminal profiles. Fredrickson and Siljander (2002) argue that criminals will alter their appearance and behavior to avoid fitting existing profiles, pointing out that an officer who sticks to static profiles is "probably missing a lot of good seizure opportunities because he or she is too narrowly defining who may be a suspect" (p. 37). As such, in order to keep up with the changing character of criminality, profiles, both formal and informal, must be updated, and contradictions are an inescapable byproduct of this process. Cole (1999:48-49) identified the following contradictions in the drug courier profiles used by federal agents to identify potential drug couriers at airports:

- *Arrival Time:* Late at night, early in the morning, in the afternoon.
- *Order of Deplaning:* One of the first to deplane, one of the last to deplane, deplaned in the middle.
- *Ticket Purchase:* Bought coach ticket, bought first class ticket, bought one-way ticket, bought round-trip ticket.
- *Luggage:* No luggage, carried one small bag, carried one medium bag, carried two heavy suitcases, carried four pieces of luggage, overly protective of luggage, disassociated self from luggage.
- *Travel Companions:* Traveled alone, traveled with a companion.
- *Dress:* Wore expensive clothing and jewelry, dressed casually.
- *Conduct:* Acted too calm, acted too nervous, made eye contact with officer, did not make eye contact with officer, walked quickly through the airport, walked slowly through the airport, walked aimlessly through the airport.
- *Post-Arrival Travel:* Left airport by taxi, by limousine, by private car, by hotel courtesy van.

Because such contradictions are inevitable, it is important to understand their overall impact on criminal profiling practices. The contradictions noted above apply exclusively to behavioral and appearance-related characteristics, mostly because these elements are regarded as the easiest for drug couriers to modify. However, as contradictions arise, the behavioral and appearance-related aspects of profiles become meaningless insofar as they offer no means for differentiation. This is particularly problematic given the fact that officers and departments are moving away from scientific profiles and towards informal ones, which means that different officers could reasonably be focusing on contradictory indicators. As a result of these contradictions within and between profiles, other factors, most notably race/ethnicity, become highly salient because they remain constant across all permutations of the profile. The effect of race/ethnicity is also magnified because the contradictions cancel out factors associated with appearance and behavior that would have previously excluded some individuals from suspicion, meaning that the number of minority suspects inevitably grows. In this sense, the officer has the discretion to identify any minority civilian and claim that he or she somehow "fits the profile" as a way of justifying the contact. With more individuals falling under the umbrella of suspicion, and with increasing contacts with minority suspects, the self-fulfilling prophecy of differential offending is reinforced and the racial/ethnic aspects of criminal profiles go unchanged.

RECONCEPTUALIZING RACIAL PROFILING

In order to bridge the gaps between these two prevailing conceptualizations, I propose an approach that more effectively balances the use of race/ethnicity in officer decision-making with concerns about racial discrimination. I start by combining the fundamental concerns captured in current understandings of racial profiling to create a base conceptualization. On this foundation, I construct three conceptual standards to differentiate racial profiling from acceptable decision-making processes related to criminal profiling. These standards are drawn from the experiences of civilians and officers and are designed to provide grounded criteria on which police action can be based and evaluated.

It is important to recognize that, even with revision, the conceptual limitations associated with decision standard approaches restrict both theory development and empirical research on racial profiling. To remedy this, I propose two new conceptual approaches. First, drawing on Skolnick's (1966) concept of the "symbolic assailant," I take the key theoretical elements used in the two current conceptualizations and develop a more expansive conceptual means for understanding racial profiling. Simply put, I argue that racial profiling exists at the conceptual nexus of race/ethnicity and suspicion, and to define, theorize, and study it we must look at the role of race/ethnicity in the social construction of suspicion and the symbolic suspect.

Second, I propose a historically and tactically oriented approach to operationalizing racial profiling. I contend that, rather than trying to read the minds of police officers, researchers should focus on identifying patterns in police practices that are indicative of the disproportionate application of pretext stop tactics to minority populations.

Reconsidering Decision Standards

As the preceding discussion illustrates, existing definitions of racial profiling are separated by a broad conceptual and theoretical expanse. However, given that both frame the problem in terms of officer decision-making, there is an opportunity for negotiation. In what could easily be mistaken as simply a minor shift in phrasing, Weitzer and Tuch (2002) provide a valuable step towards a compromise by defining racial profiling as "the use of race as a key factor in police decisions" (p. 435). Building on this core idea, I provide the following decision standard: *Racial profiling refers to instances where the race, ethnicity, or national origin of an individual is the primary factor, or is among the most important factors, considered by officers in their decision-making processes.* According to this conceptualization, criminal profiling and other law enforcement practices become racial profiling when race/ethnicity plays a central role in an officer's decision-making process. Race/ethnicity need not be the only reason or the primary reason—it need only be among the main reasons considered by an officer. Given that the relationship between race/ethnicity and crime is tenuous and mediated by a number of variables, it is a questionable practice for officers to rely heavily on race/ethnicity as a proxy for criminality in their decision-making. Furthermore, such practices threaten our Fourteenth Amendment right to equal protection. While the courts seem less interested in these protections and more interested in justifying police actions under the Fourth Amendment, a meaningful conceptualization of racial profiling should be considerate of, but not wholly determined by, the current state of legal affairs. It should be further noted that this conceptualization does not explicitly distinguish between formal and informal criminal profiling, or between reactive and proactive police action. Rather, it covers all officer decisions, including instances where officers choose not to act—an aspect of officer decision-making that has been remarkably neglected in previous research.

Taken alone, this conceptualization offers a comparative advantage over previous definitions insofar as it addresses several of the problems discussed earlier, while also providing a balance between each perspective's theoretical foundations. Conceptually, it grasps the basic distinction between racial profiling and criminal profiling, albeit at an abstract level. However, much like other decision standards, the practicality and applicability of this definition to the everyday work of police officers is questionable, especially considering the variety of contemporary police functions and responsibilities. In other words, this universal standard, like all that have come before it, does not account for the complexities of modern policing and the associated categorical differences between certain types of police work, such as the difference between reactive and proactive police action. Furthermore, this definition's utility to empirical research remains problematic insofar as social science lacks valid and reliable techniques for measuring dynamic decision-making processes. As such, an attempt to specify, focus, or even operationalize this core theme is necessary. To this end, I propose three additional standards to help illuminate the real-world implications of this conceptualization:

- *Standard One: Racial profiling occurs when race/ethnicity is used as a filter through which other indicators of suspiciousness are interpreted.* This standard demands that indicators of suspiciousness be considered independently, which addresses complaints associated with stops of minorities for being in the "wrong car" or "wrong neighborhood." If an officer considers something to be an indicator of suspiciousness only in relation to a suspect's race/ethnicity, then the officer is guilty of racial profiling. When race/ethnicity is used as a lens through which other factors are interpreted, race/ethnicity is the primary consideration, possibly even the only real consideration. Given that behavioral and appearance-related factors break down in the process of profile revision, the use of race/ethnicity in this manner is inevitably discriminatory. It is clear that such tactics and strategies are little more than hard profiling masquerading as soft profiling.

- *Standard Two: In terms of proactive police action, racial profiling occurs when race/ethnicity serves as the "tipping point" in officer decision-making.* In other words, if an officer's decision would change if the suspect's race/ethnicity were different (e.g. if the suspect were white instead of black, or vice versa), then the officer is guilty of racial profiling. This standard addresses minority drivers' claims that officers stop, interrogate, and search them because they are minorities. Some interpretations of this accusation mistakenly focus on the idea that officers base their action solely on the suspect's race/ethnicity (hard profiling), which has been classified as indefensible. However, this standard recasts these complaints as less about causal exclusivity (race/ethnicity as the only reason for an officer's actions) and more about causation within a model that includes controls for other variables (race/ethnicity as the reason for the officer's action when other relevant factors are held constant). From this perspective, instances where race/ethnicity is the "tipping point" in officer decision-making can be considered hard profiling. While race/ethnicity is not the only consideration, it is the essential element in determining the outcome.

- *Standard Three: In terms of reactive police action, racial profiling occurs when race/ethnicity is used as anything other than a confirmatory factor.* This standard refines Ramirez et. al.'s (2000) exception for using racial/ethnic information in the pursuit of suspects in known crimes, providing appropriate limitations how such information can be used. Unlike proactive action, reactive enforcement is the only condition where race/ethnicity can serve as the "tipping point" in officer decision-making. At the same time, it should not be a central factor in reactive action—information related to race/ethnicity should be considered only after other criteria have been satisfied. In the absence of other key characteristics of a description, such as sex, age, height, and weight, race/ethnicity must not be employed as the justification for police action. Given past abuses, it would seem wise for departments to embrace this standard when crafting policies related to reactive action.

When working with these standards, there are two additional points to consider. First and foremost, the fact that these standards allow for the use of race/ethnicity in officer decision-making is by no means an endorsement of such tactics, even if the use of race/ethnicity does not qualify as racial profiling. As long as officers are allowed to use race/ethnicity in their decision-making there will always be a risk of discrimination at both the individual and institutional levels. Second, none of these standards explicitly mention the role of law violation in officer decision-making. This conceptualization and the related standards are focused on identifying discrimination, and as such law violation is simply another variable in the analysis. When law violation is given special consideration, as it currently is in legal evaluations of racial profiling,[17] it can be used to conceal discriminatory acts.

The Symbolic Suspect

In his classic research on the Westville police department, Skolnick (1966) introduces the concept of the "symbolic assailant":

> The policeman [sic], because his [sic] work requires him [sic] to be occupied continually with potential violence, develops a perceptual shorthand to identify certain types of people as symbolic assailants, that is, persons who use gesture, language, and attire that the policeman has come to recognize as a prelude to violence. This does not mean that violence by the symbolic assailant is necessarily predictable. On the contrary, the policeman responds to the vague indication of danger suggested by appearance. (P. 45)

The idea of "perceptual shorthand" bears a striking similarity to criminal profiling. The pertinent issue for Skolnick is danger, and through the use of the qualities associated with symbolic assailant, officers recognize and act on indicators of potential violence. By drawing on this vocabulary of threatening characteristics, officers are better equipped to prevent violence against civilians, as well as against themselves. Of course, danger is only one of many conditions perceived by officers in the course of their daily work. In terms or criminal profiling, the pertinent issue is suspicion, or the belief that a person or a group of persons is likely to be involved in criminal activity. Alpert, MacDonald, and Dunham (2005) rightly observe that little attention has been paid to suspicion, further noting that "a police officer's initial decision to suspect that someone is involved in illegal behavior" is "at the core of the controversy surrounding issues such as racial profiling " (p. 408). Insofar as the purpose of criminal profiling is to provide officers with behavioral and demographic indicators to help them identify possible criminals, one way of understanding police actions and decision-making is to examine the qualities of "symbolic

---

[17] See *Whren v. United States*.

suspects." I am not suggesting that officers have preconceived portraits of potential perpetrators sketched out in their minds (at either the conscious or subconscious level). Like Skolnick, I argue that officers act and react based on general indicators of suspicion that are likely to be enmeshed with a number of other symbols and meanings.

The embodiment suggested by the concept of the symbolic suspect provides an excellent mode for expanding the conceptualization of racial profiling. To understand racial profiling in this conceptual framework is to explore the racial/ethnic characteristics of symbolic suspects. This strategy provides a practical means grounded in the lived experiences of officers for examining the areas of conceptual overlap between race/ethnicity and suspicion. This approach facilitates the inclusion of theory and research on criminal imagery and stereotyping. Many argue very convincingly that images of the typical criminal (which has become synonymous with street crime) and images of black and Latino males have become intertwined in contemporary American culture. In their critiques of media representations of criminality, Russell (1998) argues that "(i)mages of Black life are overridden by images of Black deviance" (p. 3), and Portillos (1998) contends that the predominant image of Latino males is the gang member.

Alpert et. al. (2005) explore the relationship between race/ethnicity and suspicion. While they draw out vital links between influences on officer decision-making, police actions in minority communities, and the cognitive structure of suspicion, their discussion is problematic insofar as it treats suspicion as a relatively simple construct focused almost exclusively on the issue of crime. While criminality is central, definitions of suspicion undoubtedly expand well beyond legal frameworks, and as such our understanding of suspicion must embrace this complexity by exploring the contours, terrain, and boundaries of this concept. A review of the literature indicates four possible dimensions of suspicion—criminal potential, danger, priority and reward—that are worthy of additional attention.

Chambliss' ([1973] 2000) classic research on the Saints and the Roughnecks introduces the dimension of criminal potential. While the Saints committed more illegal acts, and while their delinquency was arguably more serious,[18] they experienced little to no punishment. On

---

[18] Chambliss notes that the Saints often put their lives and the lives of others at risk with their pranks (p. 186).

the other hand, police and other adults frequently targeted the Roughnecks for enforcement and harassment. Chambliss attributes the differences in authorities' reactions to the Saints and the Roughnecks to bias, which is largely based on perceptions of the overall criminal potential of each group. Adults viewed the Roughnecks' conduct as evidence of "their devotion and commitment to deviance as a way of life" (p. 188), while the Saints' transgressions were dismissed as the playful indiscretions of normal boys, and as such these acts did not alter the overall positive image of the Saints. In the end, Chambliss points to social class and the positions of the Saints' families in the community as the key variables in understanding enforcement differences. Considering the interconnections between the class and racial/ethnic stratification in American society, it is likely that similar judgments of criminal potential are also made based on the suspect's race/ethnicity. Generalizations about the criminal potential of racial/ethnic groups will inevitably produce self-fulfilling prophecies like those documented by Chambliss.

Skolnick's emphasis on the symbolic assailant establishes the importance of danger as a component of suspicion. The job of law enforcement entails exposure to violence, and officers receive considerable training on how to properly respond to dangerous situations, from methods to defuse situations before they escalate (Thompson 1983) to extensive combat training (Kraska and Kappeler 1997). The use of force by officers provides an important link between danger and racial/ethnic characteristics of the symbolic suspect. Holbert and Rose (2004) argue that the police equate danger with fear and weakness, noting that these are considered liabilities in law enforcement. Considering that officers are expected maintain order and exercise control over volatile situations, feelings of fear and the appearance weakness can easily compel officers to prematurely and improperly employ forceful tactics (Herbert 1998; Hunt 1985; Waegel 1984). The fact that blacks and Latinos experience the use of force by police more frequently than whites may be, at least in part, a reflection of officers' perceptions of danger associated with these groups or areas associated with certain racial/ethnic populations (Herbert 2001).

In addition to danger as an element of suspicion, it is also important to consider the role of politics in determining and directing police action. As Becker (1963) rightly observed, moral entrepreneurs have a profound impact on the work of law enforcement officers.

What is Racial Profiling?

While the goal of moral entrepreneurship in the past was to create or modify laws, similar action in contemporary society focuses more on agenda setting and prioritization. Given that police forces around the country and at all levels lack the resources to pursue a policy of full enforcement, or to "enforce all criminal statues and city ordinances at all times and against all offenders" (Goldstein 1963:140), hierarchies of importance, both formal and informal, inevitably develop within communities and agencies. Certain violations, most likely those where there is community outrage to quell and/or political capital to reap, receive increased police attention, while others go relatively unpunished. The law enforcement priorities established as part of the War on Drugs are vital to understanding the racial profiling controversy. Marquart et. al. (1993) note that drug arrests by police in Texas rose by 69.4% from 1980 to 1989. Uniform Crime Reports note an even more dramatic increase; between 1980 and 1995, drug arrests in the United States rose by 154.1%.[19] From 1995 to 2005, the growth in arrests has continued, though at a markedly lower rate (36.6%).[20] Chiricos [1998] 2002 argues that much of the moral panic associated with the War on Drugs was related to the spread of crack cocaine from inner cities (read: black populations) into suburban neighborhoods (read: white populations), thus adding an undeniable racial/ethnic component to these priorities. UCR data further support this position. While the majority of drug arrests involved whites, a considerable, arguably disproportionate, percentage involved blacks: from 24.5% of all drug arrests in 1980 to 41.2% in 1990 and 39.1% in 1995.[21] Research on drug arrests in Seattle (WA) indicates that the prioritization of crack cocaine enforcement largely explains drug arrest disparities (Beckett, Nyrop, and Pfingst 2006).

In association with priority as a dimension of suspicion, it is important to also consider rewards to officers. When a premium is placed on a certain type of crime or criminal, then officers who are successful in enforcing the relevant laws, territories, and populations will likely receive formal rewards, possibly in the form of commendation and promotion, and informal rewards, such as the

---

[19] Retrieved April 19, 2007 (http://www.fbi.gov/filelink.html?file=/ucr/Cius_97/96CRIME/96crime5.pdf).
[20] Calculated by comparing UCR data on drug abuse violations from 1995 through 2005. Data retrieved April 19, 2007 (http://www.fbi.gov/ucr/ucr.htm).
[21] Retrieved April 19, 2007 (http://www.fbi.gov/filelink.html?file=/ucr/Cius_97/96CRIME/96crime5.pdf).

respect and adulation of other officers. As such, the priority component of suspicion works in two ways; first, it directs officers to look for suspects with characteristics that are hypothetically related to certain types of crime, and second, it establishes criteria for officer evaluation and rewards. If racial/ethnic biases are built into the prioritization hierarchy, then these inequalities will be further exacerbated by reward systems that promote discriminatory conduct.

Beyond facets of suspicion, it is important to consider race/ethnicity as a concept with multiple dimensions. Current research on racial profiling focuses almost exclusively on the officer's perception of the suspect's race/ethnicity as the key variable in determining the presence of discrimination. Using this narrow conceptualization, Nevada law enforcement agencies collected data on whether or not officers could identify the race/ethnicity of drivers prior to vehicle stops. The data demonstrated that such identifications could be made in only 16.7% of all cases (McCorkle 2003). These data could be used to argue that the issue of racial profiling is moot in 83.3% of all stops because the officer could not identify the driver's race/ethnicity before the stop. Such an argument misinterprets the underlying questions raised in association with racial profiling, which include, but are not limited to, decisions based on direct perceptions of race/ethnicity. Also of importance are officers' assumptions about race/ethnicity, which can be drawn from a number of sources. Symbols linked with certain racial/ethnic groups tap into the larger meaning structures associated with these groups. The Florida Department of Highway Safety and Motor Vehicles guidelines that directed officers to look for racial/ethnic groups associated with the drug trade also included instructions to be suspicious of drivers who wore "lots of gold" (Harris 1999), which was a clear reference to hip-hop fashion trends that gained popularity in black and Latino communities during the mid-1980s. The racial/ethnic composition of neighborhoods undoubtedly contributes to officers' judgments about who belongs and does not belong in these areas, as well as what sorts of behavior to expect from both insiders and outsiders. In terms of vehicle stops, it is also very likely that officers associate certain vehicle makes and models, after-market modifications, wheels/rims, sound systems, and music choices with certain racial/ethnic groups, most notably hip-hop and gang subcultures. These and other conceptual dimensions of race/ethnicity contribute to the overall racial/ethnic context in which officer decision-making occurs. Given the pervasiveness and power of meanings associated with race/ethnicity and the overlap between these and the dimensions of suspicion, it is vital that conceptualizations of and research on racial profiling move beyond the exclusive focus on the driver's race/ethnicity to include an analysis of the overall racial/ethnic context of police actions.

Understanding the content and conceptual dimensions of suspicion and race/ethnicity is only one aspect of the investigation into symbolic suspects; additional work is needed to understand how these meanings are constructed, modified, reinforced, and reproduced in law enforcement organizations. The characteristics of the symbolic suspect are fluid and under constant revision, a fact that is evidenced by the adjustment of federal drug courier profiles. Law enforcement as an institution undoubtedly plays a central role in this process. Organizational functions like hiring practices, officer deployment and assignments, procedures for addressing civilian complaints, rewards and job advancement opportunities, prioritization, and training all contribute to the images associated with symbolic suspects. When law enforcement agencies fail to identify the racial/ethnic biases of applicants, or when organizations fail to appropriately sanction officers who participate in discriminatory practices, the institution implicitly endorses racial discrimination. When departments reward and/or promote officers who discriminate, the endorsement is explicit. Training that instructs officers to equate race/ethnicity with suspiciousness, either directly or indirectly, defines race/ethnicity as a "master status" (Hughes 1945) of suspects. Deployment patterns that place more officers in minority communities, regardless of the justification, and priorities and assignments that instruct officers to seek out certain types of crime (e.g. drugs) can result in self-fulfilling prophecies. Not only will these conditions inevitably produce results (wherever police look for crime they will find at least some crime, regardless of the racial/ethnic composition of the community), they will also justify the future focus on minority civilians and neighborhoods. The result of these institutional processes is the further narrowing of the racial/ethnic diversity of symbolic suspects.

While institutional features of law enforcement agencies play important roles in the construction of suspicion and symbolic suspects, any analysis of such processes would be incomplete without an examination of law enforcement culture. Officers are not simply robotic extensions of law enforcement institutions; rather, they are human actors who actively interpret and redefine the world around them. Becker (1963) notes that officers "often develop their own private evaluation of the importance of various kinds of rules and infractions of them" (p. 161), adding that the officers' priorities often differ from those of the public and those of the institution or agency, specifically management. The roles of law enforcement culture and subculture are likely to reach beyond the collective redefinition of institutional features; indeed, aspects of this culture almost certainly reinforce the definition of symbolic suspects as racial/ethnic minorities. Dulaney (1996) observes that blacks have been the targets of policing and differential enforcement throughout American history, and this history is undoubtedly preserved in contemporary police culture. Bolton and Feagin (2004) note that whites have historically dominated law enforcement agencies, and that black officers have witnessed and been subjected to considerable discrimination. Stark (1972) and Kappeler, Sluder, and Alpert ([1998] 2001) contend that police culture tends to be isolationist and totalizing in the sense that officers rarely socialize with those who are not knowledgeable of and sympathetic towards police work, which means that officers are unlikely to encounter much diversity in their lives and experiences outside of work. Lipset ([1969] 1974) adds that police culture is dominated by right-wing ideology that fervently rejects progressive viewpoints of activists and social scientists, especially those that emphasize racism and social justice in their criticism.

Operationalizing Racial Profiling

Measurement problems associated with the decision standard conceptualization of racial profiling are key to understanding the content and historical course of research on racial profiling. Withrow (2006) notes that "savvy consumers of racial profiling research, including most police administrators, are quick to see the incongruence between definitions and measures" (88). Standard data collection methods (e.g. vehicle stop data, surveys of the civilian population) are unable to provide sufficient information to thoroughly examine officer decision-making. While these data capture the outcomes of officers' choices, they provide little insight into the processes through which such decisions were made. Without information on how race/ethnicity factored into officers' deliberations, decision standard conceptualizations of racial profiling prevent researchers from making reliable determinations regarding the presence and prevalence of discriminatory practices.

Withrow (2006) highlights several studies that moved away from decision standards by employing "operational definitions" of racial profiling. Rather than focusing on standards related to officer decision-making, these studies attended to disparities in stop frequency between whites and minorities, defining racial profiling as occurring "when minorities are stopped at disproportionately higher rates than they are represented within the benchmark that indicates the proportional racial representation of actual roadway users" or "population of pedestrians" (p. 84). Insofar as this approach classifies the simple presence of differences between white and minority drivers as evidence of racial profiling, these definitions fail to grasp the complex dynamics that come together to produce such differences. To conclude that the disparities between racial/ethnic groups can be attributed to discrimination (presumably by officers) and discrimination alone ignores a variety of important individual, organizational, and institutional-level explanations.

While the substance of such operational definitions is problematic, the basic approach carries with it considerable promise. By linking the conceptualization of racial profiling to real-world manifestations of discrimination, we can move beyond the empirical challenges associated with measuring decision-making processes. However, it is necessary that we move past crudely equating disparities with discrimination and towards a complex and grounded conceptualization. Considering the history of the racial profiling controversy, I propose that empirical research focus on identifying racial/ethnic disparities in the application of pretext stop practices. Pretextual vehicle stops were a central element of the criminal profiling strategies disseminated via Operation Pipeline, and this tactic remains a vital part of contemporary policing. By employing a historical and tactical conceptualization constructed around pretext stop practices, we can move beyond simplistic notions of discrimination and speculation about disparities.

Three key characteristics of pretextual traffic stops are evident in literature. First, pretext stops involve high-discretion reasons for stop, frequently taking the form of minor, subjective, or possibly even non-existent law violations. In these stops, the legal reason for the stop is little more than the requisite probable cause necessary for the stop to stand up in court—the real reason is the suspicion that serious criminal behavior may be afoot. Second, pretext stops involve increased levels of investigative attention. These investigations may include a number of tactics, including (but not limited to) a visual inspection of the passenger compartment, informal questioning of the driver and passengers regarding a number of matters (reason for travel, destination, the presence of contraband in the car), and conducting database and records checks on the driver's license and the automobile's plates.[22] While these practices are largely standard procedure for vehicle stops, what separates pretext stops from others is the thoroughness of the investigation. Finally, in cases where preliminary investigations further officers' suspicions (or at the very least fail to quell their initial misgivings), pretext stops can involve a search. While consent searches are frequently associated with pretext stops, any type of search that involves the application of discretionary standards on the part of the officer is of interest.

Identifying pretext stops is not a simple matter. While the core characteristics of these stops may seem reasonably clear—high-discretion stops that involve increased amounts of investigation and possibly searches—measurement poses a number of challenges. Much of the data collected up to now has focused on identifying racial/ethnic disparities in stop, and occasionally search, frequency and is lacking information necessary to thoroughly investigate the occurrence of pretext stops. Even in cases where sufficient data are available, indicators were not designed for this purpose, which means that investigators must retrofit elements of this operational definition to existing data. Also, when considering pretext stop practices, it is important to be attentive to historical and tactical features that differ across organizations and communities. To be clear, the specifics of pretext stop customs are likely to differ between agencies, not necessarily in their core characteristics, but rather in terms of specific practices. Furthermore, measures and data analyses must be attentive to events that may have an impact on the frequency and general qualities of pretext stop practices. In his research on the Wichita Police Department, Withrow (2004) observed that three high profile incidents—two quadruple homicides and the murder of a young girl in

---

[22] Meehan and Ponder (2002a, 2002b) examined the implications of such records checks, finding that information on black drivers was queried at a higher rate than information on white drivers.

a drive-by shooting—had a dramatic impact on the deployment of officers and their workload in the days following these events. As Withrow's experience illustrates, a standardized measurement strategy is likely neither a possibility nor desirable; rather, measures should be organic and develop alongside and in response to departmental priorities and practices.

Finally, it is important to recognize that while this operational definition provides some distinct advantages over decision standards and previous operationalization strategies, it does not account for all manifestations of discrimination. It is likely that discriminatory action by police officers and agencies is not limited to pretextual traffic stops, and this approach will not shed much, if any, light on such practices. As Fridell et. al. (2001) point out, racial profiling is only one aspect of the larger problem of race-biased policing, and future research must be attentive to the multitude of forms that discrimination can take.

CONCLUSION

In moving forward with the study of racial profiling, it is important that the conceptualization process continue. As is the case with any emerging social problem, definitions must develop alongside theoretical perspectives and with attention to empirical findings. Revisions and additions are not only inevitable; they are a vital part of the process. Since the job of law enforcement is complex and entails diverse responsibilities, there are likely relevant aspects that have not been adequately addressed in this conceptualization, especially in terms of specific standards related to officer decision-making. Furthermore, work is needed to develop empirical tests that capture the conceptual distinctions that differentiate criminal profiling from racial profiling.

In examining law enforcement data using the proposed conceptualizations, it is clear that simple group comparisons like those employed by Lamberth (1994; 1996) lack probative value, and multivariate analyses is needed to evaluate the impact of race/ethnicity relative to other influences on officer-decision-making. Fortunately, the necessity of multivariate analysis has been embraced in recent research (Alpert, Dunham, and Smith 2007; Engel 2005; Engel and Calnon 2004b; Engel et. al. 2004; Lange et. al. 2005; Lundman 2004; Lundman and Kaufman 2003; Smith and Petrocelli 2001; Withrow 2002, 2004). Of comparable importance is research into racialization of suspicion and the construction of the symbolic suspect. Given the symbolically robust world in which officers operate, and considering the significance of race/ethnicity in U.S. culture in general and the history of policing specifically, the key to achieving a complex and inclusive understanding of racial profiling lies in identifying the conceptual overlap between race/ethnicity and suspicion.

CHAPTER 3
From Disparities to Discrimination

Empirical research on racial profiling focuses primarily on the examination of data on routine contacts between police and civilians, most commonly vehicle stops. Born out of two high profile court cases and advanced by the U.S. Department of Justice (Ramirez et. al. 2000), vehicle stop data collection projects systematically gather information about stops initiated by officers. While data collection efforts have been promoted as both a community relations opportunity and as a tool for monitoring officers, the primary goal of such systems is to provide data that can be used examine claims of racial discrimination by officers and agencies. By approaching the problem of racial profiling in a scientific manner, both agencies and communities hope to move beyond anecdotal evidence and legal quarrels. To this end, over 400 law enforcement agencies have implemented vehicle stop data collection systems, and either have collected data or are in the process of collecting data (McMahon et. al. 2002).

Analyses of vehicle stop data have consistently revealed differences between white and minority drivers in terms of stop frequency, citations, arrests, searches, and other experiences with police. Determining the causes of these differences, however, has proven very challenging. Several studies (Lamberth 1994, 1996; Smith 2000; Spitzer 1999) interpreted the presence of racial/ethnic disparities in police-civilian contact data as evidence of racial profiling—a conclusion that has been rightly contested by many. As Zingraff et. al. (2000) wisely note, the presence of racial/ethnic disparities does not constitute *prima facie* evidence of racial discrimination. Numerous alternative causal theories, most of them ad-hoc and overtly political in their etiology, have been proposed as potential explanations of observed differences. Unfortunately, few of these accounts have been grounded in existing theoretical perspectives and research on racism and policing. As a result, these theories-of-convenience have failed to grasp standard conceptual distinctions (such as the difference between individuals and institutions) and lack depth and clarity (in fact, they are frequently entangled with strands of competing and occasionally contradictory perspectives). As such, the integration of theory into data collection and analysis processes has been stalled. What is needed is a clear framework that examines and incorporates the range of explanations of law enforcement disparities with attention to fundamental theoretical and conceptual considerations.

In this chapter I propose a framework for understanding and interpreting racial/ethnic disparities in law enforcement practices, specifically differences that are captured in vehicle stop data. Starting with the history of vehicle stop data collection systems, I build a six-pronged perspective that integrates and differentiates the three central causal theories suggested in previous explanations. In addition to these three primary theories, I include a complementary theory and two contextualizing factors that add a layer of depth that is currently lacking in the literature on racial profiling. In the process, I provide a conceptual mechanism for understanding how these theoretical considerations combine to produce disparities in law enforcement practices.

A BRIEF HISTORY OF VEHICLE STOP DATA COLLECTION

Civilian complaints about racial profiling were quickly integrated into legal actions. Drawing on a growing abundance of anecdotal evidence, criminal defense and civil rights lawyers accused law enforcement agencies of targeting minority drivers for stops, searches, and arrests. To establish a pattern and practice of discrimination by the police, attorneys had to move beyond the facts of a specific case and demonstrate an overarching pattern of discrimination. Two cases in particular, *State of New Jersey v. Pedro Soto* and *Wilkins v. Maryland State Police*, contributed greatly to the development of vehicle stop

From Disparities to Discrimination 43

data collection systems as a means of empirically examining enforcement patterns.

As part of the *Soto* litigation, prosecutors and defense attorneys both relied heavily on statistical experts to analyze data on the enforcement tactics of NJSP, specifically the troopers who patrolled the New Jersey Turnpike between interchanges one and three. Defense expert John Lamberth set out "to determine if the (New Jersey) State Police stop, investigate, and arrest black travelers at rates significantly disproportionate to the percentage of blacks in the traveling population" (1994:2). In his pursuit of this question, Lamberth employed a complex research strategy that relied on a number of different data sources. For data on police contacts, Lamberth consulted NJSP arrest records and patrol and communication logs for 35 randomly selected dates between April 19, 1988 and May 18, 1991. In order to contextualize and interpret enforcement differences between black and white drivers, Lamberth gathered data on the New Jersey Turnpike driving population using several observational techniques. To determine the racial/ethnic distribution of the turnpike driving population, Lamberth strategically stationed observers alongside the turnpike and instructed them to record the race/ethnicity of drivers and vehicle occupants. To test the hypothesis that black drivers may violate traffic laws more frequently than white drivers (a claim used by officers to explain disparities), Lamberth also conducted "rolling surveys" in which teams of observers drove the turnpike and identified not only the race/ethnicity of drivers, but also whether or not they were exceeding the speed limit by more than five miles-per-hour.

Lamberth (1994) found that vehicles with black drivers and/or passengers comprised 13.5% of the turnpike population in 1993. He found very little difference between the racial/ethnic distributions of the driving population and the speeding population (14.8% black). However, Lamberth identified considerable disparities between these population figures and the data derived from NJSP records and logs. Specifically, Lamberth found that vehicles with black drivers and/or passengers comprised 34.9% of turnpike stops, 44.3% of stops in between interchanges one and three (an area noted as the epicenter of the racial/ethnic discrimination in this case), and 73.2% of all drivers arrested. In terms of his study's conclusions, he wrote:

> The present study demonstrated substantially and highly statistically significant disparities between blacks in the

turnpike population (and likewise the population of turnpike violators), and the percentage of blacks subject to investigative stop...While no one can know the motivations of each individual trooper in making a stop, the statistics presented herein, representing a very broad and detailed sample of highly appropriate data, demonstrated without question a discriminatory impact on blacks...The disparities are sufficiently great that, taken as a whole, they consist strongly with and strongly support the assertion that the state police have targeted the community of black motorists or travelers for investigation, stop and arrest. (P. 29)

In *Wilkins v. Maryland State Police*, plaintiff Robert Wilkins accused MSP of violating his civil rights in the form of an unwarranted stop and K-9 search. After uncovering evidence of MSP's systematic targeting of black drivers for stops and searches (Harris 2002), the case was settled out-of-court and the records were sealed (Buerger and Farrell 2002). The most revolutionary aspect of the settlement was the requirement that MSP collect data on every vehicle stop resulting in a search for a period of three years. Lamberth was retained by the American Civil Liberties Union to analyze the data. Much like his work in New Jersey, Lamberth (1996) used observational techniques to estimate the racial/ethnic distributions of the driving and speeding population along the I-95 corridor. Lamberth's analysis showed that blacks comprised 16.9% of the drivers and 17.5% of speeders, while the MSP data indicated that black drivers were the subjects of 72.9% of all searches—a considerable disparity.

Lamberth's work in New Jersey (1994) and Maryland (1996) served as a model for future attempts to detect and measure racial profiling. Vehicle stop data collection systems require officers to collect important pieces of information on every stop, including (but not limited to) the driver's race/ethnicity, sex, age, time and location of the stop, reason for the stop, stop result, whether or not a search was conducted, contraband found during searches, and a variety of other variables. The type and amount of information collected, the collection method,[23] and coding schemes differ from project to project, but the

---

[23] Vehicle stop data are generally collected by having officers complete a paper form or "contact card" (Withrow 2002, 2006) following each stop, by

core idea of obtaining a census of officer contacts is a unifying feature of vehicle stop data collection systems. This methodology solves for the problems associated with using arrest records and patrol and communication logs as data sources, and expands on the MSP data collection project by including data on all vehicle stops, not just those involving searches.

The collection of vehicle stop data by individual law enforcement agencies has been brought about by a variety of precipitating events and legal factors. The U.S. Department of Justice integrated vehicle stop data collection systems into their negotiations with police departments under investigation for civil rights violations. Federal consent decrees and memorandums of understanding entered into by the Department of Justice and law enforcement agencies in Pittsburgh (PA) in 1997, New Jersey in 1999, Los Angeles (CA) and Montgomery County (MD) in 2000, the District of Columbia and Highland Park (IL) in 2001, Cincinnati (OH) in 2002, and Mount Prospect (IL) in 2003 included vehicle stop data collection as a tool for monitoring departmental compliance. Twenty-five states enacted legislation that requires agencies to collect data, and agencies in 21 additional states either have collected or are collecting data without legislative mandate.[24]

Vehicle stop data collection projects have gathered vast amounts of data on officer contacts, and nearly every project has noted some differences between whites and minorities in terms of their experiences. On the whole, these data have revealed several noteworthy patterns in the following areas:

- *Frequency of Stop.* Researchers frequently use U.S. Census data or observational techniques like those employed by Lamberth (1994; 1996) to construct population benchmarks to aid in the analysis of vehicle stop data. By comparing the racial/ethnic distribution of vehicle stop data to these benchmarks, researchers can estimate disparities in stop frequency. Studies in Connecticut (Cox et. al. 2001), Erie (PA) (Gamble et. al. 2002), Kansas (Lamberth 2003a), Massachusetts (Farrell et. al. 2004), Minnesota (Institute on Race

---

submitting the information electronically via computer (Smith and Petrocelli 2001), or both (Cox et. al. 2001).

[24] Retrieved April 9, 2007 (http://www.racialprofilinganalysis.neu.edu/background/jurisdictions.php).

and Poverty 2003), Missouri (Rojek, Rosenfeld, and Decker 2004), Nevada (McCorkle 2003), Overland Park (KS) (Novak 2004), Riverside (CA) (Gaines 2003), Rhode Island (Farrell et. al. 2003), San Jose (CA) (Lansdowne 2001), St. Paul (MN) (Institute on Race and Poverty 2001), Tennessee (Morgan 2002), and Texas (Steward 2004) showed that black drivers were stopped more frequently than white drivers. Vehicle stop studies in Kansas (Lamberth 2003a), Massachusetts (Farrell et. al. 2004), Nevada (McCorkle 2003), Richmond (VA) (Smith and Petrocelli 2001), Santa Cruz (CA) (Rickabaugh 2003), and Texas (Steward 2004) demonstrated that Latino drivers were stopped more frequently than white drivers.

- *Citations and Arrests.* Data on racial/ethnic disparities in the issuance of citations is conflicted. Evidence that black and Latino drivers were cited less frequently than white drivers was found in studies in Cincinnati (OH) (Eck, Liu, and Bostaph 2003), Denver (CO) (Thomas 2002), Louisville (KY) (Edwards et. al. 2002b), Nevada (McCorkle 2003), Richmond (VA) (Smith and Petrocelli 2001), Riverside (CA) (Gaines 2003), San Jose (CA) (Lansdowne 2001), St. Paul (MN) (Institute on Race and Poverty 2001), and Wichita (KS) (Withrow 2002). Studies in Massachusetts (Farrell et. al. 2004) and Overland Park (KS) (Novak 2004) found that nonwhite drivers were more likely to be cited compared to white drivers, and the Institute on Race and Poverty (2003) found that, across all Minnesota law enforcement agencies, Latino drivers were more likely than white drivers to receive citations. In terms of arrests, studies in Cincinnati (OH) (Eck et. al. 2003), Louisville (KY) (Edwards et. al. 2002b), Minnesota (MN) (Institute on Race and Poverty 2003), Missouri (Nixon 2003), Nevada (McCorkle 2003), Riverside (CA) (Gaines 2003), Tennessee (Morgan 2002), and Wichita (KS) (Withrow 2002) showed that black and Latino drivers were more likely than white drivers to be arrested.

- *Searches.* Vehicle stop data has consistently demonstrated disparities between minority drivers and white drivers in terms of search frequency. Studies in Cincinnati (OH) (Eck et. al. 2003), Connecticut (Cox et. al. 2001), Denver (CO) (Thomas 2002), Erie (PA) (Gamble et. al. 2002), Iowa City (Edwards et. al. 2002a), Lansing (MA) (Carter, Katz-Bannister, and Shafer 2002),

Massachusetts (Farrell et. al. 2004), Missouri (Rojek et. al. 2004), Nevada (McCorkle 2003), North Carolina (Zingraff et. al. 2000), Oakland (CA) (Word 2004), Pennsylvania (Engel et. al. 2004), Sacramento (CA) (Greenwald 2003), San Antonio (TX) (Lamberth 2003b), San Diego (CA) (Cordner, Williams, and Velasco 2002), St. Paul (MN) (Institute on Race and Poverty 2001), Tennessee (Morgan 2002), Texas (Steward 2004), Washington state (Lovrich et. al. 2003) and Wichita (KS) (Withrow 2002) all showed that larger percentages of black and/or Latino drivers were searched compared to white drivers.

The meaning of differences like those listed above is a matter of considerable debate. In his initial research in New Jersey (1994) and Maryland (1996), Lamberth concluded that the observed disparities were evidence of racial profiling. However, most studies have been much more guarded in their conclusions, acknowledging that:

> Racial disparities in traffic stops can be produced by a number of factors that we are just beginning to understand, only one of which is racial bias on the part of individual officers. For example, certain department enforcement strategies or allocation of patrol resources—while perhaps race neutral on their face—may result in the disparate treatment of racial groups (Farrell et. al. 2003:6).

Accounting for the influence of other relevant variables on the presence of disparities in vehicle stop data has, for the most part, been interpreted as a methodological, as opposed to a theoretical, imperative. Researchers have interpreted this as a call to employ multivariate analysis techniques in their examination of vehicle stop data (McMahon et. al. 2002). This has led agencies to collect data on a variety of demographic variables and descriptive characteristics of stops as part of their data collection projects, mostly on an ad-hoc basis and in pursuit of statistical control in regression models. However, the recognition that observed differences between racial/ethnic groups are the result of multiple influences also has profound theoretical consequences. In order to effectively design data collection systems and properly analyze vehicle stop data, it is important not only to identify factors that contribute to the emergence of racial/ethnic disparities in law enforcement practices, but also to understand how and why these variables exert their influence. Racial profiling research currently lacks a theoretical foundation that classifies these factors with attention to underlying causal themes, though some vital work has already occurred. Bernard and Engel (2001) and Engel et. al. (2002) draw out the essential distinction between three categories of factors that shape enforcement patterns: the behavior of individual actors, the behavior of specific agencies or groups, and the behavior and characteristics of the criminal justice system as a whole. In the following section, I present a framework that expands on this typology and illustrates how diverse explanations and considerations combine to produce racial/ethnic differences in law enforcement practices, and by extension vehicle stop data.

A FRAMEWORK FOR INTERPRETING DIFFERENCES IN VEHICLE STOP DATA

Explanations of racial/ethnic differences observed in law enforcement practices in general, and in vehicle stop data specifically, fall into two broad categories. Differential enforcement theories cite the asymmetrical application of the law and the uneven distribution of law enforcement resources across racial/ethnic groups as the primary source of differences, placing the majority of the blame on the police, as well as overarching aspects of the criminal justice system. In contrast, differential offending theories claim that members of different racial/ethnic groups commit crimes at varying rates, often explicitly alleging that minorities (blacks and Latinos specifically) are disproportionately involved in criminal conduct. As such, this theory maintains that the disparities reflect racial/ethnic differences in the population of criminals. Both perspectives are complex and multifaceted; however, when considering racial profiling, the components of differential enforcement are of more interest than those associated with differential offending. One distinction in particular is critical to the analysis of differential enforcement—the differentiation between individuals and institutions. As I will demonstrate throughout the following section, racial profiling critics and law enforcement agencies both have focused almost exclusively on individual officers as the problem's source, inexplicably neglecting institutional factors.

To facilitate the thorough analysis of vehicle stop data, and to guide future data collection projects, I present a six-part framework that integrates explicit and implicit explanations using the basic theoretical distinctions discussed here. In this framework, I identify three primary causal theories, one complimentary causal theory, and two contextualizing factors.

Causal Theory One: Individual Officer Beliefs and Behavior

Much of the discussion on racial profiling has pointed to racial/ethnic stereotypes held by officers as both the primary cause of differences in enforcement patterns, and the root cause of racial profiling. The fundamental causal claim of this perspective is located at the conceptual intersection between officer beliefs and discretion, asserting that officers draw on these biases in making decisions during their daily enforcement activities.

Ramirez et. al. (2000) note that officers exercise considerable discretion in their enforcement choices:

> Within the area of traffic-stops, for example, police must use reasoned judgment in deciding which cars to stop among the universe of cars being operated in violation of the law. Since many traffic enforcement and vehicle code laws apply to all cars on the road, and since more cars are being operated in violation of the local traffic laws than police have the resources to stop them, officers have a wide discretion in selecting which cars to stop. (P. 9)

Officers do not engage all violators they encounter; rather, they are afforded the power to select which violators they do and do not stop. However, this discretion is not universal—a number of considerations influence and limit the ways in which officers exercise their selection powers. Taken on the whole, officer discretion can be conceptualized as a continuum from low-discretion situations where officers' decisions *not to act* are limited, often by the seriousness or specificity of the offense, to high-discretion situations where officers have considerable selection freedom. High-discretion situations are of the greatest concern in relation to racial profiling because such circumstances readily allow for prejudices and stereotypes to enter into officers decision-making processes. Furthermore, the vast majority of vehicle stops, especially pretext stops, fall on the high-discretion end of the spectrum.

In reference to officer beliefs, there is an important distinction to be drawn between the concepts of racial/ethnic prejudice and stereotypes. In his classic work, Allport ([1954] 1979) defines prejudice:

> Ethnic prejudice is an antipathy based on faulty and inflexible generalizations. It may be felt or expressed. It may be directed toward a group as a whole, or toward an individual because he [sic] is a member of that group. The net effect of prejudice, thus defined, is to place the object of prejudice at some disadvantage not merited by his [sic] own misconduct. (P. 9)

Allport notes that prejudices are stubborn insofar as they are resistant to evidence and arguments that contradict the position. He further links prejudices to discriminatory conduct:

> It is true that any negative attitude tends somehow, somewhere, to express itself in action. Few people keep their antipathies entirely to themselves. The more intense the attitude, the more likely it is to result in vigorously hostile action. (P. 14)

Allport presents a range of negative actions associated with racial/ethnic prejudice, including antilocution (antagonistic speech), avoidance, discrimination, and violence. In sum, racial/ethnic prejudice can be understood deep-seated ideologies that inform all aspects of an individual's personality and guide his or her actions—a condition that would be labeled as racism in a common vernacular. Wilson, Dunham, and Alpert (2004) point out that the issue of prejudice has been largely ignored in racial profiling research. Police supporters and many racial profiling critics reject, either explicitly or implicitly, the idea that entrenched prejudices cause the majority of differences in enforcement practices. Most grant that there may be a small number of "bad apples" in law enforcement agencies who hold such prejudices; however, given the attention paid to racial/ethnic relations within many law enforcement agencies, the number of prejudiced officers is likely too small to produce the magnitude of differences identified in some vehicle stop data collection projects.

Furthermore, McMahon et. al. (2002) observe that those officers who are able to maintain such prejudices despite the current levels of scrutiny are likely to be resourceful enough to conceal their conduct from monitoring techniques.

Ramirez et. al. (2000) and many others argue that racial/ethnic stereotypes, as opposed to prejudices, are responsible for the differences observed in vehicle stop projects. While racial/ethnic prejudices are deeply ingrained, stereotypes tend to lack antipathy and focus more on the simplification and broad application of beliefs about the psychological and behavioral characteristics of racial/ethnic groups. Feagin ([1978] 1989) defines stereotyping as "an overgeneralization associated with a racial or ethnic category that goes beyond existing evidence" (p. 11). Allport ([1954] 1979) contends that stereotypes (racial and otherwise) are constructed through the process of categorization (which is essential to the functioning of the human mind), and that these prejudgments can develop into racial/ethnic prejudices. Paul (1974) argues that racial/ethnic prejudices, or at the very least hatred and hostility, are not a necessary element of stereotypes, noting that they are the product of normal, unavoidable, often unconscious psychological and social psychological processes. Because they are rooted in the unconscious workings of the mind, Paul notes that stereotypes can exercise a profound influence on peoples' decisions and actions, even in cases where individuals hold conscious beliefs that contradict the stereotype. This is not to say that resistance to stereotypes is impossible, but rather that it is a difficult undertaking—while aspects of the stereotype can be suppressed through conscious checks on behavior, other unconscious elements are likely to be expressed through subtle cues. When conscious barriers are lacking, or when aspects of the social world validate stereotypes (not only through evidence, but also through the reinforcement of social groups), then stereotypes can produce discriminatory conduct similar to, though not necessarily as severe or entrenched as, prejudices. Paul's contention that everyone holds stereotypes and thus has the capacity to participate in discriminatory conduct is a considerable departure from Adorno's (1950) conceptualization of the authoritarian personality, where acts of discrimination are linked to a specific personality type.

Implicit in many discussions of the links between policing, prejudice, and stereotypes is the idea that only a small group of "bad apples" rely on such beliefs about racial/ethnic groups in their enforcement practices (Tator and Henry 2006). The notion of "bad apples" and their impact on racial profiling draws heavily on research on police violence and brutality. In his research on police misconduct in minority communities, Ogletree (1995) found evidence that civilian complaints regarding the excessive use of force by officers were often concentrated around "certain officers, accompanied by a departmental failure to monitor and discipline them" (p. 46). Two studies cited by Ogletree support the contention that only a small number of officers were responsible for a significant portion of civilian complaints:

> The Christopher Commission Report found that 254 of the 1,931 (Los Angeles) police officers complained of were named in three or more incident reports and represented 30 percent of the complaints; 47 officers had five or more complaints...A 1992 investigative series in the Boston Globe found that "11 percent of all officers were named in 61.5 percent of the complaints, while two thirds of all officers had no abuse complaints." The Globe study also reported that "(f)ive officers had been investigated by the internal affairs division of the Boston Police Department one hundred times between 1981 and 1990 on complaints ranging from harassment and verbal abuse to illegal search, false arrest, and physical abuse." (P. 46-47)

While considerably more muted, this "bad apple" theme is present in the literature on racial profiling. In their resource guide on racial profiling data collection systems, Ramirez et. al. (2000) contend that "(t)he majority of police officers are hard-working public servants who perform a dangerous job with dedication and honor; however, the perceptions that some police officers are engaging in racial profiling has created resentment and distrust of the police, particularly in communities of color" (p. 3). In the process of explicitly acknowledging the good work of the "majority" of officers, the authors suggest that it is a small group of officers who employ racial profiling tactics and strategies.

It is important to note that "bad apple" theory is not simply a product of apologetic or inclusive rhetoric—it has been integrated into several vehicle stop data collection projects. The consent decree that led to the collection of vehicle stop data in New Jersey required the recording of the officer's identification number in the data for the express purpose of tracking the actions of individual officers. Walker (2001) supports using vehicle stop data collections systems as an "early warning system" to help identify "bad apples". By comparing the racial/ethnic distribution of drivers stopped by individual officers assigned to specific districts during similar shifts, Walker argues that researchers can determine which, if any, officers are responsible for racial profiling.

Causal Theory Two: Institutional Features of Law Enforcement Agencies

The impact of institutional features of law enforcement agencies on racial profiling has been neglected in the vast majority of studies, many of which have preferred to focus on issues of stereotypes and the problem of "bad apples." In fact, very few institutional explanations have developed in opposition to the popular "bad apple" perspective (Tator and Henry 2006), which essentially blames problems associated with differential enforcement on individual officers who fail to conform to the expectations of the institution. According to the "bad apple" perspective, the biased practices of a small number of officers are viewed as deviations from institutional rules and norms, thus casting the institution as bias-free, just, and part of the solution (as opposed to part of the problem). Harris (2002) argues that the institution of law enforcement is not a benevolent force that promotes bias-free policing and fights against racial/ethnic prejudices and stereotypes. To the contrary, he contends that institutional features of law enforcement agencies are at the core of differential enforcement. In contrast to the "bad apple" perspective, which defines differential enforcement as an aberration, an institutional perspective conceptualizes the occurrence of biased enforcement as a product of normal and accepted institutional functions, and a reflection of racial/ethnic biases built into the institution.

A multitude of institutional features influence when, where, and how officers enforce the law, and as such these elements can dramatically impact the presence of disparities in enforcement practices and vehicle stop data. Drawing on the historical roots of racial profiling, officer training and special enforcement programs (like drug interdiction) are of particular interest. Strangely, the fact that the initial complaints about racial profiling were directly linked to criminal profiling programs is missing from most research on racial profiling (Engel et. al. 2002). Along these lines, other departmental programs, policies, standards, rules, and procedures can have an effect on enforcement patterns. Ogletree's (1995) discussion of civilian complaint and officer disciplinary procedures illustrates how law enforcement institutions fail to address problems associated with "bad apples," and as such are at the very least complicit in these officers' crimes. Resource allocation is also likely to impact enforcement patterns, most notably in terms of officer deployment and scheduling. Resource limitations compel agencies deploy officers strategically (Cole and Smith 2007). This inevitably results in an increased number of officers and officer hours assigned to "high crime areas," which are often defined by crime rates, volume of civilian calls for assistance, general perceptions of crime (held by both the police and the public) and other social control issues. Related to resource allocation problems is the issue of prioritization. In every law enforcement agency, certain classifications of criminal behavior are given priority, meaning that officers are instructed (explicitly or implicitly) to be particularly attentive to these categories of crime and criminals. These moral enterprises (Becker 1963) frequently take the form of "wars," such as the War on Drugs, a national campaign designed to focus law enforcement attention and resources on interrupting the flow and sale of illegal drugs. Ferrell (1993) provides a detailed example of Denver's "clampdown" on graffiti, which involved a coordinated effort by city government and business leaders and resulted in a considerable investment of law enforcement resources in pursuit of a small number of local graffiti writers. Finally, the occupational culture and subculture of law enforcement plays a significant role in socializing officers (Bayley and Bittner [1984] 1999; Herbert 1998; Hunt 1985; Kappeler et. al. [1998] 2001; Sherman [1998] 1999; Terrill, Paoline III, and Manning 2003), and as such the definitions and ideologies promoted within this culture have a profound impact on officers' conduct. Given the history of racial/ethnic hostility that has characterized law enforcement culture,[25] it is possible, if not likely, that socialization processes actually produce and propagate racial/ethnic stereotypes.

When discussing the roles played by law enforcement as an institution in the production of racial/ethnic disparities in enforcement practices, it is important to address the concept of racism. Tatum

---

[25] See Chapter Two for additional discussion.

From Disparities to Discrimination

(1997) points out that many treat the terms racism and prejudice as synonyms, failing to grasp the important differences between these concepts. While prejudice can be understood as deep-seated negative feelings associated with racial/ethnic groups, Tatum notes that "racism, like other forms of oppression, is not only a personal ideology based on racial prejudice, but a system involving cultural messages and institutional policies and practices as well as the beliefs and actions of individuals" (p. 127). The institutional component of this conceptualization is very useful when considering the impact of organizational aspects of law enforcement agencies on differential enforcement. Institutional racism refers to discriminatory practices that are "generated by the way institutions function, intentionally or otherwise, rather than the individual personalities of their members" (Lea 2000:219). Institutional racism and associated discriminatory practices are generally embedded in the laws, rules, policies, norms, and standard practices of an institution, and can manifest itself in discrimination in a number of ways. Feagin ([1978] 1989) loosely organizes institutionally-based discriminatory practices into two categories—direct institutionalized discrimination, which involves the explicit and intentional targeting of certain racial/ethnic groups, and indirect institutionalized discrimination, which lacks the overt intent but nonetheless results in differential treatment. I include a third category—complicit institutionalized discrimination, where institutions allow for the unjust treatment of certain racial/ethnic groups by failing to adopt rules or policies that prevent discrimination. Each of these three categories of institutionalized racial discrimination require additional discussion. In the process, links between law enforcement and other branches of the criminal justice system will be explored, exposing the interdependencies that perpetuate inequalities both in and beyond criminal justice.

First, direct institutionalized discrimination overtly instructs or prescribes discriminatory practices based on race/ethnicity. The history of U.S. law and policy is filled with cases of state-sponsored racial discrimination, such as Jim Crow laws. While the U.S. Supreme Court was successful in striking down segregation, overtly discriminatory policies and practices still exist throughout the country. For example, accusations of blatant and explicit racial discrimination have been leveled against the War on Drugs in general, and against the DEA specifically. Many have accused the DEA of using race as part of its drug courier profile (Harris 1999). While the evidence against the

DEA is unclear, other sources have shown that law enforcement agencies have sanctioned the use of race as an indicator of suspiciousness. A memorandum uncovered as part of *Wilkins v. Maryland State Police* revealed that MSP troopers had been instructed to target black drivers for stops and searches (Harris 2002). The Florida Department of Highway Safety and Motor Vehicles published a set of drug interdiction guidelines entitled "The Common Characteristics of Drug Couriers" that specifically instructed officers to be suspicious of "ethnic groups associated with the drug trade" (Harris 1999:5).

Second, indirect institutionalized discrimination effectively targets certain racial/ethnic groups through correlates and proxies of race/ethnicity. Instead of explicitly referring to race/ethnicity, institutional rules and policies focus on characteristics associated with certain racial/ethnic groups. One of the most notable instances of indirect institutionalized discrimination is the differential sentencing guidelines for powder and crack cocaine. Kennedy (1997) offers a summary of this disparity:

> Under the federal Anti-Drug Abuse Act of 1986, a person convicted of possession with intent to distribute fifty grams or more of crack cocaine must be sentenced to no less than ten years in prison. By contrast, only if a person is convicted of possession with intent to distribute at least 5,000 grams of powder cocaine is subject to a mandatory minimum (sentence) of ten years—a 100:1 ratio in terms of intensity of punishment. Moreover, under the federal Anti-Drug Abuse Act of 1988, a person caught merely possessing one to five grams of crack cocaine is subject to a mandatory minimum sentence of five years in prison. Crack cocaine is the only drug for which there exists a mandatory minimum sentence for a first offense of simple possession. (P. 364)

Taken at face value, these laws may seem strange simply because the drugs in question appear to be the same—they are both cocaine. However, when the distribution of convictions by race/ethnicity is examined, a clear and undeniable pattern of discrimination arises from the data:

From Disparities to Discrimination

In 1992, 92.6 percent of defendants convicted for crack cocaine offenses were black and only 4.7 percent white. In comparison, 45.2 percent of defendants sentenced for powder cocaine were white, and only 20.7 percent black. (Kennedy 1997:364-365)

While many have argued that these differences are simply a reflection of the demographic characteristics of the offender population, Lockwood et. al. (1995) call into question the assertion that blacks make up the majority of the crack cocaine users. Utilizing data from the 1991 National Institute of Drug Abuse (NIDA) Household Survey, they found that 35.9% of crack users were black, 14.2% of users were Latino, and 49.9% of users were white. Kennedy (1997) links these demographic disparities between the user population and those convicted for cocaine charges to the imagery associated with crack cocaine. Said Justice Clyde S. Cahill:

Congress' decision was based in large part...on the racial imagery generated by the media which connected the crack problem with the inner city...(L)egions of newspaper articles regarding the crack cocaine epidemic depicted racial imagery of heavy involvement by blacks in crack cocaine. (P. 376)

Kennedy offers a concise analysis of this situation: "There have been laws, silent as to race, that have directly burdened only a subset of the black population but were intentionally aimed at disadvantaging blacks as a class" (p. 376).

Evidence of this type of institutionalized racial discrimination can be found in the same Florida Department of Highway Safety and Motor Vehicles publication mentioned earlier. In addition to instructing officers to target individuals of certain racial and ethnic backgrounds, the guidelines also told officers to be suspicious of drivers who wore "lots of gold" or who did not "fit the vehicle" (Harris 1999:5). The former appears to be a reference to the large gold chains (ropes), rings (including multiple finger rings), bracelets, watches, and possibly earrings on females. These are all stylistic elements that were cultivated in relation to the hip-hop subculture of the mid-1980's. While these symbols have been redefined and re-appropriated over the past 20 years, the link between race and certain types of gold jewelry appears to be quite clear for the historical period in question. The latter element of the Florida guidelines is less specific about racial proxies. Instead, this direction relies on the officer's ability to identify suspicious characteristics, magnifying the officer's biases and predispositions.

Third, unlike direct and indirect institutionalized discrimination, complicit institutionalized discrimination does not guide or instruct individual action; rather, this form focuses on the failure of institutions to check and prevent discriminatory practices. Institutional rules and policies create openings for people to exercise discretion in their decision-making. In and of itself, discretion is neither good nor bad, bias-free nor racist. However, when institutional rules and procedures lack specificity on issues of race/ethnicity, then discrimination is a relatively predictable outcome.

The United States Supreme Court's decision on the constitutionality of pretext stops serves as an example of this type of institutionalized discrimination. Pretext stops involve officers using "minor traffic infractions, real or alleged, as an excuse to stop and search a vehicle and its passengers," (Harris 1999:7). The U.S. Supreme Court affirmed this practice in 1996, and in its decision on *Whren v. United States*, the Court held that "the temporary detention of a motorist upon probable cause to believe that he [sic] has violated the traffic laws does not violate the Fourth Amendment's prohibition against unreasonable seizures, even if a reasonable officer would not have stopped the motorist absent some additional law enforcement objective," (P. 806). O'Reilly (2002) notes that, under the *Whren* decision, the test for the reasonableness of a vehicle stop under the Fourth Amendment is whether or not a traffic violation was observed by the officer, and not what actually motivated the officer to conduct the stop. The *Whren* ruling allows police discretion to go relatively unchecked in terms of racial/ethnic biases and discrimination, and Harris believes this contributes to the continued targeting and persecution of black and Latino drivers:

> In practice, the *Whren* decision has given the police virtually unlimited authority to stop and search any vehicle they want. Every driver probably violates some provision of the vehicle code at some time during even a short drive, because state traffic codes identify so many different infractions. For example, traffic codes define precisely how long a driver must

signal before turning, and the particular conditions under which a driver must use lights. Vehicle equipment is also highly regulated. A small bulb must illuminate the rear license plate...Tire tread must be at a particular depth. All equipment must be in working order at all times. If the police target a driver for a stop and search, all they have to do to come up with a pretext stop is follow the car until the driver makes an inconsequential error or until a technical violation is observed. (1999:8)

In sum, because the *Whren* decision allows for the presence of a law violation to override other considerations (at least in terms of the Fourth Amendment), the institution has preserved and protected an opportunity for racial/ethnic discrimination, and as such is complicit in the differential treatment that is almost sure to follow.

Beyond *Whren*, several additional Supreme Court decisions shed additional light on institutional complicity in perpetuating racial/ethnic discrimination both in and beyond law enforcement. *United States v. Armstrong*[26] established that defendants accusing officials of selective prosecution must demonstrate that "the Government declined to prosecute similarly situated suspects of other races" (p. 458). While *Batson v. Kentucky*[27] forbade the use of peremptory challenges to remove jurors based on race or sex, *Purkett v. Elem*[28] allowed prosecutors to "put forward silly, superstitious, an implausible reasons [for the removal of a juror] as long as the trial judge accepts the exclusion as being based on something other than race or gender" (Cole and Smith 2007:372). Despite overwhelming statistical evidence demonstrating that black defendants were more likely to receive the death penalty, the Supreme Court held in *McCleskey v. Kemp*[29] that the defendant "must prove that the decisionmakers in his [*sic*] case acted with discriminatory purpose" (p. 292).

Causal Theory Three: Civilian Behavior

This causal theory draws directly (though not exclusively) on the on the idea of differential offending. Officers consistently cite law violations

---

[26] 517 U.S. 456 (1996).
[27] 476 U.S. 79 (1986).
[28] 514 US 765 (1995).
[29] 481 U.S. 279 (1987).

as the primary, if not the sole, reason for action, and claim that racial/ethnic disparities in enforcement patterns reflect larger disparities between groups in terms of the frequency and severity of law violations. Differential offending theory is so popular among law enforcement officials that several studies have integrated complex methodologies designed to measure racial/ethnic differences in terms of moving violations, specifically speeding, into their analyses of vehicle stop data (Lamberth 1994, 1996; Lange, Blackman, and Johnson 2001; Lange et. al. 2005). Traffic law and vehicle code violations are not the only pertinent forms of offending under this theory; in fact, any law violations that are unevenly dispersed across racial/ethnic groups are of interest because these differences could be used by officers as underlying justifications for differential enforcement tactics.

While offending is at the heart of this theory, other aspects of civilian conduct that could reasonably impact law enforcement are also important when considering the totality of this perspective. For instance, the ways in which civilians interact with officers can have a profound impact on the transaction. Studies indicate that civilian demeanor can impact officers' decision-making.[30] More specifically, civilians who are impolite or disrespectful are more likely to be arrested (Black [1971] 2001). Cross-cultural differences can also impact officer decision-making, though this issue is difficult to address because the line between these differences and officer beliefs can be very complicated. Cultural elements can tap into stereotypes, and such cases clearly appeal to officer beliefs as the primary causal theory. However, there are cases where cultural differences lead to simple, relatively innocent misunderstandings between civilians and officers. In an effort to combat officer ignorance of cultural differences, many law enforcement agencies have instituted diversity training programs designed to educate their employees so that they can respond appropriately. Barlow and Barlow (1993) criticize the effectiveness of cultural diversity training programs, claiming that they fail to address larger institutional and structural issues that produce and reinforce officers' biases and ignorance. Unless conducted in a highly detailed and cautious fashion, and unless officers actually engage the materials in these programs, such trainings run the danger of not only buttressing

---

[30] See Lundman (1994) for a summary of past studies, and Klinger (1994) for a critique.

From Disparities to Discrimination

stereotypes, but also giving officers additional tools with which they can discriminate against certain racial/ethnic groups. By defining the characteristics of a racial/ethnic group with broad strokes (e.g. by identifying a unified "black perspective" or a singular "Latino culture"), those who do not fall into the presented framework could easily appear deviant, and therefore suspicious, to officers.

It is very difficult to account for the effects of differential offending, in part because of the popularity of this theory. In response to accusations of racial profiling, law enforcement officers, management, politicians, and supporters continue to rely heavily on this explanation. Coverage of racial profiling has frequently referred to the idea that different racial/ethnic groups violate laws at different rates. Additionally, there is considerable evidence that the institutional faith in this perspective predates the racial profiling controversy (Bittner 1990; Black 1980; Black and Reiss 1967; Brown 1981; Niederhoffer 1967; Skolnick 1966; Westley 1970; Wilson 1978). Therefore, it is reasonable to assume that all officers have at the very least been exposed to this theory, and it is likely that at least some officers subscribe to this perspective and refer to it in the process of enforcing the law. This is where complications arise—when officers believe in differential offending, and when this belief impacts officers' decisions and actions, the possible presence of differential offending becomes conflated with the effects of officers' beliefs. Commitment to the idea of differential offending is likely to produce self-fulfilling prophecies wherein disproportionate numbers of minority civilians are targeted for enforcement, and in turn these results serve as supporting evidence (albeit contaminated) that further perpetuate this theory. Officers' reliance on differential offending theory is no different than any other racial/ethnic stereotype that may encroach on officer decision-making processes. As such, the mere positing of this explanation casts considerable suspicion on law enforcement agencies, for any "kernel of truth" (if one exists) to differential offending theory is likely to be exaggerated considerably through the integration of differential offending theory into officers' belief systems and decision-making processes. Furthermore, the empirical task of disentangling the effects of perceptions of differential offending from any actual evidence of differential offending in vehicle stop data is a very challenging undertaking.

Complementary Causal Theory: Racism, Discrimination, and Inequality in Institutions Other Than Law Enforcement

Engel et. al. (2002) call attention to the difference between institutional factors that influence enforcement at the departmental or agency level, and characteristics of the criminal justice system as a whole. The policies and practices of the courts and corrections, as well the decisions of individual actors within these institutions, have an acute impact on the work of the police officers and agencies. As was illustrated earlier in this chapter, Supreme Court decisions like *Whren* fail to limit police discretion, providing legally defensible opportunities for discrimination. Other rulings, like *Armstrong* and *McCleskey*, establish unreasonable, even ridiculous, standards for proving discrimination, further protecting officers and agencies. Laws may place premiums on certain racialized crimes, like crack cocaine or gang violence, thus providing incentives for law enforcement to target racial/ethnic minorities. Such policies related to the War on Drugs resulted in approximately one in three black males between the ages of 20 and 29 being under some form of supervision by the criminal justice system in 1995 (Mauer 1999), increasing the suspiciousness of this group in the eyes of law enforcement. Also, the failure of the criminal justice system to appropriately punish offenders, most notably in terms of lenient plea bargains and lax prison release programs, contribute to cynicism among officers (Skolnick 1966), which serves as a justification for the use of force in the distribution of "street justice" (Waegel 1984).

The feedback loop of criminality created by law enforcement, the court system, and corrections is by no means discrete; its effects can be felt across, even amplified through, other social institutions. Consider the effects of incarceration: research by Bonczar and Beck (1997), Chiricos and Crawford (1995), and Zatz (1987) establishes that minorities are more likely than whites to be sentenced to prison. Incarceration has a profound impact families and children; Mumola's (2000) research indicates that 55.4% of all federal and state prisoners are parents of minor children. Experiences with parental incarceration were differentially distributed across racial/ethnic groups, with 7% of all black children and 2.8% of all Latino children living with at least one parent residing in prison, compared to 0.8% of white children. Incarceration not only weakens family relationships (Western, Pattillo, and Weiman 2004), it can also impact children's self-esteem and inhibit emotional and cognitive development (Travis and Waul 2003). Research further suggests that children of incarcerated parents are at higher risk for conduct problems and delinquency (Eddy and Reid 2003:251), which in turn increases the likelihood that these children will come into contact with law enforcement at some point in their lives.

Incarceration also impacts the economic security of individuals and families alike. When a parent is sent to prison, families lose a source of financial support—a burden that is disproportionately visited upon minority families (Travis and Waul 2003). Financial challenges persist even after release: changes to welfare policies have expanded the power of agencies to ban drug offenders and parole and probation violators from receiving certain types of public assistance, further exacerbating economic hardships. There is also evidence that post-release economic burdens are differential distributed across racial/ethnic groups. Pager's (2003) research examined the impact of imprisonment on employment opportunities with special attention to race; she found that blacks without criminal records, much less those with records, had fewer job opportunities that whites with criminal records. Mann (1995) observes that the links between unemployment, poverty, and crime, most notably violent crime, are well established in the literature. Considering the connections between violent crime and drugs, many of which were media constructions related to the War on Drugs (Chiricos [1998] 2002), this analysis provides yet another link back to the work of the police.

As the preceding discussion illustrates, the racial/ethnic inequalities produced through the machinations of multiple social institutions contribute to law enforcement patterns in a number of ways, two of which are especially relevant to the problem of racial profiling. First, the history of prejudice, discrimination, and systemic racism realized through and reinforced across social institutions in American society has resulted in the entrenchment of poverty and social isolation in minority communities. According to the 2000 U.S. Census, 9.1% of all whites lived below the poverty line, compared to 22.6% of all Latinos and 24.9% of all blacks.[31] Massey and Denton (1993) and Wilson (1997) describe how law, policy, culture, and other social forces have combined to (re)produce a minority underclass that is

---

[31] Retrieved April 24, 2007 (http://www.census.gov).

geographically segregated from other populations. As a result of both isolation and the persistence of poverty in these areas, social problems have become territorialized, or connected with certain locales and neighborhoods. By territorializing social issues, the causal influence of structural factors, like the breakdown of employment opportunities or enduring educational disadvantages (Kozol 1991), is minimized in favor of explanations that emphasize immediate ecological conditions; for instance, research by Fagan and Davies (2004) links neighborhood disadvantage to increases in homicide rates for blacks. In terms of policing, the net impact of such ecological and territorial perspectives is the definition of certain neighborhoods as trouble areas or "hot spots", particularly in relation to violent crime and gang and drug activity. As such, when examining enforcement patterns, particularly those related to racial profiling, it is vital to account for the influence of ecology and territory insofar as they comprise a significant portion of the milieu of police action (Parker et. al. 2004). In terms of the effects of context, Herbert (2001) notes that police are drawn to dangerous territories because they allow officers to employ hypermasculine "crime fighting" tactics. In this sense, social problems related ecologies of disadvantage become the justification for police reliance on aggressive militaristic enforcement strategies in these areas (Kraska and Kappeler 1997). In addition to setting a tactical imperative, ecological factors also dictate population expectations, or who police should encounter in certain areas, as well as who is "out of place". Meehan and Ponder (2002b) found that police surveillance of black drivers increased substantially when these drivers ventured into predominantly white neighborhoods

Second, the links between race/ethnicity and poverty influence vehicle ownership and equipment violations. First and foremost, individuals and families living in poverty are less likely to own an automobile; Engel and Calnon (2004a) cite a Federal Highway Administration study demonstrating that blacks were "considerably more likely to live in households without a vehicle" (p. 101). This means that impoverished groups are less likely to be part of the driving population. As a result, the driving population of a given area is likely to have a higher percentage of whites compared to the residential population, which means that comparisons between vehicle stop data and residential population estimates (such as U.S. Census data) inevitably underestimate the disparities between white and minority drivers. Also, people living in poverty are less likely to have sufficient funds to keep their automobiles in legal condition. Vehicle codes are notoriously complicated and detailed; they frequently include standards that address legally acceptable levels of disrepair, safety features, emissions standards, licensing, and insurance. In many jurisdictions, these standards are intertwined, meaning that vehicle registration is contingent on the automobile passing a safety inspection, the owner having proof of insurance, and/or an emissions test. As such, the financial inability to address only one of these small-scale problems will snowball and create more substantial legal issues.

Contextualizing Factor One: History

Any examination of racial profiling, theoretical or empirical, must be attentive to historical factors. History is the lens through which actions are interpreted, and as such a wide range of historical factors must be considered. A broad and deep history of race relations will provide insight into the development of cultural beliefs and customs. In addition to this, recent socially, politically, and culturally relevant events from across the nation, possibly even across the world, must also be considered in such an analysis. Modern news coverage and information technology bring events and issues from a multitude of locales to individuals all over the world, and events from hundreds, if not thousands, of miles away can have an impact on the attitudes and beliefs of civilians as well as law enforcement.

At the same time, local histories must not be neglected, for they also have an impact on the relationship between civilians and law enforcement. Relevant events, both recent and years removed, can have a profound affect on the way communities view law enforcement and vice versa. The experiences of Rodney King in Los Angeles, Amadou Diallo and Abner Louima in New York, Jonny Gammage in Pittsburgh (Harris 1999), David Bell Jr. in Louisiana (Ruiz and Woessner 2006), and John Gainer in Eugene, Oregon resonate with civilians and the police, often rising as the symbolic embodiment of racial/ethnic conflict between these groups. At the same time, it is important to recognize that knowledge of these and other high-profile incidents is not limited to local areas, illustrating the necessity of a multi-layered perspective on history. Furthermore, local historical analyses should also move beyond issues directly related to racial profiling and should examine broad-based issues of racial/ethnic relations and general issues of law enforcement. By casting a wide net the overall historical portrait will be more complete and more useful in making sense of enforcement patterns and police-community relations.

Contextualizing Factor Two: Causal Overlap and Selectivity

Causal factors that produce differences in enforcement practices are complex and interrelated, with differing levels of salience for each theory at different points in the selection process. Lieberson (1985) argues that selection bias is a cause for concern in much of social science research, and as such an analysis of the factors that impact the selection of cases for inclusion is vital to understanding patterns in the data. The lessons set forward by Lieberson can be used to aid in the interpretation of racial/ethnic disparities in vehicle stop data, not simply because vehicle stop data is social science data, but rather because systematic selection biases exercise considerable influence on who is stopped by the police.

Offending in the population as a whole is the first level of selection (see Figure 1), and civilian behavior and institutional features associated with and beyond law enforcement are highly salient at this level. While the link between civilian behavior and offending is clear, it is important to remember that offending is defined through legal codes that embody and reflect institutional imperatives and biases. Furthermore, conflict theorists point out that laws have historically been used by the dominant class to further marginalize, even persecute, subordinate groups. As such, offending cannot simply be understood as an individual behavior or choice, but rather as situated action within systems that are designed to preserve and reproduce existing power relationships. To this end, offending must be viewed as both actions that violate conduct rules as well as systems of social control that define certain actions, places, and people as violators.

There are several additional points associated with this level of selection that require clarification. The theory of differential offending proposes that the size of the violator population is different across racial/ethnic groups, claiming that larger proportions of the black and Latino populations qualify as violators. Of course, the standards used to differentiate violators from non-violators are remarkably broad. While driving behavior and vehicle code violations are the most apparent criteria, the use of vehicle stops as a drug interdiction tactic

Figure 1. Law Violation in the Driving Population

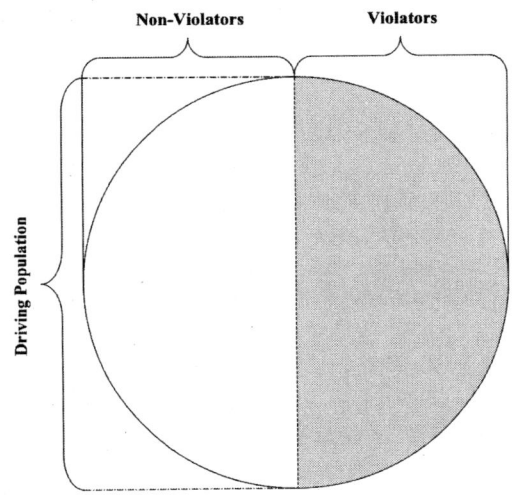

makes drug offending relevant to the determination of the violator population. Other types of crimes are likely relevant to the larger discussion of the of the overall violator population and differences between racial/ethnic groups; however, it is unclear how many of these crimes are actually relevant to the process of conducting vehicle stops. If we limit our focus to driving behavior and vehicle code violations, law enforcement officials point out that most, if not all, drivers— including police officers—violate some aspect of the rules of the road at some point during every trip (Harris 2002). This considerably decreases the importance of differential offending, though differences across racial/ethnic groups in terms of the seriousness of offenses could still be relevant.

Officer observation is the second level of selection in the vehicle stop process (see Figure 2). The selection of vehicles for stops is limited to those drivers observed by officers, and as such deployment practices and other institutional features of law enforcement are highly salient at this level. When officers and officer hours are differentially deployed to areas with higher concentrations of minority residents and/or drivers, the proportion of all stops involving minority drivers will increase regardless of officer beliefs or the presence of differential offending.

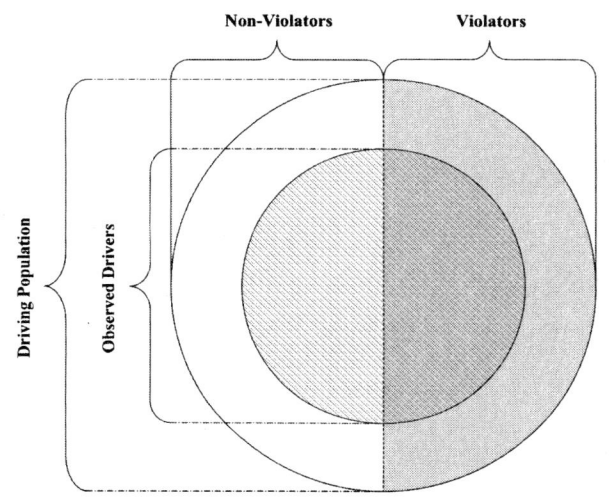

Figure 2. Law Violation in the Driving and Observed Population

The third level of selection is related to the issue of suspicion (see Figure 3). Officers do not simply stop all of those who are in overt violation of the law and ignore those drivers who are not; the decision to stop and investigate a driver involves numerous considerations. It is at this level that officers apply the complex meanings associated with suspicion to their decision-making processes. The type and seriousness of violations are undoubtedly components of suspicion, but by no means is law violation the sole consideration. Other facets of suspicion—such as location, time of day, type of car, etc.—must be addressed when discussing how officers view and act towards the civilian population. When race/ethnicity plays an important role in determining who is and is not suspicious, then racial profiling is a very real possibility.

While the action at this level is most directly related to officer beliefs, it is important not to neglect the institutional forces that contribute to the construction of suspicion. More specifically, training, prioritization, aspects of law enforcement culture and subculture, and other institutional features shape how individual officers construct and comprehend suspicion in their daily work. In order to understand larger questions associated with racial profiling, it is vital to examine

Figure 3. Law Violation and Suspicion in the Driving and Observed Populations

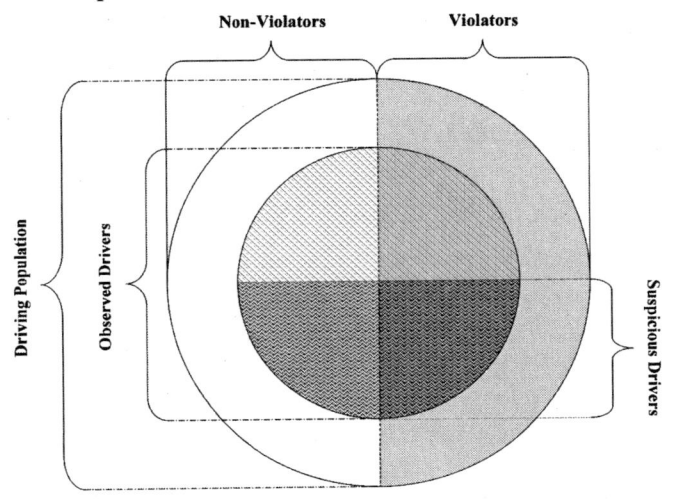

how these social forces and individual experiences come together to produce meanings associated with suspicion. The machinations are intricate and difficult to disentangle, but an understanding of the processes that generate meanings associated with suspicion is the key to designing robust research projects and progressive public policy on these matters.

Officers' decisions regarding who to stop and who not to stop constitutes the fourth level of selection (see Figure 4). As the diagram indicates, officers do not stop all violators they encounter, nor do all non-violators avoid being stopped. Furthermore, not all those individuals that officers consider to be suspicious are stopped. What is at issue in this level of selection is the threshold that separates those who are not stopped from those who are stopped. Racial profiling occurs when race/ethnicity is an important factor in the selection of who, from the observed population, is and is not stopped. To fully ascertain the impact of race/ethnicity on officers' stop decisions, it is necessary to examine information on both those who are stopped, which is captured in the form of vehicle stop data, and those who are not stopped—a population that has largely been neglected in racial profiling research.

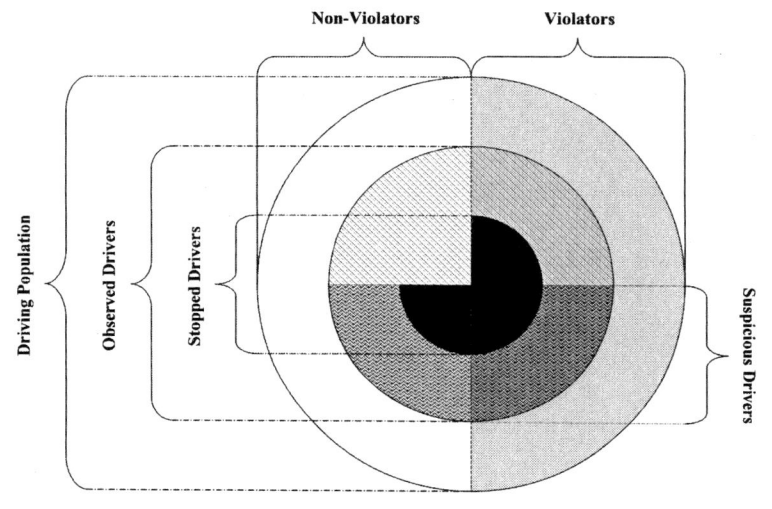

Figure 4. Law Violation, Suspicion, and the Selection of Drivers for Vehicle Stops

CONCLUSION

This chapter examines the explanations frequently used to account for racial/ethnic differences in law enforcement practices, merging existing perspectives into a theoretical framework rooted in sociological traditions. Three primary causal theories explore the dynamics that produce racial/ethnic disparities in law enforcement patterns. The first causal theory focuses on the impact of racial/ethnic prejudices and stereotypes held by officers, hypothesizing that officers' beliefs have an influence on their decision-making processes. The second causal theory centers on the idea that institutional features of law enforcement, such as hiring policies, training, deployment, scheduling, and professional culture, influence when and how officers enforce the law, and who officers come into contact with during their daily routine. The third causal theory addresses the impact of civilian behavior, most notably racial/ethnic differences in law violation, on enforcement patterns. A complementary causal theory works to include the influence of systematic racism, discrimination, and inequalities associated with institutions other than policing in the analysis of racial/ethnic differences in enforcement practices. Two contextualizing factors provide additional structure to inquiries into such disparities. First, the importance of considering a variety of historical factors is emphasized, for the history of a specific area, as well as the surrounding area and the nation as a whole, can exercise a profound influence on the workings of institutions as well as the ways in which civilians and officers view and act towards one another. Second, several important levels of selection are highlighted, demonstrating how causal theories come together to produce differences in enforcement patterns.

The theoretical framework presented in this chapter is designed to guide the analysis of existing vehicle stop data and to provide a foundation for future data collection efforts. For existing studies, theoretically relevant variables should be identified and integrated into multivariate analyses to account for explanations associated with competing perspectives. For future studies, data collection designs should focus on capturing data that can be used to compare and test these perspectives. Several factors will undoubtedly complicate matters for both existing and future research using vehicle stop data. Because the causal theories overlap and intertwine in a number of areas, isolating theoretically exclusive variables will be challenging, if not impossible in some cases. In other words, it is highly unlikely that "pure" indicators of officer beliefs, institutional features of law enforcement, or civilian behavior will be identified, which means that the theoretical interpretation of results will have to be complex, nuanced, and cautious. At this point, this theoretical framework is still in its developmental stages, and as such it should not be used for hypothesis-testing or deductive research. Instead, it commands a more inductive and exploratory approach to facilitate a broad examination of relevant issues and variables.

CHAPTER 4
Case Study: Eugene, Oregon

Located approximately 100 miles south of Portland, Oregon, in the scenic Willamette Valley, Eugene covers 41.5 square miles and is home to the University of Oregon. According to the 2000 U.S. Census, Eugene is second largest city in Oregon with a population of over 137,000, and when combined with the neighboring city of Springfield, the population of the metropolitan area is over 200,000.

The city of Eugene is frequently portrayed in the media as a liberal haven. Eugene's anarchist subculture garnered national media attention during the 1999 World Trade Organization protests in Seattle, and again in 2000 in relation to a riot in downtown Eugene. As a result of students' fervent protesting against the use of sweatshop labor by companies licensed to produce university products, Mother Jones magazine named the University of Oregon the top activist campus in the United States in 2000 (Meatto 2000). Eugene's ambitious anti-discrimination ordinance prohibits discrimination based on a number of factors, including sexual orientation and domestic partnership status. Nine-term Democratic Congressional Representative Peter DeFazio represents Oregon's fourth district, and he maintains a strong approval rating throughout his constituency in Eugene. Author and counterculture icon Ken Kesey made his home in the area, and a memorial to him stands in downtown Eugene.

While the statewide and national image of Eugene is undeniably liberal, there are active conservative forces in the city. In 1995, the Hyundai Group agreed to build a semiconductor plant in Eugene as a result of a generous tax break offer from the city government. When Hyundai expressed a desire to grow into neighboring wetlands areas, environmental critics who wished to block the expansion were met with strong resistance from mayor Ruth Bascom and her successor Jim Torrey, as well as several conservative city councilors, sparking months of public debate. The Gang of Nine, a conservative interest group, created controversy when they sponsored political cartoons in the Eugene Register-Guard that were fiercely critical of liberal city councilors. Adding to the furor was the fact that the Gang of Nine initially concealed their identities from the public. Bowing to considerable pressure, the Gang eventually revealed their members' names, including one of Eugene's most aggressive and controversial real estate developers. The Gang still produces cartoons in furtherance of their agenda, which currently focuses on requiring a citywide vote (as opposed to a ward-restricted vote) for the election of city councilors and the revival of the West Eugene Parkway, a multi-million dollar transportation project that critics assert will have dramatic environmental impacts.

Issues related to racial/ethnic diversity have proven to be problematic for the Eugene community. Like the state of Oregon as a whole, the Eugene population is predominantly white (88.1%) with small Asian (3.6%), black (1.3%), and Latino (5%) populations. Eugene is more racially/ethnically diverse than the whole of Lane County, which is approximately 91% white. Racial/ethnic relations in Oregon in general and Eugene specifically have been historically strained. The Ku Klux Klan exercised considerable power in Oregon throughout the early 20th century. In the 1940s, blacks were not allowed to live within Eugene's city limits, and as a result a cluster of black families congregated in a tent city in what is now one of the city's most popular parks (Maben 2005). More recently, Eugene's tolerant image has been challenged by the flight of black and Latino professionals from the area. These departing professionals contend that racism is rampant in Eugene, hiding just below the veneer of liberalism and diversity. Anselmo Villanueva, a local elementary school principal, informally tracked the exodus of highly educated and skilled minority educators and public servants, recording 150 cases between 1995 and 2005 (Wright 2005e). Several cited experiences with overt racism, but almost all speak of a general sense of unwelcomeness when interacting with whites in the community. Former University of

Case Study: Eugene, Oregon

Oregon law professor Robin Morris Collin, who is black, described her relationships with whites in Eugene as "a combination of shallow friendliness and social discomfort" (Wright 2005c:A14). Collin also recalled an incident at Eugene's exclusive Downtown Athletic Club where she overheard a woman use a racial epithet in the process of proclaiming her disdain for the presence of blacks in the club's membership. Chloe Veney, a professor at Northwest Christian College, and her husband Tony Veney, an assistant track coach at the University of Oregon, left Eugene after a series of racist incidents. Both recall hateful shouts, including "go back to Africa," though Chloe Veney notes that the "subtle comments and stares...could be just as hurtful" (Wright 2005d:A14). She recalled clerks asking to see her receipts when she would exit stores at local shopping malls, noting that white shoppers were spared this indignity. Many other minority residents have told similar stories, illustrating the underlying racial/ethnic tensions that exist in this community.

The Eugene Police Department (EPD) serves the city proper and several local unincorporated areas, and employs 182 sworn officers and a support staff of 122 non-sworn employees. The department promotes itself as a progressive force that subscribes to the basic principles of community policing,[32] and this commitment is captured in the department's slogan—"quality policing through partnerships"—and mission statement:

> The mission of the Eugene Police Department is to enhance the quality of life in our city by providing quality police services. We work in partnership with the community to promote safety and security, enforce laws, prevent crime and safeguard the constitutional rights of all people.[33]

In furtherance of their mission, EPD maintains several programs to engage the community. The 12-member all-civilian Eugene Police Commission provides the public with a voice in police policies and procedures, though the Commission has no oversight power and can only provide recommendations to the City Council, Chief of Police, and City Manager. EPD recently established a Citizens' Police

---

[32] See Cordner (1999) for a discussion of the basic elements of community policing.
[33] Retrieved April 29, 2005 (http://www.ci.eugene.or.us/police/index.htm).

Academy where civilians can enroll in a 13-week program and receive modified training courses on various aspects of police work.

Despite their mission and outreach efforts, EPD's relationship with the Eugene community has grown increasingly strained over recent years, as is evidenced by the repeated failure of ballot measures to fund a new downtown police station (Russo 2004a). Three incidents in particular have contributed greatly to the schism between the police and the community. First, on June 1, 1997, 22 activists were jailed by EPD for their actions during a protest against the removal of five large maple trees from a downtown area that had been designated for a multi-million dollar development project (Wright and Swanson 1997). The department and its officers were publicly criticized for their use of pepper spray, tear gas, and force on the activists as well as bystanders. Protester Brett Cole, who scaled one of the trees scheduled to be removed, claimed that officers used pepper spray on his nose, ears, and genitals (Kidd 1997). Mayor Jim Torrey, Chief Leonard Cooke, and others defended the officers' actions, noting that the protesters had been given instructions and several opportunities to disperse. An internal investigation by the Lane County District Attorney's Office cleared EPD of wrongdoing in 35 of 36 incidents related to the protest (Bishop 1998b), and the police were cleared in the remaining incident after an independent inquiry conducted by the Linn County District Attorney's Office (Mortenson 1998). Second, In June 1999, 20 protesters were arrested and eight EPD officers were injured during an anarchist parade in downtown Eugene that escalated into a riot (Mortenson 1999). The Eugene event was meant to coincide with hundreds of worldwide "street parties" promoted to reclaim the streets from corporate interests (Hartman and Mosley 1999). The police and the media both claimed that the protesters were responsible for the escalation, citing property damage to several local businesses as the catalyst. Parade participants blamed the police presence and aggression for the escalation, noting that officers closely monitored the parade from its outset, provoking the crowd into a confrontation. Finally, John Gainer's experiences with EPD, discussed in detail in Chapter One, came to symbolize racial/ethnic conflicts between Eugene's communities of color and the police.

Case Study: Eugene, Oregon 77

DATA

To examine accusations of racial profiling and differential enforcement in Eugene, Oregon, I studied vehicle stop data collected by EPD officers from January 1, 2002, through December 31, 2003. Following the recommendations set forward by the U.S. Department of Justice (Ramirez et. al. 2000), EPD convened a working group of community members and department representatives to design the data collection project. From February through June of 2001, the Racial Profiling Data Collection Task Group evaluated and discussed numerous research issues and produced the research design employed by EPD. More specifically, the task group agreed on a 19-item survey to be completed by officers for every officer-initiated vehicle stop (see Table 1 for a summary of the variables). Unlike studies conducted by other law enforcement agencies, pedestrian stops were not included in the data collection effort—only vehicle stops initiated by EPD officers were subject to reporting. The data were collected using custom printed machine-readable forms to be completed by officers after each vehicle stop. Completed cards were scanned into a database and the resulting data set was checked against the cards for errors and omissions. In order to identify problem areas in the research design, the data collection process was pretested using a select group of EPD officers from August through November 2001. The final data set included information on 36,011 stops. Internal EPD audits estimate that cards were completed for 70.4% of all stops conducted over the two-year data collection period.[34]

Common definitions of racial profiling present problems in terms of empirical evaluation. According to decision-based standards, racial profiling involves the improper use of racial/ethnic information by officers when initiating and conducting vehicle stops, and as such data on officer decision-making is necessary to evaluate the prevalence of racial profiling. Vehicle stop data is not a complete source of information on officer decision-making in two ways. First, vehicle stop data does not include data on those drivers that were not stopped. Without information on both types of choices (to stop and not to stop), the data are lacking information necessary to fully evaluate questions of

---

[34] See Chapter Six for additional information on data coverage and the potential impact of the card completion rate.

Table 1. Summary of Variables

Q1. Time of Stop

Officers identified whether the stop took place in the AM or the PM, then marked the hour (1-12) followed by the 15-minute period (00-15, 16-30, 31-45, or 46-59).

Q2. Date of Stop

Officers recorded the year (2002 or 2003), month (1-12), and date (1-31 where appropriate) of stop.

Q3. Driver's Race Identifiable Prior to Stop

Officers marked "yes" if they formed an opinion about the driver's race prior to the vehicle stop.

Q4. Reason for Stop

Officers selected all of the following reasons that applied to a given stop: Traffic violation, ORS crime, call for service, pre-existing knowledge, equipment violation, passenger violation, city ordinance violation, special detail, or other.

Q5. Driver's Race/Ethnicity

Based on visual observation only, officers selected one of the following racial/ethnic categories: White, Asian, Black, Native American, Hispanic/Latino, Middle Eastern, Pacific Islander, Indian, Alaska Native, or other/unable to categorize.

Q6. Driver's Age

Based on the driver's identification or self-report, officers selected one of the following age categories: Under 18, 18-29, 30-39, 40-59, or 60 and over.

Q7. Driver's Sex

Based on the driver's identification or self-report, officers selected one of the following categories: Male, female, or other.

Q8. District of Stop

Officers selected one of the five EPD patrol districts, or indicated that the stop occurred outside the patrol district boundaries (recorded as district zero).

Q9. Presence of a Language Barrier

Officers marked "yes" if there was a language or communication present during the stop.

Q10. Number of Passengers

Officers recoreded if there were zero, one, two, three, or four or more passengers.

Q11. Result of Stop

Officers selected all of the following results that applied to a given stop: Warning, field interview, citation, arrest, and no action.

Q12. Reason for Arrest

Officers selected all of the following reasons that applied to a given arrest: Person crime, resisting arrest, outstanding warrant, drug offense, property crime, traffic crime, behavior crime, and other. Officers also noted if the individual was taken into custody (TIC) or cited in lieu of custody (CLC).

Q13. Search Condcuted

Officers marked "yes" if a search was conducted as part of the vehicle stop.

Q14. Type of Search

Officers selected all of the follow search types that applied to a given search: Consent, reasonable suspicion, probable cause, inventory, incident to arrest, and vehicle exception.

Case Study: Eugene, Oregon

Table 1. *(continued)*

Q15. Parameters of Search

Officers selected all of the following search parameters that applied to a given search: Driver, passenger, vehicle, and property.

Q16. Contraband Found

Officers selected all of the following types of contraband that were found as a result of a search: Illegal drugs/paraphernalia, weapons, alcohol, stolen property, currency, other, or negative results (no contraband found).

Q17. Enforcement Action as a Result of a Search

Officers selected all individuals who were subject to enforcement action as a result of the search: Driver, passenger, or none.

Q18. Duration of Stop

Officers selected one of the following categories: 0-15 minutes, 16-30 minutes, or 31 minutes or more.

Q19. Driver's Residency Status

Based on the driver's identification or self-report, officers marked "yes" if the driver was a Eugene

Source: EPD Vehicle Stop Data (2002-2003).
Note: Definitions for varible categories can be found in Appendix B.

decision-making biases at this level of selection. However, vehicle stop data does contain adequate information on decisions that occurred after the initiation of the stop, such as citations, arrests, and searches. Second, vehicle stop data does not contain explicit information on how a driver's race/ethnicity was used by officers in their decision-making processes. Withrow (2002) sums up the difficulty of evaluating police decision-making:

> What we know is that policing is a dynamic and reactive process. On an average day police officers make and remake thousands of decisions based on fluid and incomplete fact situations. In order to fully understand the results of these decisions we must document the process by which these decisions are made. Unfortunately, nothing in this [vehicle stop] data set or any similar data set is capable of such an analysis. (P. 50)

While vehicle stop data cannot fully represent officer decision-making processes, it can capture important differences in enforcement patterns across racial/ethnic groups, more specifically those associated with pretext stop practices. With the proper integration of regression analysis, competing explanations can be evaluated to determine whether or not the observed group differences are in fact related to race/ethnicity or other variables. After controlling for the effects of offending, we can be confident that the remaining effects are associated with some form of differential enforcement.

The Benchmarking Problem

The comparison of vehicle stop data to demographic benchmarks has been a fundamental element of racial profiling research, primarily because one of the key charges associated with racial profiling is that police disproportionately target minority drivers for vehicle stops. While vehicle stop data provides a demographic portrait of who was stopped by the police, there is no way to determine whether or not the distribution of stops by race/ethnicity reflects a pattern of disparate treatment without an external benchmark for comparison.

The simplest benchmarking strategy involves comparing the stopped population to the racial/ethnic distribution of the residential population of a given geographic area, often using data from the U.S. Census. This strategy has been criticized for not considering variables like traffic law violation, insofar as lawbreaking increases the risk of being stopped (General Accounting Office 2000), and differences between an area's residential population and its driving population (Meehan and Ponder 2002a; Smith and Petrocelli 2001; Rojek et. al. 2004; Zingraff et. al. 2000).

The use of U.S. Census data specifically as a source of residential population data for benchmark construction has also been criticized. It is important to recognize the potential sources of error associated with Census-derived benchmarks:

- Census data are composed of civilians' self-reports of their racial/ethnic background, while vehicle stop data are commonly based on the officer's perception of a driver's race/ethnicity.[35] The difference in the way that information on race/ethnicity is collected in these two data sources is a possible source of error, the magnitude of which cannot be estimated using existing data.

---

[35] It should be noted that EPD initially attempted to collect driver self-reports on race/ethnicity during vehicle stops using a scripted question asked by officers of drivers. This practice was discontinued after complaints from both civilians and officers.

Case Study: Eugene, Oregon

- Insofar as systematic errors associated with undercounting have been identified in Census data, the impact of such errors must be considered in the comparisons made between Census-based benchmarks and vehicle stop data. Of particular concern are undercounts of certain racial/ethnic groups, which could underestimate residential population sizes and inflate estimates of stop frequency.

- Census data from the year 2000 does not account for demographic changes since the data collection period. While the Census data were collected relatively recently in comparison to the Eugene Vehicle Stop Study, it is possible that shifts have occurred, and without additional data it is impossible to ascertain the impact of these changes on the Eugene population.

Despite these criticisms, the U.S. Department of Justice contends that Census-based benchmarks can be useful in the analysis of vehicle stop data, provided that these benchmarks are constructed properly:

> First, it is important to ensure that the population data are sufficiently current. The 2000 census would be a more appropriate description of population demographics than older census estimates. Second, because the age demographics for different racial groups may vary, it is vital that the residential benchmark be applied only to individuals who are of legal driving age...Third, residential population benchmarks are least appropriate for examining the racial demographics of individuals stopped by the police who reside outside that particular jurisdiction. (Ramirez et. al. 2000:53-54)

For this study, a residential population benchmark was constructed using data from the 2000 U.S. Census. Several steps were taken in an effort to address problems with using a Census-based benchmark. First, only Eugene residents from the vehicle stop data set were compared to the benchmark.[36] This control partially solved the problem of non-residents being improperly included in the benchmark

---

[36] EPD collected data on whether or not the driver was a Eugene resident, and this variable facilitated the removal of non-residents from the benchmark comparisons.

comparison.[37] Second, only driving-age residents (ages 16 and over) were included in the benchmark. Finally, the age distributions of the Census data were adjusted to account for time differential between Census data collection and EPD's vehicle stop data collection. In other words, to ensure that the benchmark included individuals who were of driving age in 2002, two years were added to the age distribution of the 2000 Census data. This means that individuals who were 14 years of age in 2000 were included in the benchmark because they would have been 16 years of age in 2002. A similar adjustment was used in the construction of the 2003 benchmark.

In addition to the issues associated with the appropriateness of Census-based benchmarks, the method used by the U.S. Census Bureau to collect data on race/ethnicity created some difficulties. The 2000 U.S. Census measured race/ethnicity using two questions. First, all respondents were asked if they were Spanish/Hispanic/Latino. Second, all respondents were asked their race. For the second item, respondents were allowed to select all applicable categories. The U.S. Census Bureau treats race and Hispanic origin as separate concepts, noting that people who are Latino can be of any race (white, black, etc.). The two-question measurement strategy, coupled with the select-all-that-apply response option for the race question, created overlap problems across racial/ethnic categories. While some respondents fell into one category only (Asian, black, white), others selected multiple racial categories. Furthermore, each racial category could be further subdivided by Latino origin. To account for this overlap and to minimize the error associated with selecting a single estimation strategy, multiple estimates of the racial/ethnic distribution of the Eugene population were calculated for this study:

- *Exclusive Population Estimate*: This estimate included residents who selected only one racial category—mixed race residents were excluded from this benchmark. Residents who identified

---

[37] The standard for Eugene residency is not entirely clear. Because EPD jurisdiction extends beyond the formal city limits and into several unincorporated areas, it is possible that some officers classified residents of these areas as Eugene residents. Furthermore, there is anecdotal evidence that officers may not have uniformly interpreted and applied the residency standard.

themselves as Latino were removed from the estimates of the other three racial/ethnic groups (Asian, black, white).

- *Inclusive Population Estimate*: This estimate added mixed race residents by including these residents in every racial category selected (referred to as "alone or in combination" in Census notation). Latino residents were not removed from the other racial/ethnic groups.[38]

- *Population Midpoint Estimate*: This estimate was calculated by taking the midpoint between the exclusive and inclusive population estimates.

When considering all the issues associated with benchmarking vehicle stop data, it is important to recognize that there is no such thing as a perfect benchmark.[39] While benchmark comparisons can provide valuable insights into patterns of racial/ethnic differences in law enforcement practices, every benchmark design suffers from some form of error. This is not to say that benchmark comparisons are unreliable. Provided that steps are taken to ensure that benchmarks are constructed using the best available data, benchmark comparisons can provide useful information on enforcement patterns. At the same time, conclusions drawn from benchmark comparisons must be stated with caution and with attention to error sources.

METHODOLOGY

Analysis Strategy and Research Questions

The analysis of quantitative data most frequently occurs within a deductive paradigm where the primary concern is theory verification. In terms of racial profiling research, this paradigm is appealing in the sense that the foundational question asked of vehicle stop data (is racial profiling occurring?) corresponds with the general methods associated with hypothesis testing. However, deductive research is predicated on

---

[38] Since the U.S. Census collected data on Latino origin using a separate question, the size of the Latino population was constant across all population estimates.

[39] Engel and Calnon (2004a) provide an excellent discussion of the overall strengths and weaknesses of different benchmark designs.

the existence of reliable theory, and as I demonstrated in Chapters Two and Three, thinking on racial profiling has been highly fragmented and significantly lacking in terms of theoretical development. Without such theory, it is impossible to develop informed hypotheses and precise measures that address core issues related to racial profiling, and this precludes meaningful hypothesis testing. As such, many vehicle stop studies employ arbitrary thresholds in determining whether or not the data constitute evidence of racial profiling. In their comparisons of the stopped and residential populations in Washington state, Lovrich et. al. (2003) employed a five percentage point criterion, claiming that "differences are not substantively significant as long as the percentage of those contacted in any particular racial/ethnic group is not more than five percentage points larger than the percentage of that group in the resident population" (p. 40-41). Considering that blacks comprise 3.2% of the Washington state population, black drivers would have to be involved in 8.2% of all stops before the researchers would conclude that discrimination was occurring. Seen in this light, the arbitrary nature of the five percent threshold is clear.

I adopted a grounded approach in my examination of EPD's vehicle stop data. While grounded techniques are most commonly associated with qualitative methodologies, Glaser and Strauss (1967) explicitly state that the underlying principles of grounded theory can also be applied to quantitative research efforts. When quantitative researchers distance themselves from the demands of the deductive paradigm and adopt descriptive and exploratory approaches, then they:

> ...(C)an relax many rules for obtaining evidence and verifications that would otherwise limit, stultify or squelch the generation of theory. He [sic] must give himself [sic] this freedom in the flexible use of quantitative data or he will not be able to generate theory that is adequate (as we have discussed it) in terms of sampling, saturation, integration, density of property development, and so forth...The freedom and flexibility that we claim for generating theory from quantitative data will lead to new strategies and styles of quantitative analysis, with their own rules yet to be discovered. And these new styles of analyses will bring out the richness of quantitative data that is seen only implicitly while the focus remains on verification. (P. 186)

Case Study: Eugene, Oregon

I provide a detailed statistical description of enforcement patterns in Eugene. In employing a grounded strategy, it is my goal to generate conceptual, theoretical, and methodological insights through the rigorous and thorough analysis of EPD's vehicle stop data. It should be noted that the conceptualization issues discussed in Chapter Two and the theoretical framework presented in Chapter Three were developed alongside and as part of the data analysis process.[40] Of course, the discovery and development of these ideas was not purely serendipitous, but rather the product of iterative processes that synthesized aspects of the data analysis and insights from other research on racial profiling and related areas and disciplines. As I worked with the vehicle stop data, I used results to generate questions that I then used to access different areas of theory and research. These explorations produced refinements that were then integrated into data analysis procedures.

While this research relied on the principles of grounded theory, the examination of the vehicle stop data was generally organized around the concepts of differential offending and differential enforcement. Key to both of these concepts is the idea that differences exist between racial/ethnic groups in terms of law enforcement practices, and as such the first task of any racial profiling research is to identify these differences. Three research questions guided this stage of the data analysis:

- Are civilians from racial/ethnic minority groups, particularly Asian, black, and Latino drivers, stopped more or less frequently than white drivers per their representation in the population?

- Are Asian, black, and Latino drivers treated differently than white drivers during vehicle stops?

- Are there differences in the overall enforcement patterns between Asian, black, Latino, and white drivers?

The first two questions are standard in terms of racial profiling research; the first focuses on benchmark comparisons and the second on racial/ethnic group comparisons on dependent variables of interest in the vehicle stop data. The third question moves past the simple identification of differences—a limitation of many past studies—and

---

[40] The fact that this information is presented prior to the discussion of the vehicle stop data is merely a matter of sociological and academic convention.

incorporates a more holistic analysis that examines the overall racial/ethnic context of patterns observed in the data, including those patterns indicative of pretext stops. Taken together, these three questions provide for a detailed and nuanced description of enforcement patterns related to EPD vehicle stops.

However, as others have noted (Zingraff et. al. 2000), the presence of racial/ethnic differences in enforcement patterns could be the result of a number of factors, and as such these differences do not constitute proof of differential enforcement or racial profiling. To explore issues of differential enforcement and differential offending, a fourth question was formulated:

- How does race/ethnicity contribute to the production of enforcement patterns?

This question demands that variables other than race/ethnicity be included in a more thorough analysis of observed disparities. Of particular interest to racial profiling research are effects associated with offending, for officers frequently cite law violation as the primary consideration in their decision-making. Beyond race/ethnicity and offending, other variables, such as sex, age, location of the stop, and the time of day when the stop occurred, could reasonably influence officer decision-making. In order to determine whether or not observed differences are indeed related to race/ethnicity, it is necessary to control for the effects of other variables when estimating the impact of race/ethnicity on enforcement patterns.

Significance Testing

Tests of statistical significance are frequently used to generalize from random samples back to larger populations. Since vehicle stop data collection systems (including this project) are designed to include data on all vehicle stops (as opposed to a random sample of vehicle stops), these tests might seem improper. Contrary to popular belief, it is quite appropriate to use tests of statistical significance on population data like the vehicle stop data.[41] The purpose of a test of statistical

---

[41] See Winch and Campbell (1969) for a detailed discussion of the appropriate use and interpretation of tests of statistical significance.

Case Study: Eugene, Oregon

significance is to ascertain the likelihood that an observed difference could be the result of random chance. To exclude tests of statistical significance in the examination of population data is to disregard the possibility that random chance may have played a role in the observed differences.

Furthermore, considering the racial/ethnic composition of Eugene (approximately 87% of the driving age population is white according to the 2000 U.S. Census), significance testing is especially necessary to account for the comparatively small number of EPD stops involving drivers from minority groups. Since such a small percentage of all stops involved minority drivers, it is important to determine the likelihood that the observed differences may be related to random chance and not indicative of underlying enforcement patterns.

Chi-Square Tests and Logistic Regression Analysis

Research on racial profiling has frequently focused on comparisons between racial/ethnic groups in terms of key law enforcement variables, such as the percentage of each racial/ethnic group that received a citation or experienced a search. Chi-square analysis tests the statistical significance of differences between racial/ethnic groups, determining the likelihood that the observed difference was the result of random chance. Specifically, chi-square tests were used to identify differences in the experiences of Asian, black, and Latino drivers compared to white drivers on the following variables:

- Stop frequency.
- Reason(s) for stop.
- District of stop.
- Result(s) of stop (enforcement action and arrests).
- Duration of stop.
- Search occurrence.
- Search success rate (% of searches that produced contraband).
- Type(s) of contraband found in successful searches.
- Discretionary search occurrence.
- Discretionary search success rate.

These dependent variables capture vital points of the vehicle stop process, and most directly address enforcement decisions made by officers (such as the decision to stop, the decision to cite and/or arrest, the decision to search). Search success rates offer direct information on differences in offending frequency between racial/ethnic groups. District of stop is a complex variable that captures information on officer decision-making, institutional policies, and neighborhood effects. Chi-square tests were only applied to these law enforcement outcomes; racial/ethnic differences on other variables, including demographic variables, were considered descriptive and not subjected to statistical testing.

In order to isolate specific racial/ethnic group differences on dependent variables, Asian, black, and Latino drivers were each compared individually to white drivers. In addition to racial/ethnic group comparisons, all chi-square tests were subdivided to account for the effects of sex on law enforcement practices. To further refine the analysis, each dependent variable category was examined independently. For example, the drivers stopped for each individual reason for stop were compared to all drivers not stopped for that specific reason. As such, every chi-square test had a single degree of freedom, which increased the specificity of the results.

Regression analysis was employed to explore the differences observed in the bivariate comparisons in more detail. Regression analysis examined the impact of race/ethnicity on law enforcement outcomes while accounting for the effects of other relevant factors (such as sex, age, reason for stop, etc.). By creating regression models that included other potentially explanatory factors, estimates of the effects of race/ethnicity on law enforcement outcomes were much more accurate. Furthermore, by accounting for the effects of other variables, regression analysis revealed whether these factors explain differences that were originally attributed to race/ethnicity.

Because of limitations associated with the vehicle stop data, regression models were constructed to examine four dependent variables:

- Result(s) of the stop (enforcement action and arrest).
- Duration of the stop.

Case Study: Eugene, Oregon

- Search occurrence.
- Discretionary search occurrence.

Since each of these variables was dichotomous (see Table 2 for dependent variable coding), logistic regression was employed. Logistic regression is the standard regression technique when dealing with dichotomous dependent variables, and it features the exponentiated-B statistic, or odds ratio. This statistic provides a simple way to interpret the effects of independent variables. To better understand this, consider search occurrence as a dependent variable, where a value of zero equals no search and a value of one indicates that a search was conducted. An odds ratio greater than one indicates an increase in the likelihood of a search, while an odds ratio less than one indicates a decrease in the likelihood of a search. Furthermore, the odds ratio provides the factor by which the odds increase or decrease. To determine the percentage increase or decrease, subtract one from the exponentiated-B statistic and multiply by 100, or $[(e^b-1) \times 100]$. In reference to the search example, the exponentiated-B statistic associated with stops occurring in district four (1.127—see Table 34) translates into a 12.7% increase in the likelihood of that a search would be conducted. The statistic associated with stops occurring in district three (.655) translates into a 34.5% decrease in the likelihood that a search would be conducted (1-.655=.345 X 100=34.5).

Each regression table contains two models. The first model captures the effect of race/ethnicity when basic demographic characteristics (sex and age) are included. This model provides a baseline for ascertaining the impact of the control variables on the explanatory power of race/ethnicity, sex, and age. The second model captures the effect of race/ethnicity when other relevant variables are present in the model.

Because race/ethnicity is a nominal variable, dummy variables for Asian, black, and Latino drivers are used in the models. White drivers were held in the baseline (i.e. not entered into the model), and served as the reference group to which the coefficients and odds ratios for the other three racial/ethnic groups were compared. This same basic strategy (creating dummy variables for categories and entering all but one into the model, making the unentered category the reference category) was used for all independent variables in the regression models (see Table 2 for the independent variable codings).

Table 2. Variable Coding for Logistic Regression Analysis

Variable	Definition

Dependent Variables

Result of Stop: Enforcement Action

| 0 | Driver was not the subject of enforcement action. |
| 1 | Driver was cited and/or arrested as a result of the vehicle stop. |

Result of Stop: Arrest

| 0 | Driver was not arrested. |
| 1 | Driver was arrested as a result of the vehicle stop. |

Duration of Stop: 15-Minute Split

| 0 | Stop lasted 15 minutes or less. |
| 1 | Stop lasted more than 15 minutes. |

Duration of Stop: 30-Minute Split

| 0 | Stop lasted 30 minutes or less. |
| 1 | Stop lasted more than 30 minutes. |

Search Conducted

| 0 | No search. |
| 1 | Search conducted. |

Discretionary Search Conducted

| 0 | No discretionary search. |
| 1 | Discretionary search conducted. |

Independent Variables

Driver's Race/Ethnicity

WHITE	Driver's race=White (baseline).
ASIAN	Driver's race=Asian.
BLACK	Driver's race=Black.
LATINO	Driver's race=Latino.

Driver's Sex

| MALE | Driver's sex=Male (baseline). |
| FEMALE | Driver's sex=Female. |

Driver's Age

AGE1629	Driver's age=16 to 29 (baseline).
AGE3039	Driver's age=30 to 39.
AGE40OVR	Driver's age=40 to 59.

District of Stop

DIST5	Stop occurred in district five (baseline).
DIST0	Stop occurred outside EPD districts.
DIST1	Stop occurred in district one.
DIST2	Stop occurred in district two.
DIST3	Stop occurred in district three.
DIST4	Stop occurred in district four.

Case Study: Eugene, Oregon

Table 2. *(continued)*

Variable	Definition
Reason for Stop	
RFSB	Driver stopped for a traffic violation only (baseline).
RFSHID1	Driver stopped for an equipment or passenger violation only.
RFSHID2	Driver stopped for a combination of traffic, equipment, and passenger violations.
RFSLOWD	Driver stopped for a low discretion violation (ORS crime, call for service, pre-existing knowledge, city ordinance violation, special detail, or other) alone or in combination with any other reason for stop.
Number of Passengers	
PASSB	No passengers in stopped vehicle (baseline).
PASS1	One passenger in stopped vehicle.
PASS2PLS	Two or more passengers in stopped vehicle.
Language Barrier	
LANGB	No language barrier (baseline).
LANGYES	A language barrier was present during the stop.
Identify Race/Ethnicity Before Stop	
RACEB	Officer could not identify the driver's race/ethnicity prior to the stop (baseline).
RACEYES	Officer identified the driver's race/ethnicity prior to the stop.
Hour of Stop	
HRSTOPB	Stop occurred during midday hours (10:00 AM-2:59 PM Nbaseline).
HRLATE	Stop occurred during late night hours (10:00 PM-2:59 AM).
HRMORN	Stop occurred during early morning and morning commute hours (3:00 AM-9:59 AM).
HRRUSH	Stop occurred during evening rush hours (3:00 PM-5:59 PM).
HREVE	Stop occurred during evening hours (6:00 PM-9:59 PM).

Source: EPD Vehicle Stop Data (2002-2003).

Even though this research is exploratory and descriptive in its orientation, one-tailed significance tests were used in the chi-square analysis and for the race/ethnicity variables in the regression models. While theories related to differential enforcement and differential offending are not developed to the point where hypotheses can be properly formulated and tested, the underlying ideas are sufficiently clear to predict the direction of relationships between racial/ethnic groups. Both differential enforcement and differential offending theories predict that black and Latino drivers will be treated more severely than white drivers. More specifically, black and Latino drivers will experience more stops, arrests, and searches, compared to white drivers, and stops involving black and Latino drivers will last longer (because of additional investigation) and will produce more contraband in relation to searches. Enforcement action (whether or not a driver was issued a citation and/or arrested) was excluded from one-tailed tests because the literature indicates that both more severe and less severe treatment of black and Latino drivers is a possibility. If officers were singling out black and Latino drivers for harassment and punishment, or if larger percentages of black and Latino drivers were committing serious offenses compared to whites (which is a form of differential offending), then one would expect that larger percentages of black and Latino drivers would experience enforcement action. If officers were applying pretext stop tactics disproportionately to black and Latino drivers, then one would expect that smaller percentages of black and Latino drivers would experience enforcement action compared to whites, largely because these black and Latino drivers were stopped from minor violations which would likely warrant only warnings if initial investigations produced no further indications of serious crimes.

While tests for black and Latino drivers predicted more severe treatment compared to white drivers, one-tailed tests for Asian drivers predicted less severe treatment. Harris (2002) argues that the growth of Asian gangs justifies the inclusion of Asians in racial profiling studies. However, this phenomenon remains geographically isolated, and it is most definitely not an issue in Eugene. Furthermore, Asian stereotypes are complex, often varying across specific ethnicities, and when considered on the whole these stereotypes can be contradictory. Because there was little foundation in the literature or in Eugene history to justify the expectation of more severe treatment of Asian drivers, one-tailed tests predicted less severe treatment of Asian drivers in terms of stop frequency, enforcement action, arrests, and searches compared to white drivers. Furthermore, tests predicted that stops involving Asian drivers would be shorter and searches of Asian drivers would be less likely to produce contraband compared to searches of white drivers.

CHAPTER 5
Results of the EPD Vehicle Stop Study

GENERAL CHARACTERISTICS OF VEHICLE STOPS

The majority of vehicle stops involved drivers whom the officer(s) perceived as white (90.1%—see Table 3). Latino drivers accounted for 3.9%, black drivers for 2.2%, and Asian drivers for 2.1% of all stops. All other racial/ethnic groups accounted for less than 1% of all stops each. In 13% of all stops the officer(s) formed an opinion of the driver's race/ethnicity prior to the stop. Of those drivers whom the officer had formed an opinion of their race/ethnicity, 92.3% were white. In only 1.3% of all stops, or 441 total stops, a language barrier was present between the officer(s) and the driver.

In terms of the demographic characteristics of the drivers stopped by EPD, the largest percentage of vehicle stops involved drivers ages 18 to 29 (44.9%—see Table 4). Drivers ages 40 to 59 accounted for 26.5% of stops, and drivers ages 30 to 39 for 20.4% of all stops. Sixty-one percent of all stops involved male drivers, and 39% involved female drivers. The majority of stops involved Eugene residents (79.3%). Roughly two-thirds of all vehicles stopped (66.2%) had only one occupant—the driver. Approximately 23% of stops involved vehicles with a driver and a single passenger, while only 1.1% of all stops involved a vehicle with four or more passengers.

Table 3. Frequency Distribution of Driver's Race/Ethnicity, Identifiability of Driver's Race/Ethnicity, and Presence of a Language Barrier

Variable	Frequency	Percentage
Driver's Race/Ethnicity (Q5)		
White	32254	90.1%
Asian	763	2.1%
Black	783	2.2%
Native American	57	0.2%
Hispanic/Latino	1413	3.9%
Middle Eastern	136	0.4%
Pacific Islander	78	0.2%
Indian	65	0.2%
Alaska Native	13	<0.1%
Other/Unable to Categorize	240	0.7%
TOTAL	35802	-
Cases Missing Data	*209*	*0.6%*
Driver's Race Identifiable Prior to Stop (Q3)		
No	30771	87.0%
Yes	4603	13.0%
TOTAL	35374	-
Cases Missing Data	*637*	*1.8%*
Presence of a Language Barrier (Q9)		
No	34826	98.7%
Yes	441	1.3%
TOTAL	35267	-
Cases Missing Data	*744*	*2.1%*

Source: EPD Vehicle Stop Data (2002-2003).
Note: Percentage of cases missing data was calculated using the total number of stops in the vehicle stop data set (N=36,011).

In terms of when and where stops occurred, the largest percentages were conducted between the hours 10:00 AM and 2:59 PM (32.1%—see Table 5) and during late night hours of 10:00 PM and 2:59 AM (18.7%). Nearly one-third all stops occurred in patrol district five (29.9%), which includes Eugene's downtown area. A small percentage of stops (1.5%) occurred outside of EPD's patrol districts, which is legal because EPD, like all municipal police forces in Oregon, maintains statewide jurisdiction.

To obtain a complex representation of the reasons that prompted each vehicle stop, officers were allowed to select multiple categories

Results of the EPD Vehicle Stop Study 95

Table 4. Frequency Distribution of Driver's Age, Gender, Residency Status, and Number of Passengers in Vehicle

Variable	Frequency	Percentage
Driver's Age (Q6)		
Under 18	1044	2.9%
18 - 29	16100	44.9%
30 - 39	7299	20.4%
40 - 59	9520	26.5%
60 and Older	1904	5.3%
TOTAL	35867	-
Cases Missing Data	*144*	*0.4%*
Driver's Sex (Q7)		
Male	21784	61.0%
Female	13937	39.0%
TOTAL	35721	-
Cases Missing Data	*290*	*0.8%*
Driver's Residency Status (Q19)		
Not a Eugene Resident	7414	20.7%
Eugene Resident	28411	79.3%
TOTAL	35825	-
Cases Missing Data	*186*	*0.5%*
Number of Passengers (Q10)		
No Passengers	23653	66.2%
One Passenger	8313	23.3%
Two Passengers	2380	6.7%
Three Passengers	959	2.7%
Four or More Passengers	403	1.1%
TOTAL	35708	-
Cases Missing Data	*303*	*0.8%*

Source: EPD Vehicle Stop Data (2002-2003).
Note: Percentage of cases missing data was calculated using the total number of stops in the vehicle stop data set (N=36,011).

from a list of nine violations types (see Table 6). The most common reason for stop was a traffic violation, which was present in 78.1% of all stops. In 19.7% of stops an equipment violation was at least one of the reasons for the stop. In 2.5% of all stops pre-existing knowledge[42] was at least one of the reasons for the stop. All other reasons for stop

---

[42] See Appendix two for definitions of the different reasons provided for vehicle stops.

Table 5. Frequency Distribution of Time of Stop and District of Stop

Variable	Frequency	Percentage
Time of Stop (Q1)		
3:00 AM to 9:59 AM	6277	17.5%
10:00 AM to 2:59 PM	11501	32.1%
3:00 PM to 5:59 PM	6433	18.0%
6:00 PM to 9:59 PM	4881	13.6%
10:00 PM to 2:59 AM	6699	18.7%
TOTAL	35791	-
Cases Missing Data	*220*	*0.6%*
District of Stop (Q8)		
Outside of EPD Patrol Districts	537	1.5%
Patrol District One	6479	18.1%
Patrol District Two	6386	17.9%
Patrol District Three	5935	16.6%
Patrol District Four	5732	16.0%
Patrol District Five	10686	29.9%
TOTAL	35755	-
Cases Missing Data	*256*	*0.7%*

Source: EPD Vehicle Stop Data (2002-2003).
Note: Percentage of cases missing data was calculated using the total number of stops in the vehicle stop data set (N=36,011).

were present in no more than 1.1% of all stops each. A single reason for stop was provided in 95.1% of stops, while 0.5% of all stops had no reason for stop listed on the data collection form.

Officers were allowed to select multiple categories from a list of five possible results of the vehicle stop (see Table 6). The most common result was a citation, which was at least one of the results in 64.4% of all stops. In 35.9% of stops the driver was given warning, either verbal or written. In 90.7% of stops only one stop result was provided, while two stop results were listed in 8.4% of all stops.

Estimating the number of arrests was difficult. In 2.8% of all stops, or 985 total stops, the category "arrest" was selected as a stop result (see Table 6). However, in 1025 stops the officer(s) selected a reason for arrest (see Table 7). In 156 cases the officer(s) provided at least one reason for arrest but did not select "arrest" as a stop result. In 116 cases, the officer selected "arrest" as a stop result but did not provide a reason for the arrest. When the indicators were combined, and either the presence of a reason for arrest or the selection of "arrest"

Table 6. Frequency Distribution of Reason for Stop and Result of Stop

Variable	Frequency	Percentage
Reason for Stop (Q4)		
Traffic Violation	28108	78.1%
ORS Crime	144	0.4%
Call for Service	236	0.7%
Pre-Existing Knowledge	901	2.5%
Passenger Violation	380	1.1%
Equipment Violation	7085	19.7%
Violation of City Ordinance	188	0.5%
Special Detail	60	0.2%
Other	402	1.1%
TOTAL	36011	-
No Reason for Stop Provided	*186*	*0.5%*
Result of Stop (Q11)		
No Action	919	2.6%
Warning	12830	35.9%
Field Interview	1222	3.4%
Citation	23018	64.4%
Arrest	985	2.8%
TOTAL	35762	-
Cases Missing Data	*249*	*0.7%*

Source: EPD Vehicle Stop Data (2002-2003).
Note: Percentage of cases missing data was calculated using the total number of stops in the vehicle stop data set (N=36,011).

as a stop result was interpreted as evidence of an arrest then the estimated number of arrests across both years of data collection was 1141, or 3.2% of all stops. Of those arrested, a traffic crime was cited as a reason in 48.5% of all arrests (see Table 8). In 29.8% of all arrests an outstanding warrant was one of the reasons for the arrest. In 11.7% of all arrests, a drug offense was one of the reasons for the arrest.

The majority of vehicle stops lasted 15 minutes or less (88.8%—see Table 8), while 8.2% lasted between 16 and 30 minutes and 3% lasted 31 minutes or longer.

Information on Searches

Much like arrests, estimating the number of searches conducted by EPD officers was problematic. Officers were asked to provide the following information for every search:

Table 7. Arrest Estimate

Variable	Frequency	Percentage
Reason for arrest (Q12).		
No Reason for Arrest Provided	34986	97.2%
Reason for Arrest Provided	1025	2.8%
TOTAL	36011	-
Stop result (Q11).		
Arrest Stop Result Not Marked	34777	97.2%
Arrest Stop Result Marked	985	2.8%
TOTAL	35762	-
Cases Missing Data	*249*	*0.7%*
Reason for Arrest Provided and Arrest Stop Result *Not* Marked	156	0.4%
Arrest Stop Result Marked and *No* Reason for Arrest Provided	116	0.3%
Dual Indicator Arrest Estimate	1141	3.2%

Source: EPD Vehicle Stop Data (2002-2003).
Note: Percentage of cases missing data was calculated using the total number of stops in the vehicle stop data set (N=36,011).

- Search conducted (yes/no).[43]
- Type of search.
- Parameters of search.
- Contraband found.
- Enforcement action as a result of the search.

In 2247 stops, or 6.5% of all stops, the officer indicated that a search was conducted by selecting "yes" on the search conducted variable (see Table 9). In 1674 stops, or 4.6% of all stops, all five search items were completed. In 3115 stops, or 8.7% of all stops, at least one of the five search items was completed, and these cases were

---

[43] This item was to be filled out for every stop, while the other four items were to be filled out only when a search was conducted.

Results of the EPD Vehicle Stop Study

Table 8. Frequency Distribution of Reason for Arrest and Duration of Stop

Variable	Frequency	Percentage
Reason for Arrest (Q12)		
Outstanding Warrant	340	29.8%
Traffic Crime	553	48.5%
Person Crime	24	2.1%
Resisting Arrest	7	0.6%
Drug Offense	133	11.7%
Property Crime	40	3.5%
Behavior Crime	27	2.4%
Other	41	3.6%
No Reason for Arrest Marked	116	10.2%
TOTAL	1141	-
Duration of Stop (Q18)		
15 Minutes or Less	31865	88.8%
16 to 30 Minutes	2948	8.2%
31 Minutes or Longer	1082	3.0%
TOTAL	35895	-
Cases Missing Data	*116*	*0.3%*

Source: EPD Vehicle Stop Data (2002-2003).
Note: Percentage of cases missing data was calculated using the total number of stops in the vehicle stop data set (N=36,011).

coded as searches under the Any Search Indicator Present (ASIP) search definition. However, in 1441 stops, or 4% of all stops, search reporting was incomplete.[44] To address this problem, a minimum reporting threshold was established. For a stop with incomplete search information to qualify as a search under the Minimum Reporting Threshold (MRT) definition, information on at least three of the final four search indicators had to be present in the data; the search conducted variable was excluded from this calculation because this could reasonably be inferred from the subsequent items. In addition, stops where both the type of search and the type of contraband found (if any) were counted under the MRT definition. Using this definition, it

---

[44] The issue of incomplete search reporting is further complicated by 166 arrests that were missing search data. EPD officers are required to search every civilian they arrest, though this search can be a simple "pat down" or Terry search. Some officers were informally instructed not to record these searches on the data collection form.

Table 9. Search Estimate

Variable	Frequency	Percentage
Search Conducted (Q13)		
No	32323	93.5%
Yes	2247	6.5%
TOTAL	34570	-
Cases Missing Data	*1441*	*4.0%*
Search Descriptors		
Type of Search (Q14)		
Parameters of Search (Q15)		
Contraband Found (Q16)		
Enforcement Action as a Result of the Search (Q17)		
No Search Descriptors (Q14-Q17) Provided	32915	91.4%
One or More Search Descriptors	3096	8.6%
TOTAL	36011	-
All Five Search Fields Completed	1674	4.6%
Any Search Indicator Present (ASIP)		
Search Conducted	3115	8.7%
TOTAL	36011	-
Minimum Reporting Threshold (MRT)		
Search Conducted	2116	6.0%
TOTAL	35031	-
Cases Missing Data	*980*	*2.7%*

Source: EPD Vehicle Stop Data (2002-2003).
Note: Percentage of cases missing data was calculated using the total number of stops in the vehicle stop data set (N=36,011).

was estimated that searches were conducted in 2116 stops, or 6% of valid stops.[45] In order to provide a fair and complete description of the data, the results for both the Any Search Indicator Present (ASIP) and Minimum Reporting Threshold (MRT) search definitions are addressed in all following sections dealing with searches.

---

[45] Stops where the search data were incomplete were classified as missing data and were not included in the calculation of this percentage or any analysis of the Minimum Reporting Threshold search data.

Results of the EPD Vehicle Stop Study

Table 10. Frequency Distribution of Search Success Rates

Variable	Frequency	Percentage
Contraband Found (Q16)		
Any Search Indicator Present (ASIP)		
(Direct Indicator)[a]		
No Contraband	1400	67.4%
Contraband Found	678	32.6%
TOTAL	2078	-
Cases Missing Data	*1037*	*33.3%*
(Missing Data=No Contraband Found)[b]		
No Contraband	2437	78.2%
Contraband Found	678	21.8%
TOTAL	3115	-
(No Enforcement=No Contraband Found)[c]		
No Contraband	1846	73.1%
Contraband Found	678	26.9%
TOTAL	2524	-
Cases Missing Data	*591*	*19.0%*
Minimum Reporting Threshold (MRT)		
No Contraband	1379	67.1%
Contraband Found	675	32.9%
TOTAL	2054	-
Cases Missing Data	*62*	*2.9%*

Source: EPD Vehicle Stop Data (2002-2003).
[a] Includes only cases with direct information on contraband found.
[b] Cases missing data on contraband coded as no contraband found.
[c] Cases missing data where driver was not subject to enforcement action were coded as "no contraband"; cases missing data where driver was subject to enforcement action were excluded from the analysis.

Determining the percentage of ASIP searches that resulted in contraband found was difficult because of the number of searches missing contraband data (1037 searches, or 33.3% of ASIP searches—see Table 10). If the missing data is excluded, then 32.6% of ASIP searches produced contraband. If the missing data is interpreted as an unsuccessful search, then 21.8% of ASIP searches produced contraband. The missing data was analyzed to determine whether or not these cases resulted in enforcement action (i.e. the drivers were cited and/or arrested). Searches where no enforcement action occurred

Table 11. Frequency Distribution of Contraband Found in Searches

Variable	Frequency	Percentage
Contraband Found (Q16)		
Any Search Indicator Present (ASIP)		
Drugs/Paraphernalia	350	51.6%
Alcohol	207	30.5%
Stolen Property	35	5.2%
Currency	51	7.5%
Weapons	79	11.7%
Other	116	17.1%
TOTAL	678	-
Minimum Reporting Threshold (MRT)		
Drugs/Paraphernalia	350	51.9%
Alcohol	207	30.7%
Stolen Property	35	5.2%
Currency	51	7.6%
Weapons	79	11.7%
Other	113	16.7%
TOTAL	675	-

Source: EPD Vehicle Stop Data (2002-2003).

were coded as unsuccessful, while searches where enforcement occurred continued to be excluded from the analysis.[46] With this modification, officers found contraband in 26.9% of ASIP searches. In sum, the percentage of successful searches in the ASIP data was between 21.8% and 32.6%. With regard to MRT searches, officers found contraband in 32.9% of searches.

Officers were allowed to select multiple categories from a list of six types of contraband found in searches. With regard to ASIP searches that produced contraband (see Table 11), drugs and/or drug paraphernalia were found in 51.6% of all successful searches. In 30.5% of all successful ASIP searches alcohol was found.

The number of successful ASIP searches (678 searches—see Table 11) included three additional searches that were not included in the Minimum Reporting Threshold data (675 searches). The contraband found in these three additional searches was categorized as "other" on

---

[46] Searches with missing data where enforcement occurred were excluded because it is not clear whether or not the citation or arrest was related in any way to the success of the search.

the data collection forms. As such, the contraband patterns for the ASIP and MRT search data were almost identical.

RACIAL/ETHNIC GROUP COMPARISONS

Demographic Profile of Eugene, Oregon

Data from the 2000 U.S. Census was used to develop demographic profiles of the Eugene population. Demographic profiles employed both the exclusive and inclusive population estimates,[47] and separate profiles were constructed for 2002 and 2003, though the differences were minimal. This is not surprising considering that modifications for population changes, like resident deaths and migration, were not included in these profiles.

In 2002, white residents made up between 87.3% (exclusive population definition—see Table 12) and 91.8% (inclusive population definition) of the driving age population of Eugene. Asian residents made up between 3.7% and 4.5%, black residents between 1.1% and 1.6%, and Latino residents 4.3% of the driving age Eugene population.[48] The 2003 profile is almost exactly the same as the 2002 profile.

While the differences between the inclusive and exclusive population estimates for white residents were relatively small (5.3% in both 2002 and 2003—see Table 13), the differences for Asian (2002=22.8%, 2003=23.2%) and black residents (2002=44.6%, 2003=46.3%) were quite substantial. Because the U.S. Census measured Latino ethnicity using a separate question, the exclusive and inclusive population estimates were identical.

---

[47] Exclusive population estimates included only those residents who selected a single racial/ethnic category on the Census form, with Latino residents removed from other racial/ethnic categories and multi-racial residents excluded from the analysis. Inclusive population estimates included all racial/ethnic categories selected by residents on the Census form, with Latino residents included in the estimates for other racial/ethnic groups. See Chapter Four for additional discussion.

[48] Since the Latino population was measured using a separate question on the Census form, there is no variation between the exclusive and inclusive residential population estimates. See Chapter Four for additional information on the methods used to measure race/ethnicity in the U. S. Census.

Table 12. Racial/Ethnic Distribution of the Eugene (OR) Driving Age Population

	Exclusive Population	Percentage	Inclusive Population	Percentage
2002 Population				
White	101,713	87.3%	107,061	91.8%
Asian	4,286	3.7%	5,264	4.5%
Black	1,295	1.1%	1,872	1.6%
Latino	4,967	4.3%	4,967	4.3%
TOTAL		116,562		
2003 Population				
White	103,057	87.2%	108,534	91.8%
Asian	4,331	3.7%	5,337	4.5%
Black	1,312	1.1%	1,920	1.6%
Latino	5,066	4.3%	5,066	4.3%
TOTAL		118,171		
2002 Males Only				
White	49,164	86.8%	51,791	91.4%
Asian	1,925	3.4%	2,392	4.2%
Black	769	1.4%	1,052	1.9%
Latino	2,664	4.7%	2,664	4.7%
TOTAL		56,644		
2003 Males Only				
White	49,863	86.7%	52,552	91.4%
Asian	1,954	3.4%	2,434	4.2%
Black	779	1.4%	1,080	1.9%
Latino	2,721	4.7%	2,721	4.7%
TOTAL		57,491		

Profiles of the age distributions for each of the four racial/ethnic groups of interest were also developed. Unlike the previous profiles, which used both the exclusive and inclusive population estimates, these profiles only employed population midpoint estimates. Several noteworthy differences were observed. In 2002, 53.9% of the white driving age population was over 39 years of age (see Table 14), compared to 28% of the Asian population, 36% of the black population, and 28.3% of the Latino population. Also, 27.6% of the white driving age population was between the ages of 18 and 29, compared to 50.8% of the Asian population, 41% of the black population, and 43% of the Latino population. These differences were also present in the 2003 profile, with only minor changes in magnitude.

Table 12. *(continued)*

	Exclusive Population	Percentage	Inclusive Population	Percentage
2002 Females Only				
White	52,549	87.7%	55,270	92.2%
Asian	2,361	3.9%	2,872	4.8%
Black	526	0.9%	820	1.4%
Latino	2,303	3.8%	2,303	3.8%
TOTAL			59,918	
2003 Females Only				
White	53,194	87.7%	55,982	92.3%
Asian	2,377	3.9%	2,903	4.8%
Black	533	0.9%	840	1.4%
Latino	2,345	3.9%	2,345	3.9%
TOTAL			60,680	

Source: 2000 U.S. Census.

Note: Exclusive population estimates included only those residents who selected a single racial/ethnic category on the Census form, with Latino residents removed from other racial/ethnic categories and multi-racial residents excluded from the analysis. Inclusive population estimates included all racial/ethnic categories selected by residents on the Census from, with Latino residents included in the estimates for other racial/ethnic groups. See Chapter Four for additional discussion.

These general patterns were relatively consistent when the male and female residential populations were analyzed separately. A larger percentage of the white male driving age population was over 39 years of age (2002=51%, 2003=52%—see Table 15) compared to the percentages of Asian male (2002=24.8%, 2003=26%), black male (2002=38%, 2003=38.4%), and Latino male residents (2002=26.3%, 2003=27.4%) in the same age group. A smaller percentage of the white male population was between the ages of 18 and 29 (2002=29%, 2003=28.3%) compared to the percentages of Asian male (2002=52.7%, 2003=50.5%), black male (2002=38.4%, 2003=37.4%), and Latino male residents (2002=44.2%, 2003=41.8%) in the same age group.

The same basic pattern was present in the female residential population. A larger percentage of the white female driving age population was over 39 years of age (2002=56.5%, 2003=57.4%—see Table 15) compared to the percentages of Asian female (2002=30.7%, 2003=32.1%), black female (2002=33.6%, 2003=34.8%), and Latino female residents (2002=30.7%, 2003=32%) in the same age group. A

Table 13. Differences Between Exclusive and Inclusive Census Population Estimates

	White		Asian		Black	
	Difference (Inclusive-Exclusive)	Percentage Difference	Difference (Inclusive-Exclusive)	Percentage Difference	Difference (Inclusive-Exclusive)	Percentage Difference
2002						
Total Population	5,348	5.3%	978	22.8%	577	44.6%
Males Only	2,627	5.3%	467	24.3%	283	36.8%
Females Only	2,721	5.2%	511	21.6%	294	55.9%
2003						
Total Population	5,477	5.3%	1,006	23.2%	608	46.3%
Males Only	2,689	5.4%	480	24.6%	301	38.6%
Females Only	2,788	5.2%	526	22.1%	307	57.6%

Source: 2000 U.S. Census.

Note: Population estimate differences are not listed for Latino residents because the U.S. Census measures Hispanic/Latino heritage using a separate indicator. As a result, the population estimate for Latino residents remains constant throughout this analysis.

Table 14. Age Distribution of Eugene Driving Age Population By Race/Ethnicity

	White		Asian		Black		Latino	
	Population Midpoint	Percentage	Population Midpoint	Percentage	Population Midpoint	Percentage	Population Midpoint	Percentage
2002								
Ages 16-17	2,899	2.8%	97	2.0%	67	4.2%	226	4.6%
Ages 18-29	28,783	27.6%	2,424	50.8%	650	41.0%	2,137	43.0%
Ages 30-39	16,432	15.7%	917	19.2%	296	18.7%	1,197	24.1%
Ages 40-59	34,325	32.9%	1,024	21.4%	441	27.8%	1,142	23.0%
Ages 60 +	21,949	21.0%	314	6.6%	131	8.2%	265	5.3%
TOTAL	104,387		4,775		1,584		4,967	
2003								
Ages 16-17	2,818	2.7%	111	2.3%	64	3.9%	207	4.1%
Ages 18-29	28,530	27.0%	2,352	48.7%	647	40.0%	2,088	41.2%
Ages 30-39	16,544	15.6%	953	19.7%	310	19.2%	1,276	25.2%
Ages 40-59	34,800	32.9%	1,080	22.3%	455	28.2%	1,213	23.9%
Ages 60 +	23,105	21.8%	339	7.0%	141	8.7%	282	5.6%
TOTAL	105,796		4,834		1,616		5,066	

Source: 2000 U.S. Census.
Note: Population midpoint estimates were determined by taking the midpoint of the exclusive and inclusive population estimates.

Table 15. Age Distribution of Eugene Driving Age Population By Sex and Race/Ethnicity

	White		Asian		Black		Latino	
	Population Midpoint	Percentage	Population Midpoint	Percentage	Population Midpoint	Percentage	Population	Percentage

Males Only

2002

Ages 16-17	1,492	3.0%	45	2.1%	36	3.9%	100	3.8%
Ages 18-29	14,654	29.0%	1,138	52.7%	350	38.4%	1,177	44.2%
Ages 30-39	8,552	16.9%	440	20.4%	180	19.8%	687	25.8%
Ages 40-59	16,782	33.2%	416	19.2%	273	30.0%	592	22.2%
Ages 60 +	8,998	17.8%	121	5.6%	73	8.0%	108	4.1%
TOTAL	50,478		2,159		911		2,664	

2003

Ages 16-17	1,443	2.8%	55	2.5%	36	3.8%	102	3.7%
Ages 18-29	14,498	28.3%	1,109	50.5%	348	37.4%	1,137	41.8%
Ages 30-39	8,671	16.9%	461	21.0%	189	20.3%	738	27.1%
Ages 40-59	17,030	33.3%	441	20.1%	279	30.0%	628	23.1%
Ages 60 +	9,567	18.7%	129	5.9%	79	8.4%	116	4.3%
TOTAL	51,208		2,194		930		2,721	

Table 15. *(continued)*

	White		Asian		Black		Latino	
	Population Midpoint	Percentage	Population Midpoint	Percentage	Population Midpoint	Percentage	Population	Percentage

Females Only

2002

Ages 16-17	1,407	2.6%	53	2.0%	32	4.7%	126	5.5%
Ages 18-29	14,129	26.2%	1,286	49.1%	300	44.6%	960	41.7%
Ages 30-39	7,880	14.6%	477	18.2%	116	17.2%	510	22.1%
Ages 40-59	17,543	32.5%	609	23.3%	168	25.0%	550	23.9%
Ages 60 +	12,951	24.0%	193	7.4%	58	8.6%	157	6.8%
TOTAL	53,910		2,617		673		2,303	

2003

Ages 16-17	1,375	2.5%	57	2.1%	28	4.1%	105	4.5%
Ages 18-29	14,032	25.7%	1,243	47.1%	299	43.6%	951	40.6%
Ages 30-39	7,873	14.4%	492	18.6%	121	17.6%	538	22.9%
Ages 40-59	17,770	32.6%	639	24.2%	177	25.7%	585	24.9%
Ages 60 +	13,538	24.8%	210	7.9%	63	9.1%	166	7.1%
TOTAL	54,588		2,640		687		2,345	

Source: 2000 U.S. Census.
Note: Population midpoint estimates were determined by taking the midpoint of the exclusive and inclusive population estimates.

smaller percentage of the white female population was between the ages of 18 and 29 (2002=26.2%, 2003=25.7%) compared to the percentages of Asian female (2002=49.1%, 2003=47.1%), black female (2002=44.6%, 2003=43.6%), and Latino female residents (2002=41.7%, 2003=40.6%) in the same age group.

These profiles clearly demonstrate profound differences between the age distributions for Asian, black, Latino, and white residents of Eugene, Oregon. Larger percentages of the white population were in the older age categories. Larger percentages of Asian, black, and Latino populations were in the 18 to 29 age group.

Differences in Vehicle Stop Demographics

There were considerable differences in terms of the distribution of stops by sex across the four racial/ethnic groups (see Table 16). Males accounted for 59.7% of white drivers, 61.5% of Asian drivers, 74% of black drivers, and 79.5% of Latino drivers stopped by EPD.

Age differences were also present in the comparisons between these groups—59.5% of Asian drivers, 57.8% of Latino drivers, 52.5% of black drivers, and 43.7% of white drivers stopped were between the ages of 18 and 29 (see Table 16). Each of these percentages was the highest for each group. While 27.5% of white drivers stopped were between the ages of 40 and 59, only 13.3% of Latino drivers fell into this age category. Finally, 5.7% of white drivers stopped were age 60 or over, while 1.8% of black drivers and 0.6% of Latino drivers fell into this age category.

While a language barrier was present only in a small percentage of vehicle stops (1.3% of all stops—see Table 3), Asian and Latino drivers experienced a language barrier more frequently than white and black drivers (see Table 16). A language barrier was present in 22.1% of stops involving Latino drivers, 8.5% of stops involving Asian drivers, and less than 0.3% of stops involving white or black drivers.

In terms of the residency of drivers stopped, the percentage of stops involving Eugene residents was consistent across all four racial/ethnic groups (see Table 16). Eugene residents accounted for 84.6% of stops involving Asian drivers, 82.9% of black drivers, 80.6% of Latino drivers, and 79% of white drivers.

Table 16. General Demographic Characteristics of Vehicle Stops by Race/Ethnicity

	White Percentage	Asian Percentage	Black Percentage	Latino Percentage
Driver's Sex				
Male	59.7%	61.5%	74.0%	79.5%
Female	40.3%	38.5%	26.0%	20.5%
N	32,000	758	776	1,403
Driver's Age				
Ages 16 - 17	3.0%	2.0%	3.1%	2.1%
Ages 18 - 29	43.7%	59.5%	52.5%	57.8%
Ages 30 - 39	20.1%	18.8%	20.1%	26.3%
Ages 40 - 59	27.5%	17.5%	22.5%	13.3%
Ages 60 +	5.7%	2.2%	1.8%	0.6%
N	32,133	760	781	1,411
Language Barrier				
No	99.8%	91.5%	99.9%	77.9%
Yes	0.2%	8.5%	0.1%	22.1%
N	31,603	755	770	1,368
Driver's Residency Status				
Eugene Resident	21.0%	15.4%	17.1%	19.4%
Not a Resident	79.0%	84.6%	82.9%	80.6%
N	32,096	759	779	1,403
Driver's Race Identifiable Prior to Stop				
No	86.7%	93.9%	86.8%	87.5%
Yes	13.3%	6.1%	13.2%	12.5%
N	31,679	754	768	1,396
Time of Stop				
3:00 AM to 9:59 AM	17.7%	17.8%	15.1%	16.1%
10:00 AM to 2:59 PM	32.9%	28.2%	23.6%	21.8%
3:00 PM to 5:59 PM	18.2%	16.6%	13.6%	14.9%
6:00 PM to 9:59 PM	13.2%	14.6%	16.6%	20.7%
10:00 PM to 2:59 AM	18.0%	22.6%	31.1%	26.6%
N	32,071	751	779	1,401
Number of Passengers				
No Passengers	67.2%	62.7%	60.7%	52.3%
One Passenger	22.9%	24.9%	26.0%	27.8%
Two Passengers	6.4%	7.9%	7.7%	10.7%
Three Passengers	2.5%	3.7%	3.8%	5.7%
Four or More	1.0%	0.8%	1.8%	3.6%
N	31,978	756	782	1,408

Source: EPD Vehicle Stop Data (2002-2003).

Officers formed an opinion about the race/ethnicity of the driver prior the stop in 13.3% of stops involving white drivers, 6.1% of Asian drivers, 13.2% of black drivers, and 12.5% of Latino drivers (see Table 16).

In terms of the time of the vehicle stop (see Table 16), the largest percentages of white (32.9%) and Asian drivers (28.2%) were stopped between 10:00 AM and 2:59 PM. The largest percentages of black (31.1%) and Latino drivers (26.6%) were stopped between 10:00 PM and 2:59 AM. The percentage of black drivers stopped during these late night hours was nearly twice the percentage of white drivers stopped during these hours (18%).

There were also differences in terms of the number of passengers (see Table 16), and the most pronounced differences were between white and Latino drivers. In 67.2% of stops involving white drivers, there were no passengers in the vehicle, compared to 52.3% of stops involving Latino drivers. In 5.7% of stops involving Latino drivers, there were three passengers in the vehicle, compared to 2.5% of stops involving white drivers. Finally, there were four or more passengers in the vehicle in 3.6% of stops involving Latino drivers, compared to only 1% of stops involving white drivers.

Stop Frequency

In order to determine whether or not Asian, black, and Latino drivers were stopped more or less frequently than white drivers, stop rates constructed using a comparative benchmark derived from 2000 U.S. Census data. Stop rates, or the number of vehicle stops per 1000 residents, were calculated by comparing the number of vehicle stops involving Eugene residents only to the number of residents identifying themselves as members of each racial/ethnic group in the 2000 Census. The following formula was used to compute the stop rates:

Stop Rate = ((Number of Stops X 1000) / Population)

Stop rates were calculated using three different estimates of the racial/ethnic distribution of the Eugene population. The exclusive stop rate was the most conservative estimate of the number of stops per 1000 Eugene residents, excluding residents who selected multiple racial/ethnic categories, while the inclusive stop rate was the most

Results of the EPD Vehicle Stop Study

liberal estimate, "double-counting" residents who selected multiple categories. The population midpoint stop rate was an attempt to find the middle ground between the exclusive and inclusive population estimates. Chi-square tests were conducted to examine differences between white drivers and Asian, black, and Latino drivers in terms of stop rates.

All Residents. In 2002, the exclusive (79.8 stops per 1000 residents—see Table 17), inclusive (65.0), and midpoint (71.6) stop rates for Asian residents were lower than the stop rates for white residents (exclusive=119.7, inclusive=113.7, midpoint=116.6). In 2003, the exclusive (67.9—see Table 18), inclusive (55.1), and midpoint (60.8) stop rates for Asian residents remained lower than the stop rates for white residents (exclusive=125.4, inclusive=119.1, midpoint=122.2).

In 2002, the exclusive (271.0 stops per 1000 residents—see Table 17), inclusive (187.5), and midpoint (221.7) stop rates for black residents were higher than the stop rates for white residents. In 2003, the exclusive (220.3—see Table 18), inclusive (150.5), and midpoint (178.8) stop rates for black residents remained higher than the stop rates for white residents.

In 2002, the differences between stop rates for Latino residents and white residents were not statistically significant (see Table 17). In 2003, the stop rates for Latino residents (103.8 stops per 1000 residents—see Table 18) were lower than the stop rates for white residents.

The stop rates for white residents increased from 2002 to 2003 (exclusive= +5.7 stops per 1000 residents, inclusive= +5.4, midpoint= +5.6—see Table 19). The stop rates for Asian (exclusive= -11.9, inclusive= -9.9, midpoint= -10.8), black (exclusive= -50.7, inclusive= -37.0, midpoint= -42.9), and Latino residents (all rates= -16.2) all declined from 2002 to 2003.

Male Residents Only. In 2002, the exclusive (111.7 stops per 1000 residents—see Table 17), inclusive (89.9), and midpoint (99.6) stop rates for Asian male residents were lower than the stop rates for white male residents (exclusive=149.7, inclusive=142.1, midpoint=145.8). In 2003, the exclusive (87.5—see Table 18), inclusive (70.3), and

Table 17. 2002 Stop Rates

	White Exclusive Stop Rate	White Inclusive Stop Rate	White Midpoint Stop Rate	Asian Exclusive Stop Rate	Asian Inclusive Stop Rate	Asian Midpoint Stop Rate	Black Exclusive Stop Rate	Black Inclusive Stop Rate	Black Midpoint Stop Rate	Latino Exclusive Stop Rate	Latino Inclusive Stop Rate	Latino Midpoint Stop Rate
TOTAL	119.7	113.7	116.6	79.8***	65.0***	71.6***	271.0***	187.5***	221.7***	120.0	120.0	120.0
Males ONLY	149.7	142.1	145.8	111.7***	89.9***	99.6***	329.0***	240.4***	277.9***	182.1***	182.1***	182.1***
Ages 16-17	184.1	167.8	175.6	133.3	67.8*	89.9	285.7	120.0	169.0	110.0*	110.0	110.0
Ages 18-29	243.3	224.9	233.7	143.7***	114.5***	127.5***	543.2***	358.7***	432.0***	260.0	260.0**	260.0*
Ages 30-39	179.5	168.6	173.9	81.9***	69.2***	75.0***	251.6*	190.2	216.7	165.9	165.9	165.9
Ages 40-59	108.0	104.0	105.9	69.9*	56.6***	62.6**	214.6***	177.3***	194.1***	87.8	87.8	87.8
Ages 60+	45.8	44.9	45.3	63.1	53.4	57.9	58.5	51.9	55.2	18.5	18.5	18.5
Females ONLY	91.6	87.1	89.3	53.8***	44.2***	48.5***	186.3***	119.5***	145.6***	48.2***	48.2***	48.2***
Ages 16-17	122.0	110.3	115.8	78.9	44.8	57.1	235.3	87.0	127.0	31.7**	31.7**	31.7**
Ages 18-29	161.7	149.2	155.2	66.7***	53.0***	59.1***	231.5**	130.2	166.7	63.5***	63.5***	63.5***
Ages 30-39	122.1	114.7	118.3	52.5***	44.7***	48.3***	271.7***	179.9*	216.5**	58.8***	58.8***	58.8***
Ages 40-59	75.5	72.5	74.0	35.6***	30.5***	32.9***	129.3*	100.5	113.1*	25.5***	25.5***	25.5***
Ages 60+	17.7	17.4	17.5	27.2	24.8	25.9	0.0	0.0	0.0	12.7	12.7	12.7

Sources: EPD Vehicle Stop Data (2002-2003) and 2000 U.S. Census.
Note: Stop rates were calculated using the following formula: Stop Rate=((Number of Stops X 1000)/Population).
*p≤.05   **p≤.01   ***p≤.001

Table 18. 2003 Stop Rates

	White Exclusive Stop Rate	White Inclusive Stop Rate	White Midpoint Stop Rate	Asian Exclusive Stop Rate	Asian Inclusive Stop Rate	Asian Midpoint Stop Rate	Black Exclusive Stop Rate	Black Inclusive Stop Rate	Black Midpoint Stop Rate	Latino Exclusive Stop Rate	Latino Inclusive Stop Rate	Latino Midpoint Stop Rate
TOTAL	125.4	119.1	122.2	67.9***	55.1***	60.8***	220.3***	150.5***	178.8***	103.8***	103.8***	103.8***
Males ONLY	151.7	143.9	147.7	87.5***	70.3***	77.9***	283.7***	204.6***	237.8***	152.5	152.5	152.5
Ages 16-17	180.2	164.2	171.9	71.4*	44.8**	55.0*	388.9*	132.1	197.2	68.6**	68.6**	68.6**
Ages 18-29	241.7	223.3	232.1	102.1***	80.7***	90.2***	364.0***	233.5	284.5*	215.5*	215.5	215.5
Ages 30-39	180.3	168.8	174.4	93.1***	77.7***	84.7***	309.1***	239.4***	269.8***	142.3**	142.3*	142.3*
Ages 40-59	119.5	114.9	117.1	70.7**	57.6***	63.5***	239.0***	196.1***	215.4***	89.2*	89.2*	89.2*
Ages 60+	46.9	46.0	46.4	8.5*	7.1**	7.8*	54.8	47.6	51.0	17.2	17.2	17.2
Females ONLY	100.8	95.7	98.2	51.7***	42.4***	46.6***	127.6*	81.0	99.1	47.3***	47.3***	47.3***
Ages 16-17	109.7	98.8	104.0	73.2	41.7	53.1	71.4	23.8	35.7	47.6**	47.6	47.6*
Ages 18-29	163.3	150.6	156.7	49.4***	38.8***	43.4***	180.1	98.2**	127.1	49.4***	49.4***	49.4***
Ages 30-39	151.4	141.9	146.4	61.1***	52.7***	56.9***	115.8	75.3*	91.3*	65.1***	65.1***	65.1***
Ages 40-59	91.1	87.4	89.2	61.1**	52.2***	56.3**	103.2	80.8	90.7	39.3***	39.3***	39.3***
Ages 60+	20.9	20.5	20.7	10.0	9.1	9.5	34.5	29.9	32.0	6.0	6.0	6.0

Sources: EPD Vehicle Stop Data (2002-2003) and 2000 U.S. Census.
Note: Stop rates were calculated using the following formula: Stop Rate=((Number of Stops X 1000)/Population).
*$p \le .05$ **$p \le .01$ ***$p \le .001$

Table 19. Stop Rates Changes from 2002 to 2003

	White			Asian			Black			Latino		
	Exclusive Stop Rate	Inclusive Stop Rate	Midpoint Stop Rate	Exclusive Stop Rate	Inclusive Stop Rate	Midpoint Stop Rate	Exclusive Stop Rate	Inclusive Stop Rate	Midpoint Stop Rate	Exclusive Stop Rate	Inclusive Stop Rate	Midpoint Stop Rate
TOTAL	+5.7	+5.4	+5.6	-11.9	-9.9	-10.8	-50.7	-37.0	-42.9	-16.2	-16.2	-16.2
Males ONLY	+2.0	+1.8	+1.9	-24.2	-19.6	-21.7	-45.3	-35.8	-40.1	-29.6	-29.6	-29.6
Females ONLY	+9.2	+8.6	+8.9	-2.1	-1.8	-1.9	-58.7	-38.5	-46.5	-0.9	-0.9	-0.9

Sources: EPD Vehicle Stop Data (2002-2003) and 2000 U.S. Census.

midpoint (77.9) stop rates for Asian male residents remained lower than the stop rates for white male residents (exclusive=151.7, inclusive=143.9, midpoint=147.7).

The inclusion of age into this analysis reinforced this general pattern. In 2002, the exclusive, inclusive, and midpoint stop rates for Asian male residents between the ages of 18 and 59 were all lower than the stop rates for white male residents in these age groups (see Table 17). The inclusive stop rate (67.8 stops per 1000 residents) for Asian male residents ages 16 to 17 was lower than the inclusive stop rate (167.8) for white male residents in this age group. None of the other stop rate differences between Asian male and white male residents ages 16 and 17 and ages 60 and over were statistically significant in 2002. In 2003, the exclusive, inclusive, and midpoint stop rates for Asian male residents in all age categories were lower than the stop rates for white male residents (see Table 18).

In 2002, the exclusive (329.0 stops per 1000 residents—see Table 17), inclusive (240.4), and midpoint (277.9) stop rates for black male residents were higher than the stop rates for white male residents. In 2003, the exclusive (283.7—see Table 18), inclusive (204.6), and midpoint (237.8) stop rates for black male residents remained higher than the stop rates for white male residents.

The inclusion of age into the analysis revealed several interesting patterns. In 2002, the exclusive, inclusive, and midpoint stop rates for black male residents between the ages of 18 and 29 and between 40 and 59 were higher than the stop rates for white male residents in these age groups (see Table 17). The exclusive stop rate (251.6 stops per 1000 residents) for black male residents ages 30 to 39 was higher than the exclusive stop rate (179.5) for white male residents in this age group. None of the other stop rate differences between black male and white male residents ages 16 and 17, ages 30 to 39, and ages 60 and over were statistically significant in 2002. In 2003, the exclusive, inclusive, and midpoint stop rates for black male residents between the ages of 30 and 59 were higher than the stop rates for white male residents in these age groups (see Table 18). The exclusive stop rate (388.9) for black male residents ages 16 and 17, and the exclusive (364.0) and midpoint (284.5) stop rates for black male residents ages 18 to 29 were higher than the stop rates for white male residents in these age categories (exclusive for ages 16-17=180.2, exclusive for ages 18-29=241.7, midpoint for ages 18-29=232.1). None of the other stop rate differences between black male and white male residents ages 16 and

17, ages 18 to 29, and ages 60 and over were statistically significant in 2003.

In 2002, the stop rates for Latino male residents (182.1 stops per 1000 residents) were all higher than the stop rates for white male residents (see Table 17). In 2003, the differences between stop rates for Latino male residents and white male residents were not statistically significant (see Table 18).

Again, patterns related to age were observed. In 2002, the exclusive stop rate (110.0 stops per 1000 residents—see Table 17) for Latino male residents ages 16 and 17 was lower than the exclusive stop rate (184.1) for white male residents in this age group. The inclusive and midpoint (both 260.0) stop rates for Latino male residents ages 18 to 29 were higher than the stop rates for white male residents in this age category (exclusive=224.9, midpoint=233.7). None of the other stop rate differences between Latino male and white male residents ages 16 and 17, ages 18 to 29, and ages 30 and over were statistically significant in 2002. In 2003, the exclusive, inclusive, and midpoint stop rates for Latino male residents ages 16 and 17, and ages 30 to 59 were all lower than the stop rates for white male residents in the same age categories (see Table 18). The exclusive stop rate (215.5) for Latino male residents ages 18 to 29 was lower than the stop rate for white male residents (241.7) in this age group. None of the other stop rate differences between Latino male and white male residents ages 18 to 29 and ages 60 and over were statistically significant in 2003.

The stop rates for white male residents increased from 2002 to 2003 (exclusive= +2.0 stops per 1000 residents, inclusive= +1.8, midpoint= +1.9—see Table 19). The stop rates for Asian male (exclusive= -24.2, inclusive= -19.6, midpoint= -21.7), black male (exclusive= -45.3, inclusive= -35.8, midpoint= -40.1), and Latino male residents (all rates= -29.6) all declined from 2002 to 2003.

Female Residents Only. In 2002, the exclusive (53.8 stops per 1000 residents—see Table 17), inclusive (44.2), and midpoint (48.5) stop rates for Asian female residents were lower than the stop rates for white female residents (exclusive=91.6, inclusive=87.1, midpoint=89.3). In 2003, the exclusive (51.7—see Table 18), inclusive (42.4), and midpoint (46.6) stop rates for Asian female residents remained lower than the stop rates for white female residents (exclusive=100.8, inclusive=95.7, midpoint=98.2).

This general pattern was consistent once age was included in the analysis. In both 2002 and 2003, the exclusive, inclusive, and midpoint stop rates for Asian female residents between the ages of 18 and 59 were all lower than the stop rates for white female residents between these ages (see Tables 17 and 18). None of the other stop rate differences between Asian female and white female residents ages 16 and 17 and ages 60 and over were statistically significant.

In 2002, the exclusive (186.3 stops per 1000 residents—see Table 17), inclusive (119.5), and midpoint (145.6) stop rates for black female residents were higher than the stop rates for white female residents. In 2003, the exclusive stop rate (127.6—see Table 18) for black female residents was higher than the exclusive stop rate for white female residents. The differences between black female and white female residents in terms of the inclusive and midpoint stop rates in 2003 were not statistically significant.

The inclusion of age into the analysis revealed several interesting patterns. In 2002, the exclusive (271.7 stops per 1000 residents—see Table 17), inclusive (179.9), and midpoint (216.5) stop rates for black female residents ages 30 to 39 were higher than the stop rates for white female residents in this age group (exclusive=122.1, inclusive=114.7, midpoint=118.3). The exclusive stop rate (231.5) for black female residents ages 18 to 29, and the exclusive (129.3) and midpoint (113.1) stop rates for black female residents ages 40 to 59 were higher than the stop rates for white female residents in the same age categories (exclusive for ages 18-29=161.7, exclusive for ages 40-59=75.5, midpoint for ages 40-59=74.0). None of the other stop rate differences between black female and white female residents ages 16 and 17, ages 18 to 29, and ages 40 and over were statistically significant in 2002. In 2003, the inclusive stop rate (98.2—see Table 18) for black female residents ages 18 to 29, and the inclusive (75.3) and midpoint (91.3) stop rates for black female residents ages 30 to 39 were lower than the stop rates for white female residents in the same age categories (inclusive for ages 18-29=150.6, inclusive for ages 30-39=141.9, midpoint for ages 30-39=146.4). None of the other stop rate differences between black female and white female residents in 2003 were statistically significant.

In 2002, the stop rates for Latino female residents (48.2 stops per 1000 residents—see Table 17) were lower than the stop rates for white female residents. In 2003, the stop rates for Latino female residents (all

47.3—see Table 18) remained lower than the stop rates for white female residents.

The inclusion of age into this analysis reinforced this general pattern. In 2002, the exclusive, inclusive, and midpoint stop rates for Latino female residents ages 16 to 59 were lower than the stop rates for white female residents in the same age categories (see Table 17). The stop rate differences between Latino female and white female residents ages 60 and over were not statistically significant in 2002. In 2003, the exclusive, inclusive, and midpoint stop rates for Latino female residents ages 18 to 59 were lower than the stop rates for white female residents in the same age categories (see Table 18). The exclusive and midpoint stop rates (47.6 stops per 1000 residents) for Latino female residents ages 16 and 17 were lower than the exclusive (109.7) and midpoint (104) stop rates for white female residents in the same age group. None of the other stop rate differences between Latino female residents and white female residents ages 16 and 17 and ages 60 and over were statistically significant in 2003.

The stop rates for white female residents increased between 2002 and 2003 (exclusive= +9.2 stops per 1000 residents, inclusive= +8.6, midpoint= +8.9—see Table 19). The stop rates for Asian female (exclusive= -2.1, inclusive= -1.8, midpoint= -1.9), black female (exclusive= -58.7, inclusive= -38.5, midpoint= -46.5), and Latino female residents (all rates= -0.9) all declined from 2002 to 2003.

Modified Stop Rates. Using 2000 U.S. Census data to create residential population benchmarks for vehicle stops conducted in 2002 and 2003 presented a variety of problems, several of which were discussed in the Chapter Four. Two problems are of particular interest in relation to the use of Census data in the this project:

- Census data do not account for systematic errors in the data collection strategies employed by the U.S. Census Bureau.
- Census data do not account for population changes that have occurred in the time since the data collection took place.

To account for the potential impact of these sources of error, additional data sources were consulted to develop modifications for the Census population estimates. It should be noted that these modifications only address a few sources of error, and there were problems associated with the comparability[49] of the data used to calculate these modifications. As such, these estimates must be understood as attempts to capture general trends, and not as substitutes for the primary stop rates.

To address problems associated with systematic errors in Census data collection, undercount estimates provided by the U.S. Census Bureau were consulted. It is widely known that not all U.S. citizens complete and return their census forms, and research has shown that the undercount rate varies across racial/ethnic groups. At the time of this study, the undercount estimates for the 2000 Census were not available, so the estimates for Lane County, Oregon from the 1990 Census were used.[50] The undercount rate for Lane County residents 18 and over was calculated by subtracting the under-18 net undercount from the total population net undercount. This undercount rate was applied to the entire driving age population despite the fact that the undercount estimates did not include one of the age categories in the vehicle stop data (ages 16 and 17).

Two strategies were employed to address problems associated with population changes since 2000. First, 2002 Census population estimates[51] for Lane County (OR) were used to estimate Eugene population growth for each of the four racial/ethnic groups of interest. The Census population estimates allowed for separate growth calculations using exclusive and inclusive population definitions. Census estimates were available for 2002 but not for 2003, and as such the 2002 estimates were applied to both years. Second, data from the University of Oregon was used to estimate demographic changes in and growth of the student population since 2000.[52] The modification factor

---

[49] With the exception of the growth estimates for the University of Oregon population, the data used in the development of the population modifications was specific to Lane County. Data from the 2000 Census demonstrates that there are differences in the racial/ethnic distributions of Lane County and the city of Eugene.

[50] 1990 Census undercount estimates were retrieved May 6, 2005 (http://www.census.gov/dmd/www/pdf/underor.pdf)

[51] 2002 Census population estimates were retrieved May 6, 2005 (http://www.census.gov/popest/archives/2000s/vintage_2002).

[52] Student population profiles for the University of Oregon were retrieved May 6, 2005 (http://www-vms.uoregon.edu/~reoweb/profile/profle.html).

for growth in the University of Oregon population was calculated by adding these three components together:

- The raw increase in each racial/ethnic population was calculated by subtracting the mean enrolled population for 2000 from the mean enrolled populations for 2002 and 2003.

- The raw increase in multi-ethnic students only was calculated by subtracting the mean enrolled population for 2000 from the mean enrolled populations for 2002 and 2003. The raw increase was then divided in half, and the result was added to the modification factors for each of the four racial/ethnic groups.

- For international students, the ten countries with the largest number of students enrolled at the University of Oregon for each term were identified. The mean enrollment by country was calculated for both years, and students were then added to one of the four racial/ethnic group modification factors. International students from Canada and Germany were added to the white population modification factors; students from China, Hong Kong, India, Indonesia, Japan, Korea, Taiwan, and Thailand were added to the Asian population modification factors. The remaining international student populations (minus those that had already been assigned according to their home country) were divided by four and the results were added to each of the racial/ethnic modification factors. Separate modifications were calculated for 2002 and 2003.

To calculate the modified populations, the exclusive and inclusive population estimates used in the stop rate calculations were first increased according to the undercount estimate. Next, population estimates were increased by the growth factors derived from the 2002 Census population estimates. Finally, the modification factor associated with growth in the University of Oregon population was added to the population estimates. Separate modification factors were calculated for the male and female population using sex-specific data from the Census population estimates and the University of Oregon's profile of students.

The modified population estimates showed dramatic growth in the Asian, black, and Latino populations in both 2002 and 2003 (see Tables 20 and 21). The Asian population estimate increased by between 31.3% (inclusive) and 36% (exclusive) in 2002, and between 29.9% and 34.4% in 2003. The black population estimate increased by between 16.6% and 17.2% in 2002, and 17.1% and 18% in 2003. The Latino population estimates increased by roughly 19% for both years. By comparison, the increases in the white population estimates were not as substantial (see Tables 20 and 21). None of the increases to the exclusive and inclusive white population estimates were greater than 6%.

Modified stop rates were calculated using the modified population estimates. In 2002, the exclusive (58.7 stops per 1000 residents—see Table 22), inclusive (49.5), and midpoint (53.7) modified stop rates for Asian residents were lower than the modified stop rates for white residents (exclusive=113.9, inclusive=107.9, midpoint=110.8). In 2003, the exclusive (50.5), inclusive (42.4), and midpoint (46.1) modified stop rates for Asian residents remained lower than the modified stop rates for white residents (exclusive=119.0, inclusive=112.7, midpoint=115.7).

In 2002, the exclusive (231.3 stops per 1000 residents—see Table 22), inclusive (160.8), and midpoint (189.7) modified stop rates for black residents were higher than the modified stop rates for white residents. In 2003, the exclusive (186.7), inclusive (128.6), and midpoint (152.3) modified stop rates for black residents remained higher than the modified stop rates for white residents.

In 2002, the modified stop rates for Latino residents (100.8 stops per 1000 residents—see Table 22) were lower than the modified stop rates for white residents. In 2003, modified stop rates (87.2) for Latino residents remained lower than the modified stop rates for white residents.

When the analysis was limited to male residents, the patterns were generally consistent. In 2002, the exclusive (83.3 stops per 1000 residents—see Table 22), inclusive (68.3), and midpoint (75.0) modified stop rates for Asian male residents were lower than the modified stop rates for white male residents (exclusive=142.4, inclusive=134.9, midpoint=138.6). In 2003, the exclusive (65.8), inclusive (53.7), and midpoint (59.1) modified stop rates for Asian male residents remained lower than the modified stop rates for white male residents (exclusive=143.8, inclusive=136.1, midpoint=139.8).

Table 20. 2002 Population Benchmark Modifications

	Exclusive Population	Inclusive Population	1990 Census Undercount Estimate	Exclusive Population Census Growth Estimate	Inclusive Population Census Growth Estimate	University of Oregon Growth Estimate	ADJUSTED Exclusive Population	Percentage Increase	ADJUSTED Inclusive Population	Percentage Increase
TOTAL										
White	101,713	107,061	1.8%	1.4%	1.8%	+1,864.0	106,857.4	5.1%	112,813.9	5.4%
Asian	4,286	5,264	5.8%	3.6%	3.8%	+1,132.3	5,830.1	36.0%	6,913.2	31.3%
Black	1,295	1,872	2.1%	5.7%	7.9%	+120.0	1,517.6	17.2%	2,182.3	16.6%
Latino	4,967	4,967	5.5%	10.2%	10.2%	+137.0	5,911.7	19.0%	5,911.7	19.0%
Males ONLY										
White	49,164	51,791	1.8%	1.6%	1.9%	+826.9	51,676.6	5.1%	54,551.9	5.3%
Asian	1,925	2,392	5.8%	3.3%	5.6%	+477.3	2,581.2	34.1%	3,149.8	31.7%
Black	769	1,052	2.1%	3.2%	3.6%	+63.6	873.9	13.6%	1,176.4	11.8%
Latino	2,664	2,664	5.5%	9.1%	9.1%	+59.3	3,125.6	17.3%	3,125.6	17.3%
Females ONLY										
White	52,549	55,270	1.8%	1.3%	1.7%	+1,037.1	55,227.4	5.1%	58,258.5	5.4%
Asian	2,361	2,872	5.8%	3.9%	4.0%	+655.1	3,250.5	37.7%	3,815.2	32.8%
Black	526	820	2.1%	9.5%	10.9%	+56.4	644.5	22.5%	984.9	20.1%
Latino	2,303	2,303	5.5%	11.5%	11.5%	+77.8	2,786.9	21.0%	2,786.9	21.0%

Sources: 2000 U.S. Census, 1990 Census Undercount Estimates, 2002 Census Population Estimates, and University of Oregon Student Profiles.
Note: Adjusted population estimates were calculated by multiplying the original Census population estimate first by the 1990 undercount proportion estimate, then by the growth estimate derived from the 2002 Census Population estimates. Next, the University of Oregon growth estimate was added to the estimate.

Table 21. 2003 Population Benchmark Modifications

	Exclusive Population	Inclusive Population	1990 Census Undercount Estimate	Exclusive Population Census Growth Estimate	Inclusive Population Census Growth Estimate	University of Oregon Growth Estimate	ADJUSTED Exclusive Population	Percentage Increase	ADJUSTED Inclusive Population	Percentage Increase
TOTAL										
White	103,057	108,534	1.8%	1.4%	1.8%	+2,237.4	108,618.2	5.4%	114,713.8	5.7%
Asian	4,331	5,337	5.8%	3.6%	3.8%	+1,071.8	5,819.0	34.4%	6,932.9	29.9%
Black	1,312	1,920	2.1%	5.7%	7.9%	+132.4	1,548.3	18.0%	2,247.6	17.1%
Latino	5,066	5,066	5.5%	10.2%	10.2%	+142.4	6,032.2	19.1%	6,032.2	19.1%
Males ONLY										
White	49,863	52,552	1.8%	1.6%	1.9%	+1,044.9	52,617.6	5.5%	55,559.3	5.7%
Asian	1,954	2,434	5.8%	3.3%	5.6%	+463.9	2,599.5	33.0%	3,183.3	30.8%
Black	779	1,080	2.1%	3.2%	3.6%	+63.3	884.1	13.5%	1,205.7	11.6%
Latino	2,721	2,721	5.5%	9.1%	9.1%	+54.9	3,186.8	17.1%	3,186.8	17.1%
Females ONLY										
White	53,194	55,982	1.8%	1.3%	1.7%	+1,192.0	56,047.5	5.4%	59,150.5	5.7%
Asian	2,377	2,903	5.8%	3.9%	4.0%	+607.3	3,220.2	35.5%	3,801.5	31.0%
Black	533	840	2.1%	9.5%	10.9%	+68.7	664.6	24.7%	1,019.8	21.4%
Latino	2,345	2,345	5.5%	11.5%	11.5%	+87.7	2,846.2	21.4%	2,846.2	21.4%

Sources: 2000 U.S. Census, 1990 Census Undercount Estimates, 2002 Census Population Estimates, and University of Oregon Student Profiles.
Note: Adjusted population estimates were calculated by multiplying the original Census population estimate first by the 1990 undercount proportion estimate, then by the growth estimate derived from the 2002 Census Population estimates. Next, the University of Oregon growth estimate was added to the estimate.

Table 22. Modified Stop Rates

	White			Asian			Black			Latino		
	Exclusive Stop Rate	Inclusive Stop Rate	Midpoint Stop Rate	Exclusive Stop Rate	Inclusive Stop Rate	Midpoint Stop Rate	Exclusive Stop Rate	Inclusive Stop Rate	Midpoint Stop Rate	Exclusive Stop Rate	Inclusive Stop Rate	Midpoint Stop Rate
2002												
TOTAL	113.9	107.9	110.8	58.7****	49.5****	53.7****	231.3***	160.8****	189.7****	100.8***	100.8*	100.8**
Males ONLY	142.4	134.9	138.6	83.3****	68.3****	75.0****	289.5****	215.1***	246.8****	155.2*	155.2***	155.2**
Females ONLY	87.1	82.6	84.8	39.1****	33.3****	35.9****	152.1****	99.5*	120.3***	39.8****	39.8***	39.8****
2003												
TOTAL	119.0	112.7	115.7	50.5****	42.4****	46.1****	186.7****	128.6**	152.3****	87.2****	87.2***	87.2****
Males ONLY	143.8	136.1	139.8	65.8****	53.7****	59.1****	250.0***	183.3***	211.5****	130.2*	130.2	130.2
Females ONLY	95.6	90.6	93.1	38.2****	32.4****	35.0****	102.3	66.7**	80.7	39.0****	39.0***	39.0****

Sources: EPD Vehicle Stop Data (2002-2003), 2000 U.S. Census, 1990 Census Undercount Estimates, 2002 Census Population Estimates, and University of Oregon Student Profiles.
Note: Stop rates were calculated using the following formula: Stop Rate=((Number of Stops X 1000)/Population).
*$p \leq .05$ **$p \leq .01$ ****$p \leq .001$

In 2002, the exclusive (289.5 stops per 1000 residents—see Table 22), inclusive (215.1), and midpoint (246.8) modified stop rates for black male residents were higher than the modified stop rates for white male residents. In 2003, the exclusive (250.0), inclusive (183.3), and midpoint (211.5) modified stop rates for black male residents remained higher than the modified stop rates for white male residents.

In 2002, the modified stop rates for Latino male residents (155.2 stops per 1000 residents—see Table 22) were higher than the modified stop rates for white male residents. In 2003, the exclusive modified stop rate (130.2) for Latino male residents was lower than the exclusive modified stop rate for white male residents. None of the other differences between modified stop rates for Latino male residents and white male residents were statistically significant in 2003.

When the analysis was limited to female residents, several patterns of difference were observed. In 2002, the exclusive (39.1 stops per 1000 residents—see Table 22), inclusive (33.3), and midpoint (35.9) modified stop rates for Asian female residents were lower than the modified stop rates for white female residents (exclusive=87.1, inclusive=82.6, midpoint=84.8). In 2003, the exclusive (38.2), inclusive (32.4), and midpoint (35.0) modified stop rates for Asian female residents remained lower than the modified stop rates for white female residents (exclusive=95.6, inclusive=90.6, midpoint=93.1).

In 2002, the exclusive (152.1 stops per 1000 residents—see Table 22), inclusive (99.5), and midpoint (120.3) modified stop rates for black female residents were higher than the modified stop rates for white female residents. In 2003, the inclusive modified stop rate (66.7) for black female residents was lower than the inclusive modified stop rate for white female residents. None of the other differences between modified stop rates for black female residents and white female residents were statistically significant in 2003.

In 2002, the modified stop rates (39.8 stops per 1000 residents—see Table 22) for Latino female residents were lower than the modified stop rates for white female residents. In 2003, the modified stop rates for Latino female residents (39.0) remained lower than the modified stop rates for white female residents.

Summary. Stop rates for Asian residents were lower than the stop rates for white residents across both years of data collection. Asian residents experienced between 39.9 (exclusive stop rate) and 48.7 (inclusive stop rate) fewer stops per 1000 residents compared to white residents in 2002, and between 57.5 and 64.0 fewer stops in 2003. This pattern was consistent for Asian drivers of both sexes. Asian male residents experienced between 38.0 and 52.2 fewer stops compared to white male residents in 2002, and between 64.2 and 73.6 fewer stops in 2003. Asian female residents experienced between 37.8 and 42.9 fewer stops compared to white female residents in 2002, and between 49.1 and 53.3 fewer stops in 2003.

The overall stop rates for black residents were higher than the stop rates for white residents across both years of data collection. Black residents experienced between 73.8 (inclusive stop rate) and 151.3 (exclusive stop rate) more stops per 1000 residents compared to white residents in 2002, and between 31.4 and 94.9 more stops in 2003. This pattern was consistent for black male residents, who experienced between 98.3 and 179.3 more stops compared to white male residents in 2002, and between 60.7 and 132.0 more stops in 2003. The most pronounced difference between black male and white male residents in 2002 was for male residents between the ages of 18 and 29; black male residents in this age group experienced between 133.8 and 299.9 more stops than white male residents. However, in 2003 this difference diminished considerably. The difference between exclusive (122.3 more stops of black male residents) and population midpoint stop rates (52.4 more stops) for this age group were statistically significant, while the difference between inclusive stop rates was not. Black female residents experienced between 32.4 and 94.7 more stops compared to white female residents in 2002. In 2003, only the exclusive stop rate difference between black female and white female residents was statistically significant, and this stop rate indicated that black female residents experienced 26.8 more stops. However, the two other stop rates indicated that there might have been no difference between black female residents and white female residents in 2003.

In 2002, the differences between Latino and white residents in terms of overall stop rates were small and not statistically significant. In 2003, Latino drivers experienced between 15.3 (inclusive stop rate) and 21.6 (exclusive stop rate) fewer stops per 1000 residents compared to white residents. The pattern was different for Latino male residents, who experienced between 32.4 and 40.0 more stops compared to white male residents in 2002, while 2003 differences were small and not statistically significant. The stop rates for Latino female residents were consistently lower than the stop rates for white female residents.

Results of the EPD Vehicle Stop Study

Latino female residents experienced between 38.9 and 43.4 fewer stops compared to white female residents in 2002, and between 48.4 and 53.5 fewer stops in 2003.

The stop rates for white residents increased from 2002 to 2003 (population midpoint increase= +5.6), while the stop rates for Asian (-10.8), black (-42.9), and Latino residents (-16.2) declined across the two years of data collection, with the stop rates for black male (-40.1), black female (-46.5), and Latino male (-29.6) residents declining the most in terms of the number of stops per 1000 residents.

The population modifications did not have much of an impact on the general pattern of statistically significant differences with one notable exception—while the differences between Latino residents and white residents in terms of the unmodified 2002 stop rates were not statistically significant, the modified stop rates indicated that Latino drivers experienced between 7.1 (inclusive stop rate) and 13.1 (exclusive stop rate) fewer stop per 1000 residents.

The modified stop rates increased the gaps between Asian, Latino, and white residents. Using the modified stop rates, Asian residents experienced 57.1 (population midpoint) fewer stops per 1000 residents than white residents in 2002, compared to 45.0 fewer stops using the unmodified stop rates (a 12.1 stop difference). In 2003, Asian residents experienced 69.6 fewer stops than white residents using the modified stop rates, compared to 61.4 fewer stops using the unmodified stop rates (an 8.2 stop increase). Using the modified stop rates, Latino residents experienced 28.5 fewer stops than white residents in 2003, compared to 18.4 fewer stops using the unmodified stop rates (a 10.1 stop difference).

The modified stop rates decreased the differences between black residents and white residents. Using the modified stop rates, black residents experienced 78.9 (population midpoint) more stops per 1000 residents than white residents in 2002, compared to 105.1 more stops using the unmodified stop rates—a decrease of 26.2 stops. In 2003, black residents experienced 36.6 more stops than white residents using the modified stop rates, compared to 56.6 more stops using the unmodified stop rates—a difference of 20 stops per 1000 residents.

On the whole, modified stop rates showed that Asian and Latino residents may have been stopped at even lower rates than those indicated in the unmodified stop rates. The modified stop rates also demonstrated that the gaps between black and white residents might not be as large as indicated by the unmodified stop rates, though statistically significant differences persist.

Reason for Stop

Chi-square tests were conducted to examine differences between white drivers and Asian, black, and Latino drivers for each of the nine reasons for stop.

A larger percentage of Asian drivers were stopped for traffic violations (83.3%—see Table 23) compared to the percentage of white drivers (78.8%). Smaller percentages of Asian drivers were stopped for pre-existing knowledge (0.8%) and equipment violations (16.2%) compared to the percentages of white drivers (pre-existing knowledge=2.3%, equipment violation=19.6%). None of the other differences between Asian and white drivers in terms of reasons for stop were statistically significant.

Larger percentages of black drivers were stopped for ORS crimes (1.2%—see Table 23), calls for service (1.4%), pre-existing knowledge (5.9%), passenger violations (1.9%), and equipment violations (23.1%) compared to the percentages of white drivers (ORS crime=0.4%, call for service=0.6%, passenger violation=1%). A smaller percentage of black drivers were stopped for traffic violations (72.3%) compared to the percentage of white drivers. None of the other differences between black and white drivers in terms of reason for stop were statistically significant.

Larger percentages of Latino drivers were stopped for ORS crimes (0.9%—see Table 23), calls for service (1.1%), pre-existing knowledge (5.9%), and equipment violations (25.1%) compared to the percentages of white drivers. A smaller percentage of Latino drivers were stopped for traffic violations (70.1%) compared to the percentage of white drivers. None of the other differences between Latino and white drivers in terms of reason for stop were statistically significant.

Males Only. A larger percentage of Asian male drivers were stopped for traffic violations (83.2%—see Table 23) compared to the percentage of white male drivers (77.6%). Smaller percentages of Asian male drivers were stopped for pre-existing knowledge (0.9%) and equipment violations (16.6%) compared to the percentages of

Results of the EPD Vehicle Stop Study

Table 23. Reason for Stop by Race/Ethnicity

	White Percentage	Asian Percentage	Black Percentage	Latino Percentage
TOTAL				
Traffic Violation	78.8%	83.3%***	72.3%***	70.1%***
ORS Crime	0.4%	0.1%	1.2%**	0.9%**
Call for Service	0.6%	0.5%	1.4%*	1.1%*
Pre-Existing Knowledge	2.3%	0.8%**	5.9%***	5.9%***
Passenger Violation	1.0%	0.5%	1.9%*	1.3%
Equipment Violation	19.6%	16.2%*	23.1%**	25.1%***
Violation of City Ordinance	0.5%	0.1%	1.0%	0.6%
Special Detail	0.2%	0.1%	0.3%	0.2%
Other	1.1%	0.9%	0.9%	1.0%
N	32,091	760	779	1,411
Males ONLY				
Traffic Violation	77.6%	83.2%**	71.1%***	69.0%***
ORS Crime	0.5%	0.2%	1.4%**	1.1%*
Call for Service	0.8%	0.6%	1.8%**	1.3%
Pre-Existing Knowledge	2.6%	0.9%**	5.6%***	6.6%***
Passenger Violation	1.0%	0.4%	2.1%*	1.3%
Equipment Violation	20.7%	16.6%*	23.1%	25.7%***
Violation of City Ordinance	0.5%	0.2%	1.2%*	0.4%
Special Detail	0.2%	0.2%	0.2%	0.2%
Other	1.3%	0.6%	1.2%	1.1%
N	19,022	464	571	1,115
Females ONLY				
Traffic Violation	80.6%	83.5%	76.1%	74.5%**
ORS Crime	0.2%	0.0%	0.0%	0.0%
Call for Service	0.3%	0.3%	0.5%	0.0%
Pre-Existing Knowledge	2.0%	0.7%	6.5%***	3.1%
Passenger Violation	1.1%	0.7%	1.5%	1.7%
Equipment Violation	17.8%	15.5%	22.4%	22.4%*
Violation of City Ordinance	0.5%	0.0%	0.5%	1.4%
Special Detail	0.1%	0.0%	0.5%	0.0%
Other	0.9%	1.4%	0.0%	0.7%
N	10,334	291	201	286

Source: EPD Vehicle Stop Data (2002-2003).
*$p \leq .05$ **$p \leq .01$ ***$p \leq .001$ (two-tailed tests)

white male drivers (pre-existing knowledge=2.6%, equipment violation=20.7%). None of the other differences between Asian male and white male drivers in terms of reason for stop were statistically significant.

Larger percentages of black male drivers were stopped for ORS crimes (1.4%—see Table 23), calls for service (1.8%), pre-existing knowledge (5.6%), passenger violations (2.1%), and city ordinance violations (1.2%) compared to the percentages of white male drivers (ORS crime=0.5%, call for service=0.8%, passenger violation=1%, city ordinance violation=0.5%). A smaller percentage of black male drivers were stopped for traffic violations (71.1%) compared to the percentage of white male drivers. None of the other differences between black male and white male drivers in terms of reason for stop were statistically significant.

Larger percentages of Latino male drivers were stopped for ORS crimes (1.1%—see Table 23), pre-existing knowledge (6.6%), and equipment violations (25.7%) compared to the percentages of white male drivers. A smaller percentage of Latino male drivers were stopped for traffic violations (69%) compared to the percentage of white male drivers. None of the other differences between Latino male and white male drivers in terms of reason for stop were statistically significant.

Females Only. On the whole, there were no statistically significant differences between Asian female and white female drivers in terms of reason for stop (see Table 23).

A larger percentage of black female drivers were stopped for pre-existing knowledge (6.5%—see Table 23) compared to the percentage of white female drivers (2%). None of the other differences between black female and white female drivers in terms of reason for stop were statistically significant.

A larger percentage of Latino female drivers were stopped for equipment violations (22.4%—see Table 23) compared to the percentage of white female drivers (17.8%). A smaller percentage of Latino female drivers were stopped for traffic violations (74.5%) compared to the percentage of white female drivers (80.6%). None of the other differences between Latino female and white female drivers were statistically significant.

Summary. Over the two-year data collection period, a larger percentage of Asian drivers were stopped for traffic violations, and smaller percentages were stopped for pre-existing knowledge and equipment violations compared to white drivers. This pattern was consistent in the comparisons of Asian male and white male drivers, while there were no statistically significant differences between Asian female and white female drivers in terms of reason for stop.

Larger percentages of black drivers were stopped for ORS crimes, calls for service, pre-existing knowledge, equipment violations, and passenger violations, and a smaller percentage were stopped for traffic violations compared to white drivers. This pattern was consistent in the comparisons of black male and white male drivers with two exceptions—a larger percentage of black male drivers were stopped for city ordinance violations, and the difference between black male and white male drivers in terms of equipment violations was not statistically significant. A larger percentage of black female drivers were stopped for pre-existing knowledge compared to white female drivers, though none of the other differences in terms of reason for stop were statistically significant.

Larger percentages of Latino drivers were stopped for ORS crimes, calls for service, pre-existing knowledge, and equipment violations, and a smaller percentage were stopped for traffic violations compared to white drivers. This pattern was consistent in the comparisons of Latino male and white male drivers with one exception—the difference between Latino male and white male drivers in terms of calls for service was not statistically significant. A larger percentage of Latino female drivers were stopped for equipment violations, and a smaller percentage were stopped for traffic violations compared to white female drivers.

District of Stop

Chi-square tests were conducted to examine differences between white drivers and Asian, black, and Latino drivers in terms of the distribution of stops across and outside EPD's five patrol districts.

Larger percentages of Asian drivers were stopped in districts one (23.7%—see Table 24) and two (24.6%) compared to the percentages of white drivers (district one=18.3%, district two=18.1%). A smaller percentage of Asian drivers were stopped in district four (7.3%) compared to the percentage of white drivers (16%). None of the other differences between Asian and white drivers in terms of district of stop were statistically significant.

A larger percentage of black drivers were stopped in district five (38.3%—see Table 24) compared to the percentage of white drivers (29.4%). Smaller percentages of black drivers were stopped in districts two (15.1%) and four (12.8%) compared to the percentages of white drivers. None of the other differences between black and white drivers in terms of district of stop were statistically significant.

Table 24. District of Stop by Race/Ethnicity

	White Percentage	Asian Percentage	Black Percentage	Latino Percentage
TOTAL				
Outside EPD Patrol Districts	1.5%	2.2%	2.1%	1.1%
Patrol District One	18.3%	23.7%***	17.0%	11.2%***
Patrol District Two	18.1%	24.6%***	15.1%*	9.8%***
Patrol District Three	16.8%	14.6%	14.7%	14.1%**
Patrol District Four	16.0%	7.3%***	12.8%**	23.8%***
Patrol District Five	29.4%	27.6%	38.3%***	40.0%***
N	32,036	756	775	1,402
Males ONLY				
Outside EPD Patrol Districts	1.4%	3.2%**	2.1%	1.2%
Patrol District One	17.3%	23.8%***	17.3%	10.4%***
Patrol District Two	16.9%	24.9%***	13.0%**	8.9%***
Patrol District Three	16.4%	12.6%*	14.1%	13.7%**
Patrol District Four	16.9%	8.2%***	12.0%***	25.2%***
Patrol District Five	31.1%	27.3%*	41.5%***	40.6%***
N	18,980	462	568	1,107
Females ONLY				
Outside EPD Patrol Districts	1.7%	0.7%	1.5%	0.7%
Patrol District One	19.7%	23.8%	17.0%	14.3%*
Patrol District Two	20.0%	23.8%	21.0%	12.9%**
Patrol District Three	17.3%	17.9%	17.0%	15.7%
Patrol District Four	14.6%	5.5%***	15.5%	18.9%*
Patrol District Five	26.8%	28.3%	28.0%	37.4%***
N	12,814	290	200	286

Source: EPD Vehicle Stop Data (2002-2003).
*$p \leq .05$ **$p \leq .01$ ***$p \leq .001$ (two-tailed tests)

Larger percentages of Latino drivers were stopped in districts four (23.8%—see Table 24) and five (40%) compared to the percentages of white drivers. Smaller percentages of Latino drivers were stopped in districts one (11.2%), two (9.8%), and three (14.1%) compared to the percentages of white drivers (district three=16.8%). The difference between Latino and white drivers in terms of stops that occurred outside EPD patrol districts was not statistically significant.

Males Only. Larger percentages of Asian male drivers were stopped in districts one (23.8%—see Table 24) and two (24.9%), and outside the EPD patrol districts (3.2%) compared to the percentages of white male drivers (district one=17.3%, district two=16.9%, outside EPD patrol districts=1.4%). Smaller percentages of Asian male drivers were stopped in patrol districts three (12.6%), four (8.2%), and five

Results of the EPD Vehicle Stop Study 135

(27.3%) compared to the percentages of white male drivers (district three=16.4%, district four=16.9%, district five=31.1%).

A larger percentage of black male drivers were stopped in district five (41.5%—see Table 24) compared to the percentage of white male drivers. Smaller percentages of black male drivers were stopped in districts two (13%) and four (12%) compared to the percentages of white male drivers. None of the other differences between black male and white male drivers in terms of district of stop were statistically significant.

Larger percentages of Latino male drivers were stopped in districts four (25.2%—see Table 24) and five (40.6%) compared to the percentages of white male drivers. Smaller percentages of Latino male drivers were stopped in districts one (10.4%), two (8.9%), and three (13.7%) compared to the percentages of white male drivers. The difference between Latino male and white male drivers in terms of stops that occurred outside EPD patrol districts was not statistically significant.

Females Only. A smaller percentage of Asian female drivers were stopped in district four (5.5%—see Table 24) compared to the percentage of white female drivers (14.6%). None of the other differences between Asian female and white female drivers in terms of district of stop were statistically significant.

There were no statistically significant differences between black female and white female drivers in terms of district of stop (see Table 24).

Larger percentages of Latino female drivers were stopped in districts four (18.9%—see Table 24) and five (37.4%) compared to the percentages of white female drivers (district four=14.6%, district five=26.8%). Smaller percentages of Latino female drivers were stopped in districts one (14.3%) and two (12.9%) compared to the percentage of white female drivers (district one=19.7%, district two=20%). None of the other differences between Latino female and white female drivers in terms of district of stop were statistically significant.

Summary. Over the two-year data collection period, larger percentages of Asian drivers were stopped in patrol districts one and two, and a smaller percentage were stopped in patrol district four compared to white drivers. Larger percentages of Asian male drivers were stopped in patrol districts one, two, and outside EPD patrol districts, and smaller percentages were stopped in patrol districts three, four, and five compared to white male drivers. A smaller percentage of Asian female drivers were stopped in patrol district four compared to white female drivers.

A larger percentage of black drivers were stopped in patrol district five, and smaller percentages were stopped in patrol districts two and four compared to white drivers. This pattern was consistent across the comparisons between black male and white male drivers, while there were no statistically significant differences between black female and white female drivers in terms of district of stop.

Larger percentages of Latino drivers were stopped in patrol districts four and five, and smaller percentages were stopped in patrol districts one, two, and three compared to white drivers. This pattern was consistent across the comparisons between Latino and white drivers of both sexes with one exception—the difference between Latino female and white female drivers in terms of stops that occurred in patrol district three was not statistically significant.

Result of Stop

Chi-square tests were conducted to examine differences between white drivers and Asian, black, and Latino drivers group in terms of stops resulting in enforcement action (a citation and/or an arrest) and stops resulting in arrests. Logistic regression models were constructed to examine the effect of race/ethnicity on enforcement action and arrests while controlling for the effects of relevant independent variables.

Smaller percentages of black (58.1%—see Table 25) and Latino (58.5%) drivers experienced enforcement action compared to the percentage of white drivers (65.9%). The difference between Asian and white drivers in terms of enforcement action was not statistically significant.

A smaller percentage of Asian drivers (0.9%—see Table 25), and larger percentages of black (5.7%) and Latino (6.2%) drivers were arrested compared to the percentage of white drivers (3%).

Males Only. Smaller percentages of black male (58.5%—see Table 25) and Latino male (59.8%) drivers experienced enforcement

Results of the EPD Vehicle Stop Study

Table 25. Result of Stop by Race/Ethnicity

		White Percentage	Asian Percentage	Black Percentage	Latino Percentage
TOTAL					
	Enforcement Action	65.9%	65.2%	58.1%***	58.5%***
	Arrest	3.0%	0.9%***	5.7%***	6.2%***
	N	32,039	762	776	1,405
Males ONLY					
	Enforcement Action	64.9%	63.4%	58.5%***	59.8%***
	Arrest	4.0%	1.5%**	6.5%**	7.1%***
	N	18,992	465	569	1,111
Females ONLY					
	Enforcement Action	67.8%	68.2%	57.5%***	54.5%***
	Arrest	1.6%	0.0%*	2.5%	2.5%
	N	12,799	292	200	285

Source: EPD Vehicle Stop Data (2002-2003)

Note: Significance tests for arrests were one-tailed, predicitng that black and Latino drivers were more likely, and Asian drivers were less likely than white drivers to be arrested. Tests for enforcement action were two-tailed.

*$p \leq .05$ **$p \leq .01$ ***$p \leq .001$

action compared to the percentage of white male drivers (64.9%). The difference between Asian and white male drivers in terms of enforcement action was not statistically significant.

A smaller percentage of Asian male (1.5%—see Table 25), and larger percentages of black male (6.5%) and Latino male (7.1%) drivers were arrested compared to the percentage of white male drivers (4%).

Females Only. Smaller percentages of black female (57.5%—see Table 25) and Latino female (54.5%) drivers experienced enforcement action compared to the percentage of white female drivers (67.8%). The difference between Asian female and white female drivers in terms of enforcement action was not statistically significant.

A smaller percentage of Asian female drivers were arrested (0%—see Table 25) compared to the percentage of white female drivers (1.6%). The differences between black, Latino, and white female drivers in terms of arrests was not statistically significant.

Enforcement Action Regression. In these models, positive coefficients and odds ratios greater than one indicate an increase in the likelihood that a stop resulted in enforcement action, while negative coefficients and odds ratios less than one indicate a decrease in the likelihood that a stop resulted in enforcement action.

Controlling for the effects of sex and age (Model 1—see Table 26), black drivers were 28.1%[53] less likely, and Latino drivers were 23.4% less likely than white drivers to experience enforcement action. The difference between Asian drivers and white drivers was not statistically significant. Female drivers were 12.1% more likely than male drivers to experience enforcement action. Drivers ages 30 to 39 were 13.8% more likely, and drivers ages 40 and over were 22.2% more likely than drivers ages 16 to 29 to experience enforcement action.

When other variables of interest (district of stop, reason for stop, number of passengers, presence of a language barrier, identification of the driver's race prior to the stop, and hour of stop—see Model 2, Table 26) were entered into the model, several changes were observed. Black and Latino drivers were no longer less likely than white drivers to experience enforcement action. Also, the effects associated with sex and age reversed direction. In the previous model, female drivers and drivers ages 40 and over were more likely than their counterparts to experience enforcement action. When the effects of other relevant variables were included in the model, female drivers were 6.6% less likely than male drivers to experience enforcement action, while drivers ages 40 and over were 19.4% less likely than drivers ages 16 to 29 to experience enforcement action. The difference between drivers ages 30 to 39 and drivers ages 16 to 29 was no longer statistically significant in the Model 2.

The effects of offending on enforcement action were complex. The difference between drivers stopped for traffic violations only and serious, or low discretion, violations alone or in combination with other reasons (RFSLOD) was not statistically significant (see Table 26). However, there were statistically significant differences between the different categories of high discretion violations. Drivers stopped for equipment or passenger violations only (RFSHID1) were 78.2% less likely than drivers who were stopped for traffic violations only to experience enforcement action. Similarly, drivers who were stopped for a combination of traffic, equipment, and passenger violations

---

[53] Odds ratios were calculated using the following formula: $[(e^b-1) \times 100]$.

Table 26. Logistic Predictors of Enforcement Action

		Model 1			Model 2		
		B	S.E.	Exp(B)	B	S.E.	Exp(B)
Driver's Race/Ethnicity							
	ASIAN	.024	.081	1.024	-.090	.091	.914
	BLACK	-.330***	.077	0.719	-.098	.087	.907
	LATINO	-.267***	.058	0.766	-.101	.072	.904
Driver's Sex							
	FEMALE	.115***	.024	1.121	-.068**	.028	.934
Driver's Age							
	AGE3039	.129***	.031	1.138	-.053	.036	.948
	AGE40OVR	.201***	.027	1.222	-.216***	.032	.806
District of Stop							
	DIST0	-	-	-	-.303**	.118	1.354
	DIST1	-	-	-	-.240***	.040	1.271
	DIST2	-	-	-	.260***	.041	1.296
	DIST3	-	-	-	.118**	.040	1.125
	DIST4	-	-	-	-.142***	.040	.867
Reason for Stop							
	RFSHID1	-	-	-	-1.522***	.035	.218
	RFSHID2	-	-	-	-.798***	.071	.450
	RFSLOD	-	-	-	.017	.059	1.017
Number of Passengers							
	PASS1	-	-	-	-.199***	.032	.819
	PASS2PLS	-	-	-	-.083	.044	.920
Language Barrier							
	LANGYES	-	-	-	.433***	.129	1.542
Identify Race Before Stop							
	RACEYES	-	-	-	-.589***	.038	.555
Hour of Stop							
	HRLATE	-	-	-	-1.822***	.040	.162
	HRMORN	-	-	-	-.294***	.041	.745
	HRRUSH	-	-	-	-.126**	.042	.882
	HREVE	-	-	-	-1.390***	.042	.249
	Constant	.559***	.020	1.749	1.829***	.042	6.226
	N	32,592	92.6%				
	Cases Missing Data	2,621	7.4%				

Source: EPD Vehicle Stop Data (2002-2003)

Note: Significance tests for race/ethnicity were one-tailed, predicitng that black and Latino drivers were more likely, and Asian drivers were less likely than white drivers to be arrested. Tests for all other variables were two-tailed.

*$p \leq .05$ **$p \leq .01$ ***$p \leq .001$

(RFSHID2) were 55% less likely than drivers who were stopped for traffic violations only to experience enforcement action.

The regression analysis further revealed that the time and location of the stop had an impact on enforcement action. Drivers stopped in districts one (27.1%), two (29.6%), three (12.5%), and outside EPD patrol districts (35.4%) were more likely than drivers stopped in district five to experience enforcement action, while drivers stopped in district four (13.3%) were less likely than drivers stopped in district five to experience enforcement action. Compared to drivers who were stopped between 10:00 AM and 2:59 PM, drivers who were stopped during the late night hours (10:00 PM to 2:59 AM) were 83.8% less likely, drivers stopped in the early morning hours and the morning commute (3:00 AM to 9:59 AM) were 25.5% less likely, drivers stopped during evening rush hours (3:00 PM to 5:59 PM) were 11.8% less likely, and drivers stopped during evening hours (6:00 PM to 9:59 PM) were 75.1% less likely to experience enforcement action.

Several other statistically significant relationships were noted in the regression analysis:

- Stops where the vehicle had one passenger (18.1%) were less likely to result in enforcement action compared to stops where the driver was the only occupant.

- Stops where a language barrier was present were 54.2% more likely to result in enforcement action compared to stops where there was no language barrier.

- Stops where the officer could tell the race of the driver prior to the stop were 44.5% less likely to result in enforcement action compared to stops where the officer could not tell the race of the driver prior to the stop.

Arrest Regression. In these models, positive coefficients and odds ratios greater than one indicate an increase in the likelihood that a stop resulted in an arrest, while negative coefficients and odds ratios less than one indicate a decrease in the likelihood that a stop resulted an arrest.

Controlling for the effects of sex and age (Model 1—see Table 27), Asian drivers were 74.5% less likely, while black drivers were 61.3%

Table 27. Logistic Predictors of Arrests

		Model 1			Model 2		
		B	S.E.	Exp(B)	B	S.E.	Exp(B)
Driver's Race/Ethnicity							
	ASIAN	-1.367***	.412	.255	-1.309**	.418	.270
	BLACK	.478**	.167	1.613	.210	.177	1.234
	LATINO	.490***	.121	1.633	.001	.154	1.001
Driver's Sex							
	FEMALE	-.964***	.079	.381	-.826***	.082	.438
Driver's Age							
	AGE3039	.247***	.076	1.280	.397***	.081	1.487
	AGE40OVR	-.313***	.079	.731	.065	.085	1.067
District of Stop							
	DIST0	-	-	-	-.998*	.464	.368
	DIST1	-	-	-	-.418***	.109	.658
	DIST2	-	-	-	-.622***	.121	.537
	DIST3	-	-	-	-.311**	.104	.733
	DIST4	-	-	-	.142	.085	1.152
Reason for Stop							
	RFSHID1	-	-	-	-.457***	.102	.633
	RFSHID2	-	-	-	.162	.172	1.176
	RFSLOD	-	-	-	1.668***	.085	5.302
Number of Passengers							
	PASS1	-	-	-	.355***	.076	1.426
	PASS2PLS	-	-	-	.501***	.096	1.650
Language Barrier							
	LANGYES	-	-	-	.646**	.228	1.907
Identify Race Before Stop							
	RACEYES	-	-	-	.636***	.079	1.889
Hour of Stop							
	HRLATE	-	-	-	1.530***	.102	4.620
	HRMORN	-	-	-	.312*	.131	1.366
	HRRUSH	-	-	-	.296*	.128	1.345
	HREVE	-	-	-	.816***	.117	2.261
	Constant	-3.123***	.050	.044	-4.270***	.115	.014
	N	32,592	92.6%				
	Cases Missing Data	2,621	7.4%				

Source: EPD Vehicle Stop Data (2002-2003)
*$p \leq .05$ **$p \leq .01$ ***$p \leq .001$ (two-tailed tests)

more likely, and Latino drivers were 63.3% more likely than white drivers to be arrested. Female drivers were 61.9% less likely than male drivers to be arrested. Drivers ages 30 to 39 were 28% more likely, and drivers ages 40 and over were 26.9% less likely than drivers ages 16 to 29 to be arrested.

When the remaining independent variables were entered into the model (see Model 2, Table 27), several changes were observed. Black drivers and Latino drivers were no longer more likely than white drivers to be arrested. Asian drivers were still less likely than white drivers to be arrested, though only by a slightly smaller percentage (73%). Female drivers were 56.2% less likely than male drivers to be arrested, a decrease of 5.7% from the previous model. Drivers ages 30 to 39 were 48.7% more likely than drivers ages 16 to 29 to be arrested, an increase of 23.3%. The difference between drivers ages 40 and over and drivers ages 16 to 29 was not statistically significant after controlling for the effects of relevant independent variables.

Offending had a profound impact on arrests. Drivers who were stopped for low discretion violations (RFSLOD) were much more likely to be arrested (430.2%—see Table 27) compared to drivers who were stopped for traffic violations only. In terms of high discretion violations, drivers who were stopped for equipment or passenger violations (RFSHID1) were 36.7% less likely to be arrested than drivers stopped for traffic violations only, while the difference between drivers stopped for traffic violations only and drivers stopped for a combination of traffic, equipment, and passenger violations (RFSHID2) was not statistically significant.

The regression analysis further revealed that the time and location of the stop had an impact on arrests. Drivers stopped in districts one (34.2%—see Table 27), two (46.3%), three (26.7%), and outside EPD patrol districts (63.2%) were less likely than drivers stopped in district five to be arrested, while the difference between drivers stopped in districts four and five was not statistically significant. Compared to drivers who were stopped between 10:00 AM and 2:59 PM, drivers who were stopped during the late night hours (362%), early morning hours and the morning commute (36.6%), evening rush hours (35.4%), and evening hours (126.1%) were all more likely to be arrested.

Several other statistically significant relationships were noted in the regression analysis:

- Stops where the vehicle had one passenger (42.6%) or two or more passengers (65%) were more likely to result in an arrest.
- Stops where a language barrier was present were 90.7% more likely to result in an arrest.
- Stops where the officer could tell the race of the driver prior to the stop were 88.9% more likely to result in an arrest.

Summary. Over the two-year data collection period, a smaller percentage of Asian drivers were arrested compared to white drivers. The difference between Asian and white drivers in terms of enforcement action was not statistically significant. These patterns were consistent across the comparisons between Asian and white drivers of both sexes.

A smaller percentage of black drivers experienced enforcement action, and a larger percentage of were arrested compared to white drivers. This pattern was consistent across the comparisons between black male and white male drivers. A smaller percentage of black female drivers experienced enforcement action compared to white female drivers, while the difference between black female and white female drivers in terms of arrests was not statistically significant.

A smaller percentage of Latino drivers experienced enforcement action, and a larger percentage were arrested compared to white drivers. This pattern was consistent across the comparisons between Latino male and white male drivers. A smaller percentage of Latino female drivers experienced enforcement action compared to white female drivers, while the difference between Latino female and white female drivers in terms of arrests was not statistically significant.

Logistic regression analysis revealed that the effect of race/ethnicity on enforcement action was not statistically significant after controlling for the effects of relevant independent variables. In terms of predicting enforcement action, stops that occurred in districts four and five, drivers who were stopped during evening and late night hours, and drivers who were stopped for equipment or passenger violations, or for a combination of low discretion violations, were all less likely to experience enforcement action. Drivers who were stopped during midday hours (10:00 AM through 2:59 PM), stops where a language barrier was present, and stops where one or more passengers were in the vehicle were all more likely to result in enforcement action.

Logistic regression analysis revealed that Asian drivers were 73% less likely than white drivers to be arrested even after controlling for the effects of relevant independent variables, while the effects for black drivers and Latino drivers were not statistically significant in explaining arrests. Drivers stopped for serious violations, stops that occurred in district five, drivers who were stopped during evening and late night hours, and stops where a language barrier was present were all more likely to result in an arrest.

Duration of Stop

Chi-square tests were conducted to examine differences between white drivers and Asian, black, and Latino drivers in terms of stop duration. Logistic regression models were constructed to examine the effect of race/ethnicity on stop duration in terms of stops that lasted more than 15 minutes and more than 30 minutes while controlling for the effects of relevant independent variables.

Larger percentages of black (18.8%—see Table 28) and Latino (22.6%) drivers were stopped for more than 15 minutes compared to the percentage of white drivers (10.5%). The difference between Asian and white drivers in terms of stops that lasted more than 15 minutes was not statistically significant.

A smaller percentage of Asian drivers (0.8%—see Table 28), and larger percentages of black (4.7%) and Latino (6.5%) drivers were stopped for more than 30 minutes compared to the percentage of white drivers (2.9%).

Males Only. A smaller percentage of Asian male drivers (9.4%—see Table 28), and larger percentages of black male (20.5%) and Latino male (25.5%) drivers were stopped for more than 15 minutes compared to the percentage of white male drivers (12.8%). This basic pattern held true for longer stops—compared to white drivers (3.7%), a smaller percentage of Asian male (1.1%), and larger percentages of black male (5.9%) and Latino male (7.4%) drivers were stopped for more than 30 minutes.

Females Only. Larger percentages of black female (13.9%—see Table 28) and Latino female (11.5%) drivers were stopped for more

Results of the EPD Vehicle Stop Study

Table 28. Duration of Stop by Race/Ethnicity

		White Percentage	Asian Percentage	Black Percentage	Latino Percentage
TOTAL					
	15 Minutes or More	10.5%	8.9%	18.8%***	22.6%***
	30 Minutes or More	2.9%	0.8%***	4.7%**	6.5%***
	N	32,158	762	780	1,405
Males ONLY					
	15 Minutes or More	12.8%	9.4%*	20.5%***	25.5%***
	30 Minutes or More	3.7%	1.1%**	5.9%**	7.4%***
	N	19,065	466	572	1,109
Females ONLY					
	15 Minutes or More	7.3%	7.9%	13.9%***	11.5%**
	30 Minutes or More	1.7%	0.3%*	1.5%	2.8%
	N	12,846	291	201	287

Source: EPD Vehicle Stop Data (2002-2003).
Note: Significance tests for duration were one-tailed, predicitng that black and Latino drivers were more likely, and Asian drivers were less likely than white drivers to be stopped for more than 15 minutes and more than 30 minutes.
*$p \leq .05$ **$p \leq .01$ ***$p \leq .001$

than 15 minutes compare to the percentage of white female drivers (7.3%). The difference between Asian female and white female drivers in terms of stops that lasted more than 15 minutes was not statistically significant.

A smaller percentage of Asian female drivers (0.3%—see Table 28) were stopped for more than 30 minutes compared to the percentage of white female drivers (1.7%). The differences between black, Latino, and white female drivers in terms of stops that lasted more than 30 minutes were not statistically significant.

15-Minute Split Regression. In these models, positive coefficients and odds ratios greater than one indicate an increase in the likelihood that a stop lasted more than 15 minutes, while negative coefficients and odds ratios less than one indicate a decrease in the likelihood that a stop lased more than 15 minutes.

Controlling for the effects of sex and age (Model 1—see Table 29), Asian drivers were 22.6% less likely, while black drivers were 68.4% more likely, and Latino drivers were 99.6% more likely than white drivers to be stopped for more than 15 minutes. Female drivers were 46.1% less likely than male drivers to be stopped for more than 15

Table 29. Logistic Predictors of Stop Duration, 15-Minute Split

		Model 1			Model 2		
		B	S.E.	Exp(B)	B	S.E.	Exp(B)
Driver's Race/Ethnicity							
	ASIAN	-.256	.133	.774	-.161	.139	.851
	BLACK	.521***	.099	1.684	.365***	.105	1.440
	LATINO	.691***	.070	1.996	.256**	.086	1.292
Driver's Sex							
	FEMALE	-.618***	.040	.539	-.522**	.042	.594
Driver's Age							
	AGE3039	.115**	.043	1.122	.174***	.046	1.191
	AGE40OVR	-.524***	.045	.592	-.303***	.048	.738
District of Stop							
	DIST0	-	-	-	-.323	.174	.724
	DIST1	-	-	-	-.369***	.059	.691
	DIST2	-	-	-	-.611***	.064	.543
	DIST3	-	-	-	-.096	.056	.909
	DIST4	-	-	-	.107*	.051	1.113
Reason for Stop							
	RFSHID1	-	-	-	.218***	.048	1.244
	RFSHID2	-	-	-	.741***	.085	2.098
	RFSLOD	-	-	-	1.525***	.060	4.597
Number of Passengers							
	PASS1	-	-	-	.280***	.043	1.324
	PASS2PLS	-	-	-	.543***	.055	1.721
Language Barrier							
	LANGYES	-	-	-	.953***	.133	2.594
Identify Race Before Stop							
	RACEYES	-	-	-	.842***	.046	2.322
Hour of Stop							
	HRLATE	-	-	-	.670***	.054	1.954
	HRMORN	-	-	-	.175**	.062	1.191
	HRRUSH	-	-	-	.145*	.061	1.156
	HREVE	-	-	-	.471***	.059	1.602
	Constant	-1.793***	.028	.166	-2.542***	.058	.079
	N	32,698	92.9%				
Cases Missing Data		2,515	7.1%				

Source: EPD Vehicle Stop Data (2002-2003).
Note: Significance tests for race/ethnicity were one-tailed, predicitng that black and Latino drivers were more likely, and Asian drivers were less likely than white drivers to be stopped for more than 15 minutes. Tests for all other variables were two-tailed.
*$p \leq .05$ **$p \leq .01$ ***$p \leq .001$

Results of the EPD Vehicle Stop Study 147

minutes. Drivers ages 30 to 39 were 12.2% more likely, and drivers ages 40 and over were 40.8% less likely than drivers ages 16 to 29 to be stopped for more than 15 minutes.

When the remaining independent variables were entered into the model (see Model 2, Table 29), several changes were observed. Asian drivers were no longer less likely than white drivers to be stopped for more than 15 minutes. Black drivers were 14% more likely than white drivers to be stopped for more than 15 minutes, a decrease of 54.4% from the previous model. Latino drivers were 29.3% more likely than white drivers to be stopped for more than 15 minutes, a decrease of 70.4%. Female drivers were 40.6% less likely than male drivers to be stopped for more than 15 minutes, a decrease of 5.5%. Drivers ages 30 to 39 were 19.1% more likely than drivers ages 16 to 29 to be stopped for more than 15 minutes, an increase of 6.9%. Drivers ages 40 and over were 26.2% less likely than drivers ages 16 to 29 to stopped for more than 15 minutes, a decrease of 14.6%.

Offending had an impact on stop duration. Drivers who were stopped for low discretion violations (RFSLOD) were much more likely to be stopped for more than 15 minutes (357.9%—see Table 29) compared to drivers who were stopped for traffic violations only. In terms of high discretion violations, drivers who were stopped for equipment or passenger violations (RFSHID1) were 24.4% more likely, and drivers stopped for a combination of traffic, equipment, and passenger violations (RFSHID2) were 109.8% more likely to be stopped for more than 15 minutes compared to drivers who were stopped for traffic violations only.

The regression analysis further revealed that the time and location of the stop had an impact on stop duration. Drivers stopped in districts one (30.9%—see Table 29) and two (45.7%) were less likely than drivers stopped in district five to be stopped for more than 15 minutes, while the difference between drivers stopped in districts three and five was not statistically significant. Drivers stopped in district four were 11.3% more likely than drivers stopped in district five to be stopped for more than 15 minutes. Compared to drivers who were stopped between 10:00 AM and 2:59 PM, drivers who were stopped during the late night hours (95.4%), early morning hours and the morning commute (19.1%), evening rush hours (15.6%), and evening hours (60.2%) were all more likely to be stopped for more than 15 minutes.

Several other statistically significant relationships were noted in the regression analysis:

- Stops where the vehicle had one passenger (32.4%) or two or more passengers (72.1%) were more likely to last more than 15 minutes.
- Stops where a language barrier was present were 159.4% more likely to last more than 15 minutes.
- Stops where the officer could tell the race of the driver prior to the stop were 132.2% more likely to last more than 15 minutes.

30-Minute Split Regression. In these models, positive coefficients and odds ratios greater than one indicate an increase in the likelihood that a stop lasted more than 30 minutes, while negative coefficients and odds ratios less than one indicate a decrease in the likelihood that a stop lasted more than 30 minutes.

Controlling for the effects of sex and age (Model 1—see Table 30), Asian drivers were 81.6% less likely, while black drivers were 47.1% more likely, and Latino drivers were 92.9% more likely than white drivers to be stopped for more than 30 minutes. Female drivers were 55.4% less likely than male drivers to be stopped for more than 30 minutes. Drivers ages 30 to 39 were 25.2% more likely, and drivers ages 40 and over were 19.1% less likely than drivers ages 16 to 29 to be stopped for more than 30 minutes.

When the remaining variables were entered into the model (see Model 2, Table 30), several changes were observed. Asian drivers were 79.5% less likely than white drivers to be stopped for more than 30 minutes, a slight decrease of 2.1%. Black drivers and Latino drivers were no longer more likely than white drivers to be stopped for more than 30 minutes. Female drivers were 48.2% less likely than male drivers to be stopped for more than 30 minutes, a decrease of 7.2% from the previous model. Drivers ages 30 to 39 were 37.1% more likely than drivers ages 16 to 29 to be stopped for more than 30 minutes, an increase of 11.9%. The difference between drivers ages 40 and over and drivers ages 16 to 29 was no longer statistically significant.

As was the case with the 15-minute split models, offending had an impact on stop duration. Drivers who were stopped for low discretion violations (RFSLOD) were much more likely to be stopped for more than 30 minutes (376.5%—see Table 30) compared to drivers who

Table 30. Logistic Predictors of Stop Duration, 30-Minute Split

		Model 1			Model 2		
		B	S.E.	Exp(B)	B	S.E.	Exp(B)
Driver's Race/Ethnicity							
	ASIAN	-1.693***	.502	.184	-1.585**	.505	.205
	BLACK	.386*	.180	1.471	.146	.187	1.157
	LATINO	.657***	.119	1.929	.172	.150	1.188
Driver's Sex							
	FEMALE	-.806***	.078	.446	-.658***	.080	.518
Driver's Age							
	AGE3039	.225**	.079	1.252	.315***	.083	1.371
	AGE4OOVR	-.212**	.079	.809	.108	.084	1.114
District of Stop							
	DIST0	-	-	-	-.905*	.459	.404
	DIST1	-	-	-	-.264*	.109	.768
	DIST2	-	-	-	-.561***	.124	.571
	DIST3	-	-	-	-.208*	.105	.812
	DIST4	-	-	-	.269**	.086	1.309
Reason for Stop							
	RFSHID1	-	-	-	.021	.093	1.021
	RFSHID2	-	-	-	.640***	.153	1.896
	RFSLOD	-	-	-	1.561***	.090	4.765
Number of Passengers							
	PASS1	-	-	-	.230**	.078	1.258
	PASS2PLS	-	-	-	.440***	.097	1.553
Language Barrier							
	LANGYES	-	-	-	.751***	.220	2.119
Identify Race Before Stop							
	RACEYES	-	-	-	.713***	.079	2.041
Hour of Stop							
	HRLATE	-	-	-	1.182***	.101	3.262
	HRMORN	-	-	-	.201	.128	1.223
	HRRUSH	-	-	-	.367**	.120	1.444
	HREVE	-	-	-	.729***	.113	2.073
	Constant	-3.244***	.052	.039	-4.328***	.115	.013
	N	32,698	92.9%				
	Cases Missing Data	2,515	7.1%				

Source: EPD Vehicle Stop Data (2002-2003).
Note: Significance tests for race/ethnicity were one-tailed, predicitng that black and Latino drivers were more likely, and Asian drivers were less likely than white drivers to be stopped for more than 30 minutes. Tests for all other variables were two-tailed.
*p≤.05   **p≤.01   ***p≤.001

were stopped for traffic violations only. In terms of high discretion violations, drivers who were stopped for a combination of traffic, equipment, and passenger violations (RFSHID2) were 89.6% more likely to be stopped for more than 30 minutes compared to drivers who were stopped for traffic violations only, while the difference between drivers stopped for equipment or passenger violations only (RFSHID1) and drivers stopped for traffic violations only was not statistically significant.

The regression analysis further revealed that the time and location of the stop had an impact on stop duration. Drivers stopped in districts one (23.2%—see Table 29), two (42.9%), three (18.8%), and outside EPD patrol districts (59.6%) were less likely than drivers stopped in district five to be stopped for more than 30 minutes, while drivers stopped in district four were 30.9% more likely than drivers stopped in district five to be stopped for more than 30 minutes. Compared to drivers who were stopped between 10:00 AM and 2:59 PM, drivers who were stopped during the late night hours (226.2%), evening rush hours (44.4%), and evening hours (107.3%) were more likely to be stopped for more than 30 minutes.

Several other statistically significant relationships were noted in the regression analysis:

- Stops where the vehicle had one passenger (25.8%) or two or more passengers (55.3%) were more likely to last more than 30 minutes.
- Stops where a language barrier was present were 111.9% more likely to last more than 30 minutes.
- Stops where the officer could tell the race of the driver prior to the stop were 104.1% more likely to last more than 30 minutes.

Summary. Over the two-year data collection period, a smaller percentage of Asian drivers were stopped for more than 30 minutes compared to white drivers. The difference between Asian and white drivers in terms of stops that lasted more than 15 minutes was not statistically significant. This pattern was consistent across the comparisons between Asian female and white female drivers. Smaller percentages of Asian male drivers were stopped for more than 15 minutes and more than 30 minutes compared to white male drivers.

Larger percentages of black drivers were stopped for more than 15 minutes and more than 30 minutes compared to white drivers. This pattern was consistent across the comparisons between black male and white male drivers. A larger percentage of black female drivers were stopped for more than 15 minutes compared to white female drivers, while the difference between black female and white female drivers in terms of stops that lasted more than 30 minutes was not statistically significant.

Larger percentages of Latino drivers were stopped for more than 15 minutes and more than 30 minutes compared to white drivers. This pattern was consistent across the comparisons between Latino male and white male drivers. A larger percentage of Latino female drivers were stopped for more than 15 minutes compared to white female drivers, while the difference between Latino female and white female drivers in terms of stops that lasted more than 30 minutes was not statistically significant.

Logistic regression analysis revealed that black drivers were 14% more likely, and Latino drivers were 29.2% more likely than white drivers to be stopped for more than 15 minutes even after controlling for the effects of other relevant variables, while the effect for Asian drivers were not statistically significant in explaining stops that lasted more than 15 minutes. Drivers who were stopped for low discretion violations, as well as drivers who were stopped for equipment and passenger violations and combinations of low discretion violations were more likely to last more than 15 minutes. Drivers stopped during evening and late night hours, and stops where a language barrier was present were also more likely to last more than 15 minutes.

Logistic regression analysis revealed that Asian drivers were 79.5% less likely than white drivers to be stopped for more than 30 minutes even after controlling for the effects of relevant independent variables, while the effects for black drivers and Latino drivers were not statistically significant in explaining stops that lasted more than 30 minutes. Much like the 15-minute split, drivers who were stopped during evening and late night hours, and stops where a language barrier was present were more likely to last more than 30 minutes. Drivers stopped for a combination of low discretion violations and stops that occurred in districts four and five were also more likely to last more than 30 minutes.

Demographic Characteristics of EPD Searches[54]

The majority of searches involved male drivers (see Tables 31 and 32). Using the Any Search Indicator Present (ASIP) definition, 72.6% of white drivers searched, 81.8% of Asian drivers searched, 85.2% of black drivers searched, and 91.2% of Latino drivers searched were male. Using the Minimum Reporting Threshold (MRT) definition, the percentage male increased across all four racial/ethnic categories— 75.3% of white drivers searched, 93.8% of Asian drivers searched, 92.8% of black drivers searched, and 93.2% of Latino drivers searched were male.

Across all four racial/ethnic categories, drivers between the ages of 18 and 29 (see Tables 31 and 32) were most likely to experience a search, though there were several differences. For ASIP searches, 49.6% of white drivers searched, 73.5% of Asian drivers searched, 50% of black drivers searched, and 65.7% of Latino drivers searched fell into the 18 to 29 age group. Differences were also observed in the 40 to 59 age group—20.6% of white drivers searched, 2.9% of Asian drivers searched, 22.4% of black drivers searched, and 6% of Latino drivers searched fell into this age group. These patterns were generally consistent across the MRT search definition, though larger differences were observed in the 30 to 39 age group—28.1% of white drivers searched, 5.9% of Asian drivers searched, 19.7% of black drivers searched, and 22.8% of Latino drivers searched fell into this age group.

For stops that included a search, officers were able to identify the race of the driver prior to the stop more frequently for white drivers (ASIP=33.1%, MRT=35.9%—see Tables 31 and 32), compared to Asian (ASIP=14.7%, MRT=11.8%), black (ASIP=24.6%, MRT= 27.9%), and Latino drivers (ASIP=22.3%, MRT=24.2%).

The patrol district with the highest percentage of searches for all four racial/ethnic groups was district five (see Tables 31 and 32). For ASIP searches, 38.6% of searches involving white drivers, 35.3% of searches involving Asian drivers, 34.2% of searches involving black drivers, and 46.4% of searches involving Latino drivers occurred in district five. For MRT searches, 42.5% of searches involving white

---

[54] Insofar as the purpose of this section is to review the demographic characteristics of those drivers searched by EPD officers, tests of statistical significance were not applied to these comparisons.

Table 31. General Demographic Characteristics of Any Search Indicator Present (ASIP) Searches by Race/Ethnicity

		White Percentage	Asian Percentage	Black Percentage	Latino Percentage
Driver's Sex					
	Male	72.6%	81.8%	85.2%	91.2%
	Female	27.4%	18.2%	14.8%	8.8%
	N	2,599	33	115	262
Driver's Age					
	Ages 16 - 17	2.9%	2.9%	1.7%	3.0%
	Ages 18 - 29	49.6%	73.5%	50.0%	65.7%
	Ages 30 - 39	25.2%	20.6%	24.1%	24.5%
	Ages 40 - 59	20.6%	2.9%	22.4%	6.0%
	Ages 60 and Over	1.6%	0.0%	1.7%	0.8%
	N	2,613	34	116	265
Driver's Race Identifiable Prior to Stop					
	No	66.9%	85.3%	75.4%	77.7%
	Yes	33.1%	14.7%	24.6%	22.3%
	N	2,583	34	114	260
District of Stop					
	Outside EPD Patrol Districts	0.6%	0.0%	1.7%	1.5%
	Patrol District One	13.2%	20.6%	16.2%	9.2%
	Patrol District Two	10.0%	17.6%	13.7%	5.0%
	Patrol District Three	12.7%	8.8%	13.7%	12.6%
	Patrol District Four	24.9%	17.6%	20.5%	25.3%
	Patrol District Five	38.6%	35.3%	34.2%	46.4%
	N	2,594	34	117	261
Time of Stop					
	3:00 AM to 9:59 AM	13.9%	6.3%	13.8%	13.0%
	10:00 AM to 2:59 PM	20.1%	21.9%	21.6%	14.9%
	3:00 PM to 5:59 PM	13.1%	15.6%	12.9%	14.1%
	6:00 PM to 9:59 PM	18.4%	15.6%	12.1%	24.4%
	10:00 PM to 2:59 AM	34.5%	40.6%	39.7%	33.6%
	N	2,590	32	116	262
Number of Passengers					
	No Passengers	53.8%	72.7%	53.8%	51.9%
	One Passenger	30.9%	15.2%	27.4%	28.0%
	Two Passengers	9.6%	9.1%	12.0%	9.1%
	Three Passengers	3.9%	3.0%	4.3%	6.4%
	Four or More Passengers	1.9%	0.0%	2.6%	4.5%
	N	2,594	33	117	264

Source: EPD Vehicle Stop Data (2002-2003).

Table 32. General Demographic Characteristics of Minimum Reporting Threshold (MRT) Searches by Race/Ethnicity

	White Percentage	Asian Percentage	Black Percentage	Latino Percentage
Driver's Sex				
Male	75.3%	93.8%	92.8%	93.2%
Female	24.7%	6.3%	7.2%	6.8%
N	1,776	16	69	191
Driver's Age				
Ages 16 - 17	2.4%	5.9%	2.8%	3.1%
Ages 18 - 29	49.0%	88.2%	49.3%	68.9%
Ages 30 - 39	28.1%	5.9%	19.7%	22.8%
Ages 40 - 59	19.6%	0.0%	25.4%	5.2%
Ages 60 and Over	0.9%	0.0%	2.8%	0.0%
N	1,777	17	71	193
Driver's Race Identifiable Prior to Stop				
No	64.1%	88.2%	72.1%	75.8%
Yes	35.9%	11.8%	27.9%	24.2%
N	1,756	17	68	190
District of Stop				
Outside EPD Patrol Districts	0.3%	0.0%	1.4%	1.1%
Patrol District One	11.1%	5.9%	18.3%	6.9%
Patrol District Two	8.6%	23.5%	14.1%	5.8%
Patrol District Three	13.3%	5.9%	15.5%	12.7%
Patrol District Four	24.2%	23.5%	21.1%	25.9%
Patrol District Five	42.5%	41.2%	29.6%	47.6%
N	1,766	17	71	189
Time of Stop				
3:00 AM to 9:59 AM	11.9%	0.0%	18.6%	11.6%
10:00 AM to 2:59 PM	18.4%	26.7%	22.9%	12.6%
3:00 PM to 5:59 PM	12.5%	20.0%	12.9%	14.7%
6:00 PM to 9:59 PM	19.8%	13.3%	5.7%	29.5%
10:00 PM to 2:59 AM	37.4%	40.0%	40.0%	31.6%
N	1,766	15	70	190
Number of Passengers				
No Passengers	54.0%	76.5%	53.5%	53.4%
One Passenger	30.3%	11.8%	29.6%	29.5%
Two Passengers	10.3%	11.8%	12.7%	9.8%
Three Passengers	3.5%	0.0%	4.2%	3.1%
Four or More Passengers	1.9%	0.0%	0.0%	4.1%
N	1,768	17	71	193

Source: EPD Vehicle Stop Data (2002-2003).

Results of the EPD Vehicle Stop Study

drivers, 41.2% of searches involving Asian drivers, 29.6% of searches involving black drivers, and 47.6% of searches involving Latino drivers occurred in district five. With the exception of searches involving Asian drivers, the second largest percentage of searches of white (ASIP=24.9%, MRT=24.2%), black (ASIP=20.5%, MRT=21.1%), and Latino drivers (ASIP=25.3%, MRT=25.9%) occurred in district four. For ASIP searches, the second largest percentage of searches involving Asian drivers occurred in patrol district one (20.6%). For MRT searches, the second largest percentage of searches involving Asian drivers occurred in patrol districts two (23.5%) and four (23.5%).

The largest percentage of searches involving Asian (ASIP=40.6%, MRT=40%—see Tables 31 and 32), black (ASIP=39.7%, MRT=40%), Latino (ASIP=33.6%, MRT=31.6%), and white drivers (ASIP=34.5%, MRT=37.4%) occurred during late night hours (10:00 PM to 2:59 AM). There were several noteworthy differences between the time distributions of searches involving Latino and white drivers. A larger percentage of searches involving Latino drivers (ASIP=24.4%, MRT=29.5%) were conducted between the hours of 6:00 PM and 9:59 PM compared to the percentage of searches involving white drivers (ASIP=18.4%, MRT=19.8%), while a smaller percentage of searches involving Latino drivers (ASIP=14.9%, MRT=12.6%) were conducted between the hours of 10:00 AM and 2:59 PM compared the percentage of searches involving white drivers (ASIP=20.1%, MRT=18.4%).

The majority of searches involved vehicles with no passengers (see Tables 31 and 32). For ASIP searches, 53.8% of white drivers searched, 72.7% of Asian drivers searched, 53.8% of black drivers searched, and 51.9% of Latino drivers searched had no passengers in the vehicle. For MRT searches, 54% of white drivers searched, 76.5% of Asian drivers searched, 53.5% of black drivers searched, and 53.4% of Latino drivers searched had no passengers in the vehicle. Also, the percentage of searches where two or more passengers were in the vehicle was similar for white (ASIP=15.4%, MRT=15.7%), Asian (ASIP=12.1%, MRT=11.8%), black (ASIP=18.9%, MRT=16.9%), and Latino drivers (ASIP=20%, MRT=17%).

Search Conducted—Any Search Indicator Present

Chi-square tests were conducted to examine differences between white drivers and Asian, black, and Latino drivers in terms of search occurrence using the Any Search Indicator Present search definition. Logistic regression models were constructed to examine the effect of race/ethnicity on search occurrence while controlling for the effects of relevant independent variables.

A smaller percentage of Asian drivers were searched (4.5%—see Table 33) compared to the percentage of white drivers (8.1%). Larger percentages of black (14.9%) and Latino drivers (18.8%) were searched compared to the percentage of white drivers.

Males Only. A smaller percentage of Asian male drivers were searched (5.8%—see Table 33) compared to the percentage of white male drivers (9.9%). Larger percentages of black male (17.1%) and Latino male drivers (21.4%) were searched compared to the percentage of white male drivers.

Females Only. A smaller percentage of Asian female drivers were searched (2.1%—see Table 33) compared to the percentage of white female drivers (5.5%). A larger percentage of Latino female drivers were searched (8%) compared to the percentage of white female drivers. The difference between the percentage of black female and white female drivers who were searched was not statistically significant.

Search Conducted (ASIP) Regression. In these models, positive coefficients and odds ratios greater than one indicate an increase in the likelihood that a search was conducted, while negative coefficients and odds ratios less than one indicate a decrease in the likelihood that a search was conducted.

Controlling for the effects of sex and age (Model 1—see Table 34), Asian drivers were 53.8% less likely, while black drivers were 77.3% more likely, and Latino drivers were 108.5% more likely than white drivers to be searched. Female drivers were 48.8% less likely than male drivers to be searched. Drivers ages 30 to 39 were 10.5% more likely, and drivers ages 40 and over were 43.6% less likely than drivers ages 16 to 29 to be searched.

When the remaining variables were entered into the model (see Model 2, Table 34), several changes were observed. Asian drivers were 47.6% less likely than white drivers to be searched, a decrease of 6.2% from the previous model. Black drivers were 51.1% more likely than white drivers to be searched, a decrease of 26.2%. Latino drivers

Results of the EPD Vehicle Stop Study

Table 33. Search Conducted by Race/Ethnicity

		White Percentage	Asian Percentage	Black Percentage	Latino Percentage
Any Search Indicator Present					
TOTAL	Search Conducted	8.1%	4.5%***	14.9%***	18.8%***
	N	32,254	763	783	1,413
Males ONLY	Search Conducted	9.9%	5.8%**	17.1%***	21.4%***
	N	19,118	466	574	1,116
Females ONLY	Search Conducted	5.5%	2.1%**	8.4%	8.0%*
	N	12,882	292	202	287
Minimum Reporting Threshold					
TOTAL	Search Conducted	5.7%	2.3%***	9.6%***	14.4%***
	N	31,429	747	737	1,342
Males ONLY	Search Conducted	7.2%	3.3%***	11.9%***	16.9%***
	N	18,574	455	540	1,056
Females ONLY	Search Conducted	3.5%	0.3%***	2.6%	4.7%
	N	12,610	287	190	277

Source: EPD Vehicle Stop Data (2002-2003).
Note: Significance tests for whether or not a search was conducted were one-tailed, predicitng that black and Latino drivers were more likely, and Asian drivers were less likely than white drivers to be searched.
*$p \leq .05$ **$p \leq .01$ ***$p \leq .001$

were 48.5% more likely than white drivers to be searched, a decrease of 60% from the previous model. Female drivers were 42.8% less likely than male drivers to be searched, a decrease of 6%. Drivers ages 30 to 39 were 18.4% more likely than drivers ages 16 to 29 to be searched, an increase of 7.9%. Drivers ages 40 and over were 28.7% less likely than drivers ages 16 to 29 to be searched, a decrease of 14.9%.

Offending had a profound impact on searches. Drivers who were stopped for low discretion violations (RFSLOD) were much more likely to be searched (335%—see Table 34) compared to drivers who were stopped for traffic violations only. In terms of high discretion

Table 34. Logistic Predictors of Any Search Indicator Present (ASIP) Searches

		Model 1			Model 2		
		B	S.E.	Exp(B)	B	S.E.	Exp(B)
Driver's Race/Ethnicity							
	ASIAN	-.772***	.188	.462	-.647***	.194	.524
	BLACK	.573***	.107	1.773	.412***	.114	1.511
	LATINO	.735***	.075	2.085	.395***	.093	1.485
Driver's Sex							
	FEMALE	-.670***	.046	.512	-.558***	.048	.572
Driver's Age							
	AGE3039	.099*	.049	1.105	.169***	.052	1.184
	AGE4OOVR	-.572***	.051	.564	-.338***	.054	.713
District of Stop							
	DIST0	-	-	-	-.680**	.227	.506
	DIST1	-	-	-	-.368***	.066	.692
	DIST2	-	-	-	-.651***	.073	.522
	DIST3	-	-	-	-.424***	.067	.655
	DIST4	-	-	-	.120*	.056	1.127
Reason for Stop							
	RFSHID1	-	-	-	.050	.055	1.051
	RFSHID2	-	-	-	.211	.108	1.235
	RFSLOD	-	-	-	1.470***	.063	4.350
Number of Passengers							
	PASS1	-	-	-	.265***	.049	1.304
	PASS2PLS	-	-	-	.373***	.063	1.452
Language Barrier							
	LANGYES	-	-	-	.629***	.149	1.876
Identify Race Before Stop							
	RACEYES	-	-	-	.936***	.050	2.549
Hour of Stop							
	HRLATE	-	-	-	.915***	.061	2.496
	HRMORN	-	-	-	.242***	.072	1.274
	HRRUSH	-	-	-	.135	.072	1.144
	HREVE	-	-	-	.520***	.068	1.682
	Constant	-2.070***	.031	.126	-2.821***	.066	.060
	N	32,780	93.1%				
	Cases Missing Data	2,433	6.9%				

Source: EPD Vehicle Stop Data (2002-2003).

Note: Significance tests for race/ethnicity were one-tailed, predicitng that black and Latino drivers were more likely, and Asian drivers were less likely than white drivers to be searched. Tests for all other variables were two-tailed.

*p≤.05   **p≤.01   ***p≤.001

violations, the differences between drivers stopped for traffic violations only, equipment or passenger violations only (RFSHI1), or a combination of traffic, equipment, and passenger violations (RFSHID2) were not statistically significant.

The regression analysis further revealed that the time and location of the stop had an impact on searches. Drivers stopped in districts one (30.8%—see Table 34), two (47.8%), three (34.5%), and outside EPD patrol districts (49.4%) were less likely than drivers stopped in district five to be searched, while drivers stopped in district four were 12.7% more likely than drivers stopped in district five to be searched. Compared to drivers that were stopped between 10:00 AM and 2:59 PM, drivers who were stopped during the late night hours (149.6%), early morning hours and the morning commute (27.4%), and evening hours (68.2%) were more likely to be searched.

Several other statistically significant relationships were noted in the regression analysis:

- Stops where the vehicle had one passenger (30.4%) or two or more passengers (45.2%) were more likely to involve a search.
- Stops where a language barrier was present were 87.6% more likely to involve a search.
- Stops where the officer could tell the race of the driver prior to the stop were 154.9% more likely to involve a search.

Summary. Using the Any Search Indicator Present search definition, a smaller percentage of Asian drivers were searched compared to white drivers. This pattern was consistent for Asian and white drivers of both sexes.

A larger percentage of black drivers were searched compared to white drivers. This pattern was consistent across the comparisons between black male and white male drivers. The difference between black female and white female drivers in terms of search occurrence was not statistically significant.

A larger percentage of Latino drivers were searched compared to white drivers. This pattern was consistent for Latino and white drivers of both sexes.

Logistic regression analysis revealed that Asian drivers were 47.6% less likely, black drivers were 51.1% more likely, and Latino drivers were 48.5% more likely than white drivers to be searched even after controlling for the effects of relevant independent variables. In addition to the effects of race/ethnicity, drivers who were stopped for low discretion violations, stops that occurred in districts four and five, drivers stopped during evening and late night hours, and stops where a language barrier was present were all more likely to include a search.

Search Conducted—Minimum Reporting Threshold

Chi-square tests were conducted to examine differences between white drivers and Asian, black, and Latino drivers in terms of search occurrence using the Minimum Reporting Threshold search definition. Logistic regression models were constructed to examine the effect of race/ethnicity on search occurrence while controlling for the effects of relevant independent variables.

A smaller percentage of Asian drivers were searched (2.3%—see Table 33) compared to the percentage of white drivers (5.7%). Larger percentages of black (9.6%) and Latino drivers (14.4%) were searched compared to the percentage of white drivers.

Males Only. A smaller percentage of Asian male drivers were searched (3.3%—see Table 33) compared to the percentage of white male drivers (7.2%). Larger percentages of black male (11.9%) and Latino male (16.9%) drivers were searched compared to the percentage of white male drivers.

Females Only. A smaller percentage of Asian female drivers were searched (0.3%—see Table 33) compared to the percentage of white female drivers (3.5%). There were no statistically significant differences between the percentages of black, Latino, and white female drivers who were searched.

Search Conducted (MRT) Regression. In these models, positive coefficients and odds ratios greater than one indicate an increase in the likelihood of a search, while negative coefficients and odds ratios less than one indicate a decrease in the likelihood of a search.

Controlling for the effects of sex and age (Model 1—see Table 35), Asian drivers were 69% less likely, while black drivers were 47.8% more likely, and Latino drivers were 113.4% more likely than white

Table 35. Logistic Predictors of Minimum Reporting Threshold (MRT) Searches

		Model 1			Model 2		
		B	S.E.	Exp(B)	B	S.E.	Exp(B)
Driver's Race/Ethnicity							
	ASIAN	-1.171***	.272	.310	-1.052***	.278	.349
	BLACK	.391**	.135	1.478	.174	.145	1.191
	LATINO	.758***	.086	2.134	.326**	.110	1.385
Driver's Sex							
	FEMALE	-.827***	.056	.437	-.707***	.059	.493
Driver's Age							
	AGE3039	.178**	.056	1.195	.264***	.061	1.302
	AGE4OOVR	-.646***	.063	.524	-.388***	.067	.679
District of Stop							
	DIST0	-	-	-	-1.192***	.344	.304
	DIST1	-	-	-	-.599***	.083	.549
	DIST2	-	-	-	-.837***	.091	.433
	DIST3	-	-	-	-.432***	.078	.649
	DIST4	-	-	-	.020	.066	1.021
Reason for Stop							
	RFSHID1	-	-	-	-.057	.068	.945
	RFSHID2	-	-	-	.257*	.127	1.294
	RFSLOD	-	-	-	1.705***	.070	5.501
Number of Passengers							
	PASS1	-	-	-	.223***	.058	1.250
	PASS2PLS	-	-	-	.350***	.075	1.420
Language Barrier							
	LANGYES	-	-	-	.830***	.168	2.293
Identify Race Before Stop							
	RACEYES	-	-	-	.962***	.058	2.617
Hour of Stop							
	HRLATE	-	-	-	.983***	.073	2.674
	HRMORN	-	-	-	.128	.091	1.137
	HRRUSH	-	-	-	.153	.087	1.165
	HREVE	-	-	-	.597***	.081	1.816
	Constant	-2.406***	.037	.090	-3.151***	.079	.043
	N	31,923	90.7%				
	Cases Missing Data	3,290	9.3%				

Source: EPD Vehicle Stop Data (2002-2003).
Note: Significance tests for race/ethnicity were one-tailed, predicitng that black and Latino drivers were more likely, and Asian drivers were less likely than white drivers to be searched. Tests for all other variables were two-tailed.
*$p \leq .05$ **$p \leq .01$ ***$p \leq .001$

drivers to be searched. Female drivers were 56.3% less likely than male drivers to be searched. Drivers ages 30 to 39 were 19.5% more likely, and drivers ages 40 and over were 47.6% less likely than drivers ages 16 to 29 to be searched.

When the remaining variables were entered into the model (see Model 2, Table 35), several changes were observed. The difference between black drivers and white drivers was no longer statistically significant. Asian drivers were 65.1% less likely than white drivers to be searched, a decrease of 3.9% from the previous model. Latino drivers were 38.5% more likely than white drivers to be searched, a decrease of 74.9%. Female drivers were 50.7% less likely than male drivers to be searched, a decrease of 5.6%. Drivers ages 30 to 39 were 30.2% more likely than drivers ages 16 to 29 to be searched, an increase of 10.7%. Drivers ages 40 and over were 32.1% less likely than drivers ages 16 to 29 to be searched, a decrease of 15.5%.

As was the case with ASIP searches, offending had an impact on MRT searches. Drivers who were stopped for low discretion violations (RFSLOD) were much more likely to be searched (450.1%—see Table 35) compared to drivers who were stopped for traffic violations only. In terms of high discretion violations, drivers stopped for a combination of traffic, equipment, and passenger violations (RFSHID2) were 29.4% more likely to be searched than drivers stopped for traffic violations only. The difference between drivers stopped for equipment or passenger violations only (RFSHID1) and drivers stopped for traffic violations only was not statistically significant.

The regression analysis further revealed that the time and location of the stop had an impact on searches. Drivers stopped in districts one (45.1%—see Table 35), two (56.7%), three (35.1%), and outside EPD patrol districts (69.6%) were less likely than drivers stopped in district five to be searched, while the difference between drivers stopped in district four and district five was not statistically significant. Compared to drivers that were stopped between 10:00 AM and 2:59 PM, drivers who were stopped during the late night hours (167.4%) and evening hours (81.6%) were more likely to be searched.

Several other statistically significant relationships were noted in the regression analysis:

- Stops where the vehicle had one passenger (25%) or two or more passengers (42%) were more likely to involve a search.

- Stops where a language barrier was present were 129.3% more likely to involve a search.
- Stops where the officer could tell the race of the driver prior to the stop were 161.7% more likely to involve a search.

Summary. Using the Minimum Reporting Threshold search definition, a smaller percentage of Asian drivers were searched compared to white drivers. This pattern was consistent for Asian and white drivers of both sexes.

A larger percentage of black drivers were searched compared to white drivers. This pattern was consistent across the comparisons between black male and white male drivers. The difference between black female and white female drivers in terms of search occurrence was not statistically significant.

A larger percentage of Latino drivers were searched compared to white drivers. This pattern was consistent across the comparisons between Latino male and white male drivers. The difference between Latino female and white female drivers in terms of search occurrence was not statistically significant.

Logistic regression analysis revealed that Asian drivers were 65.1% (see Table 35, Model 2) less likely, and Latino drivers were 38.5% more likely than white drivers to be searched even after controlling for the effects of relevant independent variables. In addition to the effects of race/ethnicity, drivers who were stopped for low discretion violations, stops that occurred in district five, drivers stopped during evening and late night hours, and stops where a language barrier was present were all more likely to involve a search.

Search Success Rates—Any Search Indicator Present

Chi-square tests were conducted to examine differences between white drivers and Asian, black, and Latino drivers in terms of the three search success rate measures developed for the Any Search Indicator Present search definition.

A smaller percentage of searches involving Asian drivers resulted in contraband (missing data indicator=5.9%, no enforcement indicator 8.7%—see Table 36) compared to the percentage of searches involving white drivers (missing data indicator=21.4%, no enforcement indicator=26.4%). There were no statistically significant differences

Table 36. Search Success Rates for Any Search Indicator Present (ASIP) Searches by Race/Ethnicity

	White Percentage	Asian Percentage	Black Percentage	Latino Percentage
TOTAL				
Direct Indicator				
Contraband Found	32.2%	11.8%	31.5%	32.3%
N	1,744	17	73	189
Missing Data =No Contraband				
Contraband Found	21.4%	5.9%*	19.7%	23.0%
N	2,620	34	117	265
No Enforcement=No Contraband				
Contraband Found	26.4%	8.7%*	26.1%	27.6%
N	2,128	23	88	221
Males ONLY				
Direct Indicator				
Contraband Found	34.2%	13.3%	30.3%	32.0%
N	1,311	15	66	173
Missing Data =No Contraband				
Contraband Found	23.8%	7.4%*	20.4%	23.8%
N	1,887	27	98	239
No Enforcement=No Contraband				
Contraband Found	28.8%	11.1%	26.7%	28.4%
N	1,560	18	75	201
Females ONLY				
Direct Indicator				
Contraband Found	25.7%	0.0%	40.0%	21.4%
N	421	1	5	14
Missing Data =No Contraband				
Contraband Found	15.2%	0.0%	11.8%	13.0%
N	712	6	17	23
No Enforcement=No Contraband				
Contraband Found	19.6%	0.0%	18.2%	16.7%
N	551	4	11	18

Source: EPD Vehicle Stop Data (2002-2003).
*p^2.05   ** p^2.01   *** p^2.001 (two-tailed tests)

between searches involving black, Latino, and white drivers in terms of search success rates.

Males Only. A smaller percentage of searches involving Asian male drivers produced contraband (missing data indicator=7.4%—see Table 36) compared to the percentage of successful searches involving white male drivers (missing data indicator=23.8%). There were no statistically significant differences between searches involving black, Latino, and white male drivers in terms of search success rates.

Females Only. There were no statistically significant differences between search success rates for searches involving female drivers from any of the racial/ethnic groups (see Table 36).

Summary. Using the Any Search Indicator Present search definition, a smaller percentage of searches involving Asian drivers produced contraband compared to searches involving white drivers. This pattern was generally consistent, yet not as substantial, across the comparisons of searches involving Asian male and white male drivers. The differences between searches involving Asian female and white female drivers in terms of search success rate were not statistically significant.

The differences between searches involving black, Latino, and white drivers in terms of search success rates were not statistically significant. This pattern was consistent across comparisons of searches involving black, Latino, and white drivers of both sexes.

Search Success Rate—Minimum Reporting Threshold

Chi-square tests were conducted to examine differences between white drivers and Asian, black, and Latino drivers in terms of search success rate using the Minimum Reporting Threshold search definition.

In terms of search success rates, there were no statistically significant differences between searches involving Asian, black, Latino, and white drivers of both sexes (see Table 37).

Table 37. Search Success Rates for Minimum Reporting Threshold (MRT) Searches by Race/Ethnicity

		White Percentage	Asian Percentage	Black Percentage	Latino Percentage
TOTAL					
	Contraband Found	32.4%	11.8%	32.9%	32.3%
	N	1,726	17	70	186
Males ONLY					
	Contraband Found	34.5%	13.3%	31.7%	32.7%
	N	1,297	15	63	171
Females ONLY					
	Contraband Found	25.9%	0.0%	40.0%	23.1%
	N	417	1	5	13

Source: EPD Vehicle Stop Data (2002-2003).
*$p \leq .05$ **$p \leq .01$ ***$p \leq .001$ (two-tailed tests)

Contraband Found in Successful Searches

Chi-square tests were conducted to examine differences between white drivers and Asian, black, and Latino drivers in terms of the types of contraband found in successful searches. Since the findings for the different search definitions were almost identical, both Any Search Indicator Present and Minimum Reporting Threshold results will be discussed in this section.

There were no statistically significant differences between Asian, black, and white drivers who were searched in terms of the types of contraband found in successful searches (see Tables 38 and 39).

A larger percentage of successful searches involving Latino drivers yielded currency (ASIP=13.1%, MRT=13.3%—see Tables 38 and 39) compared to the percentage of successful searches involving white drivers (ASIP and MRT=5%). A smaller percentage of successful searches involving Latino drivers yielded drugs and/or paraphernalia (ASIP=36.1%, MRT=36.7%) compared to the percentage of successful searches involving white drivers (ASIP=53.3%, MRT=53.5%).

Results of the EPD Vehicle Stop Study

Table 38. Contraband Found in Productive Any Search Indicator Present (ASIP) Searches by Race/Ethnicity

		White Percentage	Asian Percentage	Black Percentage	Latino Percentage
TOTAL					
	Drugs/Paraphernalia	53.3%	50.0%	34.8%	36.1%**
	Alcohol	31.4%	0.0%	26.1%	31.1%
	Stolen Property	5.2%	0.0%	13.0%	4.9%
	Currency	5.0%	0.0%	13.0%	13.1%*
	Weapons	11.6%	0.0%	8.7%	9.8%
	Other	15.7%	50.0%	17.4%	24.6%
	N	561	2	23	61
Males ONLY					
	Drugs/Paraphernalia	52.1%	50.0%	35.0%	35.1%*
	Alcohol	32.7%	0.0%	25.0%	33.3%
	Stolen Property	5.1%	0.0%	15.0%	5.3%
	Currency	4.7%	0.0%	15.0%	12.3%*
	Weapons	11.6%	0.0%	10.0%	8.8%
	Other	14.9%	50.0%	15.0%	26.3%*
	N	449	2	20	57
Females ONLY					
	Drugs/Paraphernalia	58.3%	n/a	50.0%	66.7%
	Alcohol	25.0%	n/a	50.0%	0.0%
	Stolen Property	5.6%	n/a	0.0%	0.0%
	Currency	5.6%	n/a	0.0%	33.3%
	Weapons	12.0%	n/a	0.0%	0.0%
	Other	19.4%	n/a	0.0%	0.0%
	N	108	0	2	3

Source: EPD Vehicle Stop Data (2002-2003).
*$p \leq .05$ **$p \leq .01$ ***$p \leq .001$ (two-tailed tests)

Males Only. There were no statistically significant differences between Asian, black, and white male drivers in terms of the types of contraband found in successful searches (see Tables 38 and 39).

Larger percentages of successful searches involving Latino male drivers yielded currency (ASIP=12.3%, MRT=12.5%—see Tables 38 and 39) and/or other contraband (ASIP=26.3%, MRT=25%) compared to the percentages of successful searches involving white male drivers (currency: ASIP and MRT=4.7%; other contraband: ASIP=14.9%, MRT=14.5%). A smaller percentage of successful searches involving Latino male drivers yielded drugs and/or paraphernalia (ASIP=35.1%, MRT=35.7%) compared to the percentage of successful searches involving white male drivers (ASIP=52.1%, MRT=52.3%).

Table 39. Contraband Found in Productive Minimum Reporting Threshold (MRT) Searches by Race/Ethnicity

		White Percentage	Asian Percentage	Black Percentage	Latino Percentage
TOTAL					
	Drugs/Paraphernalia	53.5%	50.0%	34.8%	36.7%**
	Alcohol	31.5%	0.0%	26.1%	31.7%
	Stolen Property	5.2%	0.0%	13.0%	5.0%
	Currency	5.0%	0.0%	13.0%	13.3%*
	Weapons	11.6%	0.0%	8.7%	10.0%
	Other	15.4%	50.0%	17.4%	23.3%
	N	559	2	23	60
Males ONLY					
	Drugs/Paraphernalia	52.3%	50.0%	35.0%	35.7%*
	Alcohol	32.9%	0.0%	25.0%	33.9%
	Stolen Property	5.1%	0.0%	15.0%	5.4%
	Currency	4.7%	0.0%	15.0%	12.5%*
	Weapons	11.6%	0.0%	10.0%	8.9%
	Other	14.5%	50.0%	15.0%	25.0%*
	N	447	2	20	56
Females ONLY					
	Drugs/Paraphernalia	58.3%	n/a	50.0%	66.7%
	Alcohol	25.0%	n/a	50.0%	0.0%
	Stolen Property	5.6%	n/a	0.0%	0.0%
	Currency	5.6%	n/a	0.0%	33.3%
	Weapons	12.0%	n/a	0.0%	0.0%
	Other	19.4%	n/a	0.0%	0.0%
	N	108	0	2	3

Source: EPD Vehicle Stop Data (2002-2003).
*$p \leq .05$ **$p \leq .01$ ***$p \leq .001$ (two-tailed tests)

Females Only. There were no statistically significant differences between Asian, black, Latino, and white female drivers in terms of the types of contraband found in successful searches (see Tables 38 and 39).

Summary. Regardless of the search definition, there were no differences between productive searches involving Asian, black, and white drivers in terms of the type of contraband found. These patterns were consistent across comparisons of productive searches involving Asian, black, and white drivers of both sexes.

A larger percentage of productive searches involving Latino drivers yielded currency, while a smaller percentage yielded drugs and/or paraphernalia compared to white drivers. This pattern was consistent across comparisons of productive searches involving Latino male and white male drivers with one addition—a larger percentage of productive searches involving Latino male drivers yielded other contraband compared to white male drivers. The differences between productive searches involving Latino female and white female drivers in terms of the type of contraband found were not statistically significant.

Discretionary Searches

The use of discretion by officers has been identified as an area of interest in past research on racial profiling (Ramirez et. al. 2000), and as such, it is important to identify areas where officer discretion can impact vehicle stop processes. One area where officer discretion can play an important role is in the decision to search; at the same time, it is important to note that officer discretion does not have an influence on two of the six search categories—searches that occur incident to arrest and inventory searches do not involve discretionary choices made by officers. These types of searches are products of police procedure, scripted into the policies that officers are required to follow in the process of executing specific duties. Analyses of these searches do not provide direct information about officers' use of discretion.

Four of the six search categories in the vehicle stop data do involve the exercise of discretion by officers. Consent searches, probable cause searches, reasonable suspicion searches, and vehicle exception searches all rely on officers' discretionary evaluations and choices. However, it would be a mistake to consider these decisions to be purely and entirely the product of officers' discretion. To the contrary, there are rules that govern each of these types of searches, most notably established standards and tests that officers apply to situations in order to judge if a search is appropriate.[55] In the end, these searches rest on officer judgment, and are therefore in need of independent evaluation.[56]

---

[55] See Appendix Two for additional details on the standards for discretionary searches.

[56] Cases where officers selected both discretionary and non-discretionary search types were coded as discretionary searches and included in the analysis. Cases where only non-discretionary search types were present were coded as missing data.

Discretionary Search Conducted—Any Search Indicator Present

Chi-square tests were conducted to examine differences between white drivers and Asian, black, and Latino drivers in terms of discretionary search occurrence using the Any Search Indicator Present search definition. Logistic regression models were constructed to examine the effect of race/ethnicity on discretionary search occurrence while controlling for the effects of relevant independent variables.

A smaller percentage of Asian drivers experienced a discretionary search (1.1%—see Table 40) compared to the percentage of white drivers (2.4%). Larger percentages of black (4.2%) and Latino (6.7%) drivers experienced a discretionary search compared to the percentage of white drivers.

Males Only. A smaller percentage of Asian male drivers experienced a discretionary search (1.8%—see Table 40) compared to the percentage of white male drivers (3.3%). Larger percentages of black male (5.4%) and Latino male (8.3%) drivers experienced a discretionary search compared to the percentage of white male drivers.

Females Only. A smaller percentage of Asian female drivers experienced a discretionary search (0%—see Table 40) compared to the percentage of white female drivers (1.1%). There were no statistically significant differences between black, Latino, and white female drivers in terms of discretionary search occurrence.

Discretionary Search (ASIP) Regression. In these models, positive coefficients and odds ratios greater than one indicate an increase in the likelihood of a discretionary search, while negative coefficients and odds ratios less than one indicate a decrease in the likelihood of a discretionary search.

Controlling for the effects of sex and age (Model 1—see Table 41), Asian drivers were 63.6% less likely, while black drivers were 49.7% more likely, and Latino drivers were 105.7% more likely than white drivers to experience a discretionary search. Female drivers were 69.4% less likely than male drivers to experience a discretionary search. Drivers ages 40 and over were 51.2% less likely than drivers

Results of the EPD Vehicle Stop Study

Table 40. Discretionary Search Conducted by Race/Ethnicity

		White Percentage	Asian Percentage	Black Percentage	Latino Percentage
Any Search Indicator Present					
TOTAL					
	Search Conducted	2.4%	1.1%*	4.2%**	6.7%***
	N	30,377	737	695	1,231
Males ONLY					
	Search Conducted	3.3%	1.8%*	5.4%**	8.3%***
	N	17,826	447	503	956
Females ONLY					
	Search Conducted	1.1%	0.0%*	1.1%	0.8%
	N	12,311	286	187	266
Minimum Reporting Threshold					
TOTAL					
	Search Conducted	2.4%	1.1%*	4.2%**	6.6%***
	N	30,374	738	695	1,230
Males ONLY					
	Search Conducted	3.2%	1.8%*	5.4%**	8.1%***
	N	17,821	448	503	955
Females ONLY					
	Search Conducted	1.1%	0.0%*	1.1%	0.8%
	N	12,313	286	187	266

Source: EPD Vehicle Stop Data (2002-2003).
Note: Significance tests for whether or not a discretionary search was conducted were one-tailed, predicitng that black and Latino drivers were more likely, and Asian drivers were less likely than white drivers to experience a discretionary search.
*$p \leq .05$ **$p \leq .01$ ***$p \leq .001$

ages 16 to 29 to experience a discretionary search. The difference between drivers ages 30 to 39 and drivers ages 16 to 29 was not statistically significant.

When the remaining variables were entered into the model (see Model 2, Table 41), several changes were observed. The differences between black, Latino, and white drivers were no longer statistically significant. Asian drivers were 58.4% less likely than white drivers to experience a discretionary search, a decrease of 5.2% from the previous

Table 41. Logistic Predictors of Any Search Indicator Present (ASIP) Discretionary Searches

		Model 1			Model 2		
		B	S.E.	Exp(B)	B	S.E.	Exp(B)
Driver's Race/Ethnicity							
	ASIAN	-1.011**	.382	.364	-.877*	.390	.416
	BLACK	.404*	.198	1.497	.143	.209	1.154
	LATINO	.721***	.127	2.057	.155	.164	1.168
Driver's Sex							
	FEMALE	-1.183***	.095	.306	-1.060***	.098	.347
Driver's Age							
	AGE3039	.074	.086	1.077	.226*	.092	1.253
	AGE40OVR	-.718***	.096	.488	-.336***	.102	.715
District of Stop							
	DIST0	-	-	-	-1.348*	.586	.260
	DIST1	-	-	-	-.828***	.137	.437
	DIST2	-	-	-	-.784***	.137	.456
	DIST3	-	-	-	-.355**	.113	.701
	DIST4	-	-	-	-.003	.096	.997
Reason for Stop							
	RFSHID1	-	-	-	.064	.100	1.066
	RFSHID2	-	-	-	.195	.194	1.215
	RFSLOD	-	-	-	1.756***	.099	5.787
Number of Passengers							
	PASS1	-	-	-	.534***	.086	1.706
	PASS2PLS	-	-	-	.722***	.105	2.059
Language Barrier							
	LANGYES	-	-	-	.744**	.241	2.105
Identify Race Before Stop							
	RACEYES	-	-	-	.926***	.085	2.525
Hour of Stop							
	HRLATE	-	-	-	1.196***	.113	3.308
	HRMORN	-	-	-	.088	.153	1.092
	HRRUSH	-	-	-	.143	.143	1.154
	HREVE	-	-	-	.769***	.125	2.157
	Constant	-3.161***	.053	.042	-4.234***	.125	.014
	N	30,790	87.4%				
	Cases Missing Data	4,423	12.6%				

Source: EPD Vehicle Stop Data (2002-2003).

Note: Significance tests for race/ethnicity were one-tailed, predicitng that black and Latino drivers were more likely, and Asian drivers were less likely than white drivers to experience a discretionary search. Tests for all other variables were two-tailed.

*p≤.05   **p≤.01   ***p≤.001

model. Female drivers were 65.3% less likely than male drivers to experience a discretionary search, a decrease of 4.1%. Drivers ages 40 and over were 28.5% less likely than drivers ages 16 to 29 to experience a discretionary search, a decrease of 22.7%. Drivers ages 30 to 39 were now 25.3% more likely than drivers ages 16 to 29 to experience a discretionary search, and this effect was statistically significant unlike the effect in Model 1.

Offending had an impact on discretionary searches. Drivers who were stopped for low discretion violations (RFSLOD) were much more likely experience a discretionary search (478.7%—see Table 41) compared to drivers who were stopped for traffic violations only. In terms of high discretion violations, the differences between drivers stopped for traffic violations only, equipment or passenger violations only (RFSHI1), or a combination of traffic, equipment, and passenger violations (RFSHID2) were not statistically significant.

The regression analysis further revealed that the time and location of the stop had an impact on discretionary searches. Drivers stopped in districts one (56.3%—see Table 41), two (54.4%), three (29.9%), and outside EPD patrol districts (74%) were less likely than drivers stopped in district five to experience a discretionary search, while the difference between drivers stopped in district four and district five was not statistically significant. Compared to drivers that were stopped between 10:00 AM and 2:59 PM, drivers who were stopped during the late night hours (230.8%) and evening hours (115.7%) were more likely to experience a discretionary search.

Several other statistically significant relationships were noted in the regression analysis:

- Stops where the vehicle had one passenger (70.6%) or two or more passengers (105.9%) were more likely to involve a discretionary search.

- Stops where a language barrier was present were 110.5% more likely to involve a discretionary search.

- Stops where the officer could tell the race of the driver prior to the stop were 152.5% more likely to involve a discretionary search.

These results indicate that once relevant independent variables were included in the regression analysis, the effects for black and Latino drivers were not statistically significant. However, a potential problem was observed with regard to the amount of missing data in the regression models (12.6%—see Table 41). This is important because cases missing data on any of the independent variables were automatically excluded from the logistic regression models.

An analysis of the distribution of missing data across racial/ethnic groups was conducted to examine the potential impact of the excluded cases (see Table 42). Chi-square tests indicated that there were differences between racial/ethnic groups in terms of partial reporting. Larger percentages of stops involving black (16.2%) and Latino drivers (15.1%) were missing data on one or more of the 19 vehicle stop items compared to the percentage of stops involving white drivers (11.7%). The difference between white drivers and Asian drivers was not statistically significant. Furthermore, tests indicated that there were differences between racial/ethnic groups in terms of partial reporting of search data. Larger percentages of stops involving black drivers (8%) and Latino drivers (7.8%) were missing data on one or more of the five search indicators (see Table 9 for a list of search variables) compared to the percentage of stops involving white drivers (3.8%). Once again, the difference between white drivers and Asian drivers was not statistically significant.

Of particular interest were the percentages of cases missing data on the independent variables used in the regression models (see Table 42). On the whole, there were no statistically significant differences between Asian, black, Latino, and white drivers in terms of the percentages of cases missing data. However, there were statistically significant differences between Latino drivers and white drivers in terms of the percentages of discretionary searches that were missing data on one or more of the independent variables. A larger percentage of discretionary searches involving Latino drivers (9.8%) were missing data on the independent variables compared to the percentage of discretionary searches involving white drivers (2.1%). This means that a disproportionate number of discretionary searches involving Latino drivers were excluded from the regression analysis because of missing data.

To account for the effect of this missing data, additional regression models were constructed (see Table 43). In these models, missing data

Results of the EPD Vehicle Stop Study

Table 42. Partial Reporting by Race/Ethnicity

	White	Asian	Black	Latino
	Percentage	Percentage	Percentage	Percentage
Vehicle Stop Data Reporting				
Complete Reporting	88.3%	90.2%	83.8%	84.9%
Partial Reporting	11.7%	9.8%	16.2%***	15.1%***
N	32,254	763	783	1,413
Partial Reporting on Searches	3.8%	2.8%	8.0%***	7.8%***
Partial Reporting on Independent Variables in Regression Models	6.9%	6.6%	6.8%	6.8%
Any Search Indicator Present				
Percentage of Discretionary Searches w/Partial Reporting on Independent Variables in Regression Models	2.1%	2.1%	2.2%	9.8%***
Number of Searches	44	1	1	8
Minimum Reporting Threshold				
Percentage of Discretionary Searches w/Partial Reporting on Independent Variables in Regression Models	2.1%	2.1%	2.2%	9.8%***
Number of Searches	43	1	1	8

Source: EPD Vehicle Stop Data (2002-2003).
*$p \leq .05$ **$p \leq .01$ ***$p \leq .001$ (two-tailed tests)

for each of the independent variables were entered into the models as a set of dummy variables with a value of "unknown",[57] signified in the regression tables by the label suffix "NV." While none of the unknown value categories proved to be statistically significant, the inclusion of

---

[57] The most common technique for dealing with missing data problems involves inferring values for the cases missing data using the other data in the set. While such "guessing" can most definitely be educated and take into account the distributions of other pertinent variables, it is "guessing" nonetheless. The goal of this project is to describe the vehicle stop data in detail, and the unknown value dummy variable technique achieves this goal.

Table 43. Logistic Predictors of Any Search Indicator Present (ASIP) Discretionary Searches Including Cases Missing Data on Independent Variables

		Model 1			Model 2		
		B	S.E.	Exp(B)	B	S.E.	Exp(B)
Driver's Race/Ethnicity							
	ASIAN	-.931**	.358	.394	-.769*	.365	.463
	BLACK	.387*	.194	1.472	.131	.205	1.140
	LATINO	.777***	.121	2.174	.276*	.153	1.318
Driver's Sex							
	FEMALE	-1.150***	.092	.317	-1.031***	.095	.357
	SEXNV	.100	.343	1.105	.011	.353	1.011
Driver's Age							
	AGE3039	.079	.083	1.082	.229*	.089	1.257
	AGE4OOVR	-.714***	.093	.490	-.338***	.099	.713
	AGENV	-3.627	3.279	.027	-3.706	5.227	.025
District of Stop							
	DIST0	-	-	-	-1.385*	.588	.250
	DIST1	-	-	-	-.846***	.136	.429
	DIST2	-	-	-	-.768***	.133	.464
	DIST3	-	-	-	-.364***	.111	.695
	DIST4	-	-	-	.035	.093	1.036
	DISTNV	-	-	-	-.129	.416	.879
Reason for Stop							
	RFSHID1	-	-	-	.031	.097	1.031
	RFSHID2	-	-	-	.127	.193	1.136
	RFSLOD	-	-	-	1.748***	.095	5.744
	RFSNV	-	-	-	-.787	1.009	.455
Number of Passengers							
	PASS1	-	-	-	.529***	.083	1.698
	PASS2PLS	-	-	-	.721***	.101	2.056
	PASSNV	-	-	-	-.959	.722	.383
Language Barrier							
	LANGYES	-	-	-	.591*	.236	1.806
	LANGNV	-	-	-	-.331	.238	.719
Identify Race Before Stop							
	RACEYES	-	-	-	.917***	.083	2.502
	RACENV	-	-	-	-.368	.364	.692
Hour of Stop							
	HRLATE	-	-	-	1.214***	.110	3.367
	HRMORN	-	-	-	.155	.147	1.167
	HRRUSH	-	-	-	.131	.141	1.140
	HREVE	-	-	-	.772***	.122	2.163
	HRNV	-	-	-	.744	.413	2.105
	Constant	-3.182***	.052	.041	-4.248***	.123	.014
	N	33,040	93.8%				
	Cases Missing Data	2,173	6.2%				

Source: EPD Vehicle Stop Data (2002-2003).

Note: Significance tests for race/ethnicity were one-tailed, predicitng that black and Latino drivers were more likely, and Asian drivers were less likely than white drivers to experience a discretionary search. Tests for all other variables were two-tailed.

Note: Unknown value dummy variables are signified by NV suffix.

*p≤.05   **p≤.01   ***p≤.001

the missing cases did have an effect on the statistical significance of race/ethnicity in the case of Latino drivers. With the additional cases returned to the analysis, the new models indicated that Latino drivers were 31.8% more likely than white drivers to experience a discretionary search even after accounting for the influence of other variables. Furthermore, the only difference worth noting between the models with the missing data included and the models excluding the missing data was a small decline in the odds ratio associated with the presence of a language barrier.

Summary. Using the Any Search Indicator Present search definition, a smaller percentage of Asian drivers experienced a discretionary search compared to white drivers. This pattern was consistent for Asian and white drivers of both sexes.

A larger percentage of black drivers experienced a discretionary search compared to white drivers. This pattern was consistent across the comparisons between black male and white male drivers. The difference between black female and white female drivers in terms of whether or not a discretionary search was discretionary search occurrence was not statistically significant.

A larger percentage of Latino drivers experienced a discretionary search compared to white drivers. This pattern was consistent across the comparisons between Latino male and white male drivers. The difference between Latino female and white female drivers in terms of discretionary search occurrence was not statistically significant.

Logistic regression analysis revealed that Asian drivers were 58.4% (see Table 43, Model 2) less likely than white drivers to experience a discretionary search. The effects for black and Latino drivers were not statistically significant in explaining discretionary searches in the first set of models, but after problems with missing data were addressed, the analysis revealed that Latino drivers were 31.8% more likely than white drivers to experience a discretionary search. Much like the results for all searches, drivers who were stopped for low discretion violations, stops that occurred in district five, drivers stopped during evening and late night hours, and stops where a language barrier was present were all more likely to involve a discretionary search.

Discretionary Search Conducted—Minimum Reporting Threshold

Chi-square tests were conducted to examine differences between white drivers and Asian, black, and Latino drivers terms of discretionary search occurrence using the Minimum Reporting Threshold search definition. Logistic regression models were constructed to examine the effect of race/ethnicity on discretionary search occurrence while controlling for the effects of relevant independent variables.

A smaller percentage of Asian drivers experienced a discretionary search (1.1%—see Table 40) compared to the percentage of white drivers (2.4%). Larger percentages of black (4.2%) and Latino (6.6%) drivers experienced a discretionary search compared to the percentage of white drivers.

Males Only. A smaller percentage of Asian male drivers experienced a discretionary search (1.8%—see Table 40) compared to the percentage of white male drivers (3.2%). Larger percentages of black male (5.4%) and Latino male (8.1%) drivers experienced a discretionary search compared to the percentage of white male drivers.

Females Only. A smaller percentage of Asian female drivers experienced a discretionary search (0%—see Table 40) compared to the percentage of white female drivers (1.1%). There were no statistically significant differences between black, Latino, and white female drivers in terms of discretionary search occurrence.

Discretionary Search (MRT) Regression. In these models, positive coefficients and odds ratios greater than one indicate an increase in the likelihood of a discretionary search, while negative coefficients and odds ratios less than one indicate a decrease in the likelihood of a discretionary search.

Controlling for the effects of sex and age (Model 1—see Table 44), Asian drivers were 62.7% less likely, while black drivers were 54.1% more likely, and Latino drivers were 105.8% more likely than white drivers to experience a discretionary search. Female drivers were 68.9% less likely than male drivers to experience a discretionary search. Drivers ages 40 and over were 51.7% less likely than drivers ages 16 to 29 to experience a discretionary search. The difference between drivers ages 30 to 39 and drivers ages 16 to 29 was not statistically significant.

When the remaining variables were entered into the model (see Model 2, Table 44), several changes were observed. The differences

Table 44. Logistic Predictors of Minimum Reporting Threshold (MRT) Discretionary Searches

		Model 1			Model 2		
		B	S.E.	Exp(B)	B	S.E.	Exp(B)
Driver's Race/Ethnicity							
	ASIAN	-.986*	.383	.373	-.859*	.391	.424
	BLACK	.432*	.198	1.541	.168	.209	1.183
	LATINO	.722***	.129	2.058	.137	.167	1.146
Driver's Sex							
	FEMALE	-1.168***	.096	.311	-1.044***	.099	.352
Driver's Age							
	AGE3039	.074	.087	1.077	.231*	.093	1.260
	AGE40OVR	-.728***	.097	.483	-.339***	.104	.712
District of Stop							
	DIST0	-	-	-	-1.333*	.588	.264
	DIST1	-	-	-	-.837***	.139	.433
	DIST2	-	-	-	-.776***	.138	.460
	DIST3	-	-	-	-.388***	.115	.678
	DIST4	-	-	-	-.014	.097	.986
Reason for Stop							
	RFSHID1	-	-	-	.047	.101	1.048
	RFSHID2	-	-	-	.222	.194	1.248
	RFSLOD	-	-	-	1.758***	.100	5.798
Number of Passengers							
	PASS1	-	-	-	.521***	.087	1.684
	PASS2PLS	-	-	-	.704***	.107	2.022
Language Barrier							
	LANGYES	-	-	-	.788***	.242	2.200
Identify Race Before Stop							
	RACEYES	-	-	-	.937***	.086	2.552
Hour of Stop							
	HRLATE	-	-	-	1.235***	.115	3.440
	HRMORN	-	-	-	.096	.157	1.101
	HRRUSH	-	-	-	.160	.146	1.174
	HREVE	-	-	-	.806***	.127	2.239
	Constant	-3.190***	.054	.041	-4.280***	.128	.014
	N	30,786	87.4%				
	Cases Missing Data	4,427	12.6%				

Source: EPD Vehicle Stop Data (2002-2003).
Note: Significance tests for race/ethnicity were one-tailed, predicitng that black and Latino drivers were more likely, and Asian drivers were less likely than white drivers to experience a discretionary search. Tests for all other variables were two-tailed.
*$p \leq .05$ **$p \leq .01$ ***$p \leq .001$

between black, Latino, and white drivers were no longer statistically significant. Asian drivers were 57.6% less likely than white drivers to experience a discretionary search, a decrease of 5.1% from the previous model. Female drivers were 64.8% less likely than male drivers to experience a discretionary search, a decrease of 4.1%. Drivers ages 30 to 39 were now 26% more likely than drivers ages 16 to 29 to experience a discretionary search. Drivers ages 40 and over were 28.8% less likely than drivers ages 16 to 29 to experience a discretionary search, a decrease of 22.9%.

Offending had an impact on discretionary searches. Drivers who were stopped for low discretion violations (RFSLOD) were much more likely to experience a discretionary search (479.8%—see Table 44) than drivers who were stopped for traffic violations only. In terms of high discretion violations, the differences between drivers stopped for traffic violations only, equipment or passenger violations only (RFSHI1), or a combination of traffic, equipment, and passenger violations (RFSHID2) were not statistically significant.

The regression analysis further revealed that the time and location of the stop had an impact on discretionary searches. Drivers stopped in districts one (56.7%—see Table 44), two (54%), three (32.2%), and outside EPD patrol districts (73.6%) were less likely than drivers stopped in district five to experience a discretionary search, while the difference between drivers stopped in district four and district five was not statistically significant. Compared to drivers that were stopped between 10:00 AM and 2:59 PM, drivers who were stopped during the late night hours (244%) and evening hours (123.9%) were more likely to experience a discretionary search.

Several other statistically significant relationships were noted in the regression analysis:

- Stops where the vehicle had one passenger (68.4%) or two or more passengers (102.2%) were more likely to involve a discretionary search.

- Stops where a language barrier was present were 120% more likely to involve a discretionary search.

- Stops where the officer could tell the race of the driver prior to the stop were 155.2% more likely to involve a discretionary search.

Results of the EPD Vehicle Stop Study

Missing data problems similar to those noted in the ASIP discretionary search models were found in the MRT models (see Table 42). To account for the effects of the missing data, additional regression models were constructed (see Table 45) employing the same methods used to address missing data issues in the ASIP data. While none of the unknown value categories were statistically significant, the inclusion of the missing cases did have an effect on the statistical significance of race/ethnicity in the case of Latino drivers. With the additional cases returned to the analysis, the new models indicated that Latino drivers were 30.5% more likely than white drivers to experience a discretionary search even after accounting for the influence of other variables. Furthermore, much like the ASIP data, the only other difference between the models with the missing data included and the models excluding the missing data was a small decline in the odds ratio associated with the presence of a language barrier.

Summary. Under the Minimum Reporting Threshold search definition, a smaller percentage of Asian drivers experienced a discretionary search compared to white drivers. This pattern was consistent for Asian and white drivers of both sexes.

A larger percentage of black drivers experienced a discretionary search compared to white drivers. This pattern was consistent across the comparisons between black male and white male drivers. The difference between black female and white female drivers in terms of discretionary search occurrence was not statistically significant.

A larger percentage of Latino drivers experienced a discretionary search compared to white drivers. This pattern was consistent across the comparisons between Latino male and white male drivers. The difference between Latino female and white female drivers in terms of discretionary search occurrence was not statistically significant.

Logistic regression analysis revealed that Asian drivers were 58.4% (see Table 44, Model 2) less likely than white drivers to experience a discretionary search. The effects for black drivers and Latino drivers were not statistically significant in explaining discretionary searches in the first set of models, but after problems with missing data were addressed, the analysis revealed that Latino drivers were 30.5% more likely than white drivers to experience a discretionary search. In addition to the effects of race/ethnicity, drivers who were stopped for low discretion violations, stops that occurred in

Table 45. Logistic Predictors of Minimum Reporting Threshold (MRT) Discretionary Searches Including Cases Missing Data on Independent Variables

		Model 1			Model 2		
		B	S.E.	Exp(B)	B	S.E.	Exp(B)
Driver's Race/Ethnicity							
	ASIAN	-.905*	.358	.405	-.748*	.366	.473
	BLACK	.415*	.194	1.515	.157	.206	1.170
	LATINO	.780***	.122	2.181	.266*	.155	1.305
Driver's Sex							
	FEMALE	-1.134***	.093	.322	-1.012***	.096	.364
	SEXNV	.130	.343	1.139	.038	.354	1.039
Driver's Age							
	AGE3039	.081	.084	1.085	.237**	.090	1.267
	AGE4OOVR	-0.721***	.094	.486	-.339***	.100	.713
	AGENV	-3.609	3.279	.027	-3.684	5.224	.025
District of Stop							
	DIST0	-	-	-	-1.362*	.588	.256
	DIST1	-	-	-	-.850***	.137	.427
	DIST2	-	-	-	-.757***	.134	.469
	DIST3	-	-	-	-.392***	.113	.676
	DIST4	-	-	-	.029	.094	1.029
	DISTNV	-	-	-	-.113	.416	.893
Reason for Stop							
	RFSHID1	-	-	-	.007	.099	1.007
	RFSHID2	-	-	-	.152	.193	1.164
	RFSLOD	-	-	-	1.749***	.096	5.747
	RFSNV	-	-	-	-.765	1.009	.466
Number of Passengers							
	PASS1	-	-	-	.516***	.084	1.675
	PASS2PLS	-	-	-	.695***	.103	2.004
	PASSNV	-	-	-	-.943	.723	.390
Language Barrier							
	LANGYES	-	-	-	.630**	.237	1.877
	LANGNV	-	-	-	-.304	.238	.738
Identify Race Before Stop							
	RACEYES	-	-	-	.927***	.084	2.527
	RACENV	-	-	-	-.469	.388	.626
Hour of Stop							
	HRLATE	-	-	-	1.253***	.112	3.500
	HRMORN	-	-	-	.150	.151	1.162
	HRRUSH	-	-	-	.146	.143	1.157
	HREVE	-	-	-	.808***	.124	2.243
	HRNV	-	-	-	.796	.414	2.218
	Constant	-3.213***	.052	.040	-4.293***	.125	.014
	N	33,037	93.8%				
	Cases Missing Data	2,176	6.2%				

Source: EPD Vehicle Stop Data (2002-2003).

Note: Significance tests for race/ethnicity were one-tailed, predicitng that black and Latino drivers were more likely, and Asian drivers were less likely than white drivers to experience a discretionary search. Tests for all other variables were two-tailed.

Note: Unknown value dummy variables are signified by NV suffix.

*p≤.05   **p≤.01   ***p≤.001

district five, drivers stopped during evening and late night hours, and stops where a language barrier was present were all more likely to involve a search.

Discretionary Search Success Rate—Any Search Indicator Present

Chi-square tests were conducted to examine differences between white drivers and Asian, black, and Latino drivers in terms of the three search success rate measures developed for the Any Search Indicator Present search definition. These search success rates were limited to discretionary searches only.

A smaller percentage of discretionary searches involving Asian drivers produced contraband (12.5% on all three indicators—see Table 46) compared to the percentage of successful discretionary searches involving white drivers (direct indicator=51.1%, missing data indicator=48.5%, no enforcement indicator=50.4%). There were no statistically significant differences between search success rates for discretionary searches involving black, Latino, and white drivers.

Males Only. A smaller percentage of discretionary searches involving Asian male drivers produced contraband (12.5% on all three indicators—see Table 46) compared to the percentage of successful discretionary searches involving white male drivers (direct indicator=52.1%, missing data indicator=49.2%, no enforcement indicator=51.3%). There were no statistically significant differences between search success rates for discretionary searches involving black, Latino, and white male drivers.

Females Only. There were no statistically significant differences between search success rates for discretionary searches involving Asian, black, Latino, and white female drivers (see Table 46).

Summary. Using the Any Search Indicator Present search definition, a smaller percentage of discretionary searches involving Asian drivers produced contraband compared to discretionary searches involving white drivers. This pattern was consistent across the comparisons of discretionary searches involving Asian male and white male drivers. The differences between discretionary searches involving Asian female and white female drivers in terms of search success rates were not statistically significant.

Table 46. Discretionary Search Success Rates for Any Search Indicator Present (ASIP) Discretionary Searches by Race/Ethnicity

	White Percentage	Asian Percentage	Black Percentage	Latino Percentage
TOTAL				
Direct Indicator				
Contraband Found	51.1%	12.5%*	44.8%	46.2%
N	704	8	29	78
Missing Data =No Contraband				
Contraband Found	48.5%	12.5%*	44.8%	43.4%
N	743	8	29	83
No Enforcement=No Contraband				
Contraband Found	50.4%	12.5%*	44.8%	45.6%
N	714	8	29	79
Males ONLY				
Direct Indicator				
Contraband Found	52.1%	12.5%*	44.4%	44.6%
N	562	8	27	74
Missing Data =No Contraband				
Contraband Found	49.2%	12.5%*	44.4%	41.8%
N	597	8	27	79
No Enforcement=No Contraband				
Contraband Found	51.3%	12.5%*	44.4%	44.0%
N	571	8	27	75
Females ONLY				
Direct Indicator				
Contraband Found	47.4%	n/a	50.0%	100.0%
N	135	0	2	2
Missing Data =No Contraband				
Contraband Found	45.4%	n/a	50.0%	100.0%
N	141	0	2	2
No Enforcement=No Contraband				
Contraband Found	47.1%	n/a	50.0%	100.0%
N	136	0	2	2

Source: EPD Vehicle Stop Data (2002-2003).
*$p \leq .05$ **$p \leq .01$ ***$p \leq .001$ (two-tailed tests)

The differences between discretionary searches involving black, Latino, and white drivers in terms of search success rates were not statistically significant. These patterns were consistent across comparisons of discretionary searches involving black, Latino, and white drivers of both sexes.

Discretionary Search Success Rate—Minimum Reporting Threshold

Chi-square tests were conducted to examine differences between white drivers and Asian, black, and Latino drivers in terms of discretionary search success rate using the Minimum Reporting Threshold search definition.

A smaller percentage of discretionary searches involving Asian drivers produced contraband (12.5%—see Table 47) compared to the percentage of successful discretionary searches involving white drivers (51.4%). There were no statistically significant differences between search success rates for discretionary searches involving black, Latino, and white drivers.

Males Only. A smaller percentage of discretionary searches involving Asian male drivers produced contraband (12.5%—see Table 47) compared to the percentage of successful discretionary searches involving white male drivers (52.4%). There were no statistically significant differences between search success rates for discretionary searches involving black, Latino, and white male drivers.

Females Only. There were no statistically significant differences between search success rates for discretionary searches involving Asian, black, Latino, and white female drivers (see Table 47).

Summary. Using the Minimum Reporting Threshold search definition, a smaller percentage of discretionary searches involving Asian drivers produced contraband compared to white drivers. This pattern was consistent across the comparisons of discretionary searches involving Asian male and white male drivers. The difference between discretionary searches involving Asian female and white female drivers in terms of search success rate was not statistically significant.

Table 47. Discretionary Search Success Rates for Minimum Reporting Threshold (MRT) Discretionary Searches by Race/Ethnicity

		White Percentage	Asian Percentage	Black Percentage	Latino Percentage
TOTAL					
	Contraband Found	51.4%	12.5%*	44.8%	46.2%
	N	700	8	29	78
Males ONLY					
	Contraband Found	52.4%	12.5%*	44.4%	44.6%
	N	559	8	27	74
Females ONLY					
	Contraband Found	47.8%	n/a	50.0%	100.0%
	N	134	0	2	2

Source: EPD Vehicle Stop Data (2002-2003).
*$p \leq .05$ **$p \leq .01$ ***$p \leq .001$ (two-tailed tests)

The differences between discretionary searches involving black, Latino, and white drivers in terms of search success rates were not statistically significant. These patterns were consistent across comparisons of discretionary search success rates involving black, Latino, and white drivers of both sexes.

CHAPTER 6
Making Sense of the Disparities

REVIEW OF KEY FINDINGS

Finding One: EPD Contacts

The majority of EPD vehicle stops, searches, enforcement actions, and arrests involved white drivers. White drivers accounted for 90.1% of all vehicle stops in 2002 and 2003 (see Table 48). Taken another way, EPD conducted 36,011 stops during the two-year data collection period, or 49.3 stops per day. In terms of the racial/ethnic distribution of these stops, 44.2 stops per day involved white drivers, 1.0 involved Asian drivers, 1.1 involved black drivers, 1.9 involved Latino drivers, and 0.8 involved drivers of other racial/ethnic backgrounds. Furthermore, white drivers accounted for between 84.3% (MRT) and 84.4% (ASIP) of searches, 90.9% of stops where enforcement action occurred, and 85.8% of arrests.

That the majority of vehicle stops involved white drivers does not prove that EPD is free of racial profiling, but it is important to note the rough similarities between racial/ethnic distributions of the vehicle stop data and the Eugene population. These similarities can reasonably be interpreted to mean that any racial profiling problems that may exist are not as pronounced and pervasive as those discovered in New Jersey (Lamberth 1994), Maryland (Lamberth 1996), and other communities across the United States. This is not to say that observed differences are not substantial and worthy of further analysis. For instance, Latino

Table 48. Summary of Racial/Ethnic Distribution of EPD Contacts

	Vehicle Stops		ASIP Searches		MRT Searches		Enforcement Action		Arrests	
	Frequency	Percentage	Frequency	Percentage	Frequency	Percentage	Frequency	Percentage	Frequency	Percentage
White	32,254	90.1%	2,620	84.4%	1,778	84.3%	21,122	90.9%	974	85.8%
Asian	763	2.1%	34	1.1%	17	0.8%	497	2.1%	7	0.6%
Black	783	2.2%	117	3.8%	71	3.4%	451	1.9%	44	3.9%
Latino	1,413	3.9%	265	8.5%	193	9.1%	822	3.5%	87	7.7%
Other	589	1.6%	69	2.2%	51	2.4%	353	1.5%	23	2.0%

Source: EPD Vehicle Stop Data (2002-2003).

Making Sense of the Disparities

drivers, who accounted for 3.9% of all stops (see Table 48), were the subjects of between 8.5% (ASIP) and 9.1% (MRT) of all searches, and made up 7.7% of all arrests.

Finding Two: Stop Frequency

There were differences between racial/ethnic groups in terms of stop frequency. Asian residents were stopped at a lower rate per 1000 residents than white residents in both 2002 and 2003, and this applied to both males and females. These patterns were consistent across the modified stop rates.

On the whole, Latino and white residents were stopped at roughly the same rate in 2002[58] (see Table 17), and Latinos were stopped at a lower rate than white residents in 2003 (see Table 18). When stop rates were broken down by sex, the analysis revealed that Latino female residents were stopped at a lower rate than white female residents in both 2002 and 2003. As a group, Latino male residents were stopped at a higher rate than white male residents in 2002, while in 2003 the differences between Latino male and white male residents were not statistically significant. Of particular interest in the 2002 data was the fact that the differences between Latino male and white male residents lost statistical significance (with a few exceptions) once age was factored into the analysis. This can be attributed to differences between the age distributions of the Latino male and white male populations (see Table 15). A larger percentage of the Latino male population fell into the 18 to 29 age category (44.2%) compared to the percentage of the white male population in this age group (29%), which is important because majority of stops of Latino male residents involved drivers in this category. While 46.5% of stops involving white male residents involved drivers between the ages of 18 and 29, 63.1% of stops involving Latino male residents fell into this age category. The variations in the residential population age distributions balanced out most of the stop rate differences between Latino male and white male residents.

The most pronounced differences in stop rates were between black and white residents. Compared to white residents, black residents

---

[58] The modified stop rates for Latino residents were lower than the modified stop rates for white residents in 2002, and these differences were statistically significant.

experienced between 73.8 (inclusive stop rate—see Table 17) and 151.3 (exclusive stop rate) more stops per 1000 residents in 2002. In 2003, black residents experienced between 31.4 (inclusive—see Table 18) and 94.9 (exclusive) more stops—a substantial decline from 2002 (inclusive=42.4 fewer stops, exclusive=56.4 fewer stops). This pattern was particularly pronounced for black male residents, who experienced between 98.3 (inclusive) and 179.3 (exclusive) more stops compared to white male residents in 2002. In 2003, black male residents experienced between 60.7 (inclusive) and 132.0 (exclusive) more stops. Compared to the 2002 stop rates, the 2003 stop rates for black male residents declined between 37.6 (inclusive) and 47.3 (exclusive) stops. Despite these drops in stop rates for black residents on the whole, and for black male residents in particular, the differences between black and white residents remained statistically significant. Furthermore, these differences persisted even after modification factors were incorporated to adjust the population estimates (see Table 22).

The stop rates for Asian, black, and Latino residents all declined from 2002 to 2003. There are two reasons for this reduction. First, the number of Asian, black, and Latino residents stopped by EPD decreased from 2002 to 2003.[59] Second, the population estimates increased from 2002 to 2003. This increase was related solely to the manner in which the benchmarks were calculated. The inclusion of age as a variable in the population estimates allowed for the inclusion of residents in the benchmark as they entered the driving age population. As such, residents who were 15 years of age in 2002 were excluded from that year's benchmark; however, because these individuals were 16 years of age in 2003, they were included in that year's benchmark, thus increasing the overall size of the driving age population (see Table 12). Also, it is important to remember that the unmodified Census benchmark does not include estimates of deaths and migration (both to and from Eugene), and these factors would undoubtedly have an impact on the population estimates. For instance, the fact that the benchmark did not account for deaths means that the population estimates for older

---

[59] It is unclear why EPD stopped fewer Asian, black, and Latino drivers (and residents) in 2003. It is possible that this reduction was a reaction to the findings of the 2002 data, most notably the stop rates, which were delivered to EPD in early 2003. However, there is no direct evidence to justify this supposition. Furthermore, other racial profiling studies have found little evidence to support suspicions of reactivity (Withrow 2006).

Making Sense of the Disparities

segments of Eugene's residential population were likely inflated, and as such the stop rates for these segments of the population (60 and over) underestimate the actual rate.

Modified stop rates were calculated to address changes in the population size (related to deaths, migration, etc.), changes in the University of Oregon population, and Census data collection problems. In theory, accounting for these changes should improve the accuracy of the population estimates and stop rates. However, the use of multiple data sources in the modified benchmark calculation also introduced additional errors to the process. The Census undercount estimates used in the calculation of the modified stop rates were from the 1990 Census, not the 2000 Census.[60] Furthermore, the undercount estimates and the population growth estimates were both for Lane County as a whole, not Eugene specifically. The Census population growth estimates for Lane County were for 2002, not 2003. With regard to changes in the University of Oregon population, there were problems associated with students who chose not to report their race/ethnicity. Given these known problems, not to mention the unknown problems, in the benchmark modifications, it is difficult to judge whether the resulting stop rates are superior or inferior to those calculated using the Census-only benchmark. As such, the modified stop rates should be considered tests of possible population changes. Comparisons between the standard and modified stop rates should focus on the magnitude of the differences between these rates, as well as the overall patterns of statistical significance.

While these results provide some insight into the frequency of vehicle stops for Asian, black, Latino, and white Eugene residents, it is important to recognize that all benchmarks used in this research are only estimates of the actual population. In any research examining vehicle stop data, the population of interest is the driving population in a given area or jurisdiction. The benchmarks used in this study focus on the residential population, and while there is most definitely overlap between these populations, there are also important differences. As the vehicle stop data shows, 20.7% of drivers stopped by EPD were not Eugene residents (see Table 4), and while these stops were excluded from the stop rate analysis (because the benchmark was only applicable to Eugene residents), they are part of the population of interest.

---

[60] Undercount estimates for the 2000 Census were not available at the time of this analysis.

Census-derived or otherwise, residential population benchmarks like those used in this study are limited because they only describe the population that lives in a given area. Information pertinent to the question of whether or not minority drivers are stopped more frequently than white drivers is missing from this benchmark, including:

- Percentage of the local population that possess drivers' licenses (by race/ethnicity, sex, and age).
- Racial/ethnic composition of local driving population.
- Frequency of driving (total miles) in jurisdiction by race/ethnicity.
- Areas most frequently driven in the jurisdiction by race/ethnicity (to compare to common patrol and traffic enforcement areas as a means of assessing risk of stop).
- Common driving times by race/ethnicity (to compare to officer scheduling and deployment).
- Differences in driving behavior by race/ethnicity (most notably in terms of traffic violations).
- Differences in automobiles by race/ethnicity (most notably in terms of equipment violations).

This list is not exhaustive. It is likely that other important elements will be identified in the future by researchers, law enforcement professionals, and civilians.

While the Census-based benchmark used in this study does provide valuable information, it is important to recognize that it does not provide a complete picture. At the same time, the refinements introduced in this study (limiting the benchmark comparison to Eugene residents only, age adjustments, and the population modifications and modified stop rates) make the products of these comparisons valuable and more informative than previous studies in other jurisdictions.

Finding Three: Reason for Stop

There were differences between racial/ethnic groups in terms of the reasons for vehicle stops. Over the two-year data collection period, a larger percentage of Asian drivers were stopped for traffic violations,

Making Sense of the Disparities

and smaller percentages were stopped for pre-existing knowledge and equipment violations compared to white drivers. Larger percentages of black drivers were stopped for ORS crimes, calls for service, pre-existing knowledge, equipment violations, and passenger violations, and a smaller percentage were stopped for traffic violations compared to white drivers. Larger percentages of Latino drivers were stopped for ORS crimes, calls for service, pre-existing knowledge, and equipment violations, and a smaller percentage were stopped for traffic violations compared to white drivers.

While the vehicle stop data indicates that there are differences between Asian, black, Latino, and white drivers in terms of reasons for vehicle stops, it is difficult to interpret these findings. Vehicle stop data alone is not an adequate data source to address two of the questions most pertinent to the problem of racial profiling:

- Do Asian, black, and Latino drivers commit certain crimes (most notably traffic and equipment violations) at different rates than white drivers?
- Are larger or smaller proportions of all Asian, black, and Latino drivers who are in violation of the law stopped by the police, compared to the proportion of white drivers?

To answer these questions, data on the driving behavior of those drivers who were *not* stopped is needed. Each of these questions appeals to information that is only partially captured in the vehicle stop data, and it is necessary to examine additional data sources to fully answer these questions.

In terms of determining whether or not Asian, black, and Latino drivers committed certain crimes more or less frequently than whites, vehicle stop data alone is not an adequate indicator because of the potential for bias in data collection. The racial/ethnic differences in the vehicle stop data could be an unbiased estimate of offending in the jurisdiction, they could be an indicator of racial profiling, or they could be related to other factors, such as the time and location of the stop. Using only vehicle stop data it is impossible to prove or disprove any of these theories—data on those drivers who were *not* stopped is needed to construct a complete picture of offending in the jurisdiction.

Similarly, in terms of determining whether larger or smaller percentages of the Asian, black, and Latino driving population who were in violation of the law were stopped, data on the population that was not stopped is once again necessary for comparison. As it stands, the vehicle stop data only allows for comparisons of drivers who were stopped to other drivers who were also stopped. It is impossible to determine if the percentage of the offending population who was stopped by EPD is equal across racial/ethnic groups using only vehicle stop data. For example, the vehicle stop data indicates that 180 black drivers (23.1% of all black drivers stopped—see Table 23), 354 Latino drivers (25.1%), and 6,287 white drivers (19.6%) were stopped for equipment violations. While it is possible to determine the percentage of the stopped population for which an equipment violation was at least one of the reasons provided for the stop, we do not know the percentages of the overall violating population that was stopped. It is possible that these numbers show that roughly the same percentage of all black, Latino, and white drivers who committed equipment violations were stopped by EPD. These numbers could be evidence that a larger percentage of all black and Latino drivers who committed equipment violations were stopped compared to white drivers. It is also possible that these numbers could demonstrate that, compared to white drivers, a smaller percentage of all black and Latino drivers who committed equipment violations were stopped. It is not possible to draw any conclusions in terms of these claims without data on equipment violations committed by those drivers who were not stopped.

It is for the reasons noted in the preceding paragraphs that regression models were not constructed to examine the differences in reason for stop. These models would have inevitably compared those drivers who were stopped for certain reasons to drivers who were stopped for other reasons. Such models would not address the question of whether or not race/ethnicity played a role in the decision to stop (or not to stop) a driver/vehicle for a specific type of violation. Once again data on drivers and vehicles that were in violation but not stopped is necessary to answer this question.

In addition to the problems associated with the need for additional data, it is difficult to interpret these findings without more information on the practical meaning of each of these categories. The categories used reflect legal and administrative elements of police officers' daily work. In order to effectively analyze and interpret this data, it is important to understand what these categories mean in the everyday lives and routines of officers. To be clear, it is necessary to obtain

Making Sense of the Disparities

information on what these violations look like from officers' viewpoints, including how certain violations are identified, prioritized, and handled by officers.

Furthermore, it is essential to address issues relevant to the problem of racial profiling in these categories, most notably officer discretion. More specifically, the coding scheme used for reason for stop does not allow for a complex and multifaceted analysis of officer discretion. For example, traffic violations accounted for 78.1% of all stops (see Table 6), equipment violations accounted for 19.7% of all stops, and each of the other reasons accounted for no more than 2.5% of all stops. This lack of variation indicates that traffic and equipment violations needed to be broken down into more specific categories that addressed issues of officer discretion and seriousness of the offense. Using the current coding scheme, drivers who exceeded the speed limit by five miles-per-hour and drivers who exceeded the speed limit by 25 miles-per-hour are grouped in the same category. Clearly, these two situations would be perceived differently in terms of seriousness and would involve different levels of officer discretion, and as such they should be measured separately.

Finally, it is important to note that it is impossible to determine whether or not the reasons for stop recorded in the vehicle stop data are valid. In other words, there is no way to identify cases where the reason for stop may not have been legitimate. All that was captured in the vehicle stop data was the officer's accusation.

Finding Four: Location of Stop

There were differences between racial/ethnic groups in terms of district of stop. Over the two-year data collection period, larger percentages of Asian drivers were stopped in districts one and two, and a smaller percentage were stopped in district four compared to white drivers. A larger percentage of black drivers were stopped in district five, and smaller percentages were stopped in districts two and four compared to white drivers. Larger percentages of Latino drivers were stopped in districts four and five, and smaller percentages were stopped in districts one, two, and three compared to white drivers.

Regression models were not constructed for this analysis because of comparison issues similar to those identified in the reason for stop discussion. Using only the vehicle stop data, regression models would compare those drivers stopped in a specific district to those stopped in other districts. These models would be meaningless because only the stopped population would be included in the comparisons. These data do not get at the main question of interest to racial profiling: are drivers from certain racial/ethnic groups stopped at a higher rate than white drivers in certain patrol districts? To answer this question, a comparative benchmark for each district is necessary. District-level stop rates were not calculated because the specific district of residence for stopped drivers was not included in the vehicle stop data. As such, it was not possible to compare drivers who were stopped in their district of residence to the residential population of the district where the stop occurred, introducing an unacceptable level of error to the stop rate calculation process. While regression models and stop rates were not used in the analysis of differences in district of stop, population estimates for each of the five patrol districts were used in the interpretation of district of stop differences (see Table 49).

There are several factors that should be considered when analyzing differences in district of stop, and officer deployment is one of those variables. On average, EPD assigned two patrol officers each to districts one through four, while five officers were typically assigned to district five. The reason for this uneven deployment was related to call volume—EPD noted that the largest percentage of calls for police service came from district five. This uneven deployment explains, at least in part, why the largest percentages of stops involving Asian (27.6%—see Table 24), black (38.3%), Latino (40%), and white drivers (29.4%) occurred in district five.

With regard to these differences, the residential population within each patrol district provides some additional insight. The residential population demographics within each patrol district are of interest for several reasons. First, if the residential population within a district is more likely to travel within that district, then the demographic makeup of each district is important for understanding the racial/ethnic distribution of stops. Second, the percentage of minority groups within a given district may have an impact on how officers view that district.[61] In terms of racial profiling, officers could see areas where racial/ethnic

---

[61] See Chapter Three.

Table 49. Racial/Ethnic Distribution of Eugene Population by Patrol District

	District One[a] Exclusive Population	District One[a] Percentage	District Two[b] Exclusive Population	District Two[b] Percentage	District Three[c] Exclusive Population	District Three[c] Percentage	District Four[d] Exclusive Population	District Four[d] Percentage	District Five[e] Exclusive Population	District Five[e] Percentage
2002										
White	24795	89.1%	17888	90.2%	17809	87.0%	18522	88.0%	15657	81.5%
Asian	1043	3.7%	575	2.9%	794	3.9%	241	1.1%	1251	6.5%
Black	280	1.0%	161	0.8%	274	1.3%	180	0.9%	304	1.6%
Latino	824	3.0%	627	3.2%	729	3.6%	1223	5.8%	1105	5.8%
TOTAL	27826		19829		20468		21050		19202	
2003										
White	25150	89.1%	18128	90.2%	18133	86.9%	18808	87.9%	15720	81.5%
Asian	1053	3.7%	585	2.9%	805	3.9%	246	1.1%	1254	6.5%
Black	283	1.0%	163	0.8%	283	1.4%	183	0.9%	305	1.6%
Latino	843	3.0%	633	3.1%	753	3.6%	1253	5.9%	1116	5.8%
TOTAL	28234		20099		20860		21406		19287	

Source: 2000 U.S. Census.
Note: District populations were calculated by matching census tracts to a map of EPD patrol districts. In cases where a tract fell into two or more patrol districts, the population of that tract was divided and distributed evenly. Two tracts (37 and 54) fell into two patrol districts, and one tract (42) fell into three patrol districts.

[a] Tracts included in District One: 22.01, 22.02, 29.01, 29.02, 30, 31.01, and 31.02.
[b] Tracts included in District Two: 36, 37, 47, 48, 49, 50, 51, 52, and 54.
[c] Tracts included in District Three: 25.02, 42, 43, 44.01, 44.02, 44.03, 46, 53, and 54.
[d] Tracts included in District Four: 23, 24.01, 24.03, 24.04, 25.01, 25.02, 26, 27, 28, 41, 42, and 43.
[e] Tracts included in District Five: 37, 38, 39, 40, 42, and 45.

minority groups comprise a larger percentage of the residential population as more suspicious, and this could impact enforcement patterns.

Compared to the other patrol districts, district five had the largest percentage of Asian (6.5%—see Table 49) and black residents (1.6%), and the largest percentages of all stops involving Asian and black drivers occurred in this district. In 2002, districts four and five had equal percentages of Latino residents (5.8%), while in 2003 the percentage of district four Latino residents (5.9%) was slightly greater than district five (5.8%). Regardless of these slight variations, it is vital to note that the largest percentages of stops involving Latino drivers occurred in districts four and five. In addition, district four had the smallest percentage of Asian residents (1.1%), and the smallest percentage of all stops involving Asian drivers occurred in this district (7.3%—see Table 24). Contrary to this pattern, district two, the patrol district with the second lowest percentage of Asian residents (2.9%—see Table 49) had the second highest percentage of all stops involving Asian drivers (24.6%—see Table 24).

On the whole, these results offer some support for the idea that residential population demographics are related to the distribution of stops across districts. Larger percentages of all stops involving Asian, black, and Latino drivers occurred in areas with more racial/ethnic diversity.

It is important to reiterate that it was not possible to determine a driver's district of residence using the vehicle stop data. While it is possible to determine whether or not the driver was a Eugene resident, the specific district of residence is not included in the data. This makes it impossible to directly test the theory that drivers who reside within a specific district are more likely to travel within that district, and are therefore more likely to be stopped in that district.

Furthermore, this part of the analysis was not limited to Eugene residents. This analysis included both residents and non-residents, and as a result it can be used to explore the impact of the racial/ethnic population distribution of a specific district on perceptions of criminality. At the same time, it is also important to consider officer deployment patterns in this analysis. While district five was the most racially/ethnically diverse patrol district (81.5% white—see Table 49), and while it featured the highest percentages of all stops involving Asian, black, and Latino drivers, it also had the highest percentage of

Making Sense of the Disparities

all stops involving white drivers despite the fact that it had the smallest percentage of white residents when compared to the other patrol districts.[62] As this research demonstrates, disentangling the effects of officer deployment and residential population demographics is a difficult proposition.

Finding Five: Result of Stop

There were differences between racial/ethnic groups in terms of stop results, and most of these differences were explained by variables other than race/ethnicity. Over the two-year data collection period, a smaller percentage of Asian drivers were arrested compared to white drivers. Smaller percentages of black and Latino drivers experienced enforcement action, while larger percentages of black and Latino drivers were arrested compared to white drivers.

Regression analysis revealed that the effects of race/ethnicity on enforcement action were not statistically significant after controlling for the effects of other relevant variables (see Table 26, Model 2). While Asian drivers were 73% less likely than white drivers to be arrested even after controlling for the effects of other factors (see Table 27, Model 2), the effects for black and Latino drivers were not statistically significant in explaining arrests or enforcement action. That only one of the racial/ethnic categories was statistically significant in the two regression models for stop results indicates that variables other than race/ethnicity were more useful in explaining stop results.

The effects of offending were among the most interesting noted in the regression analyses. In terms of the likelihood of enforcement action, there was no difference between drivers stopped for traffic violations only and drivers stopped for more serious, low discretion violations (see Table 26, Model 2). However, drivers stopped for other high discretion violations were less likely to experience enforcement action compared to drivers stopped for traffic violations only. Assuming that offending is a key determinant of enforcement actions and arrests (as officers and police officials have argued), this finding indicates that drivers stopped for equipment or passenger violations only or for a combination of traffic, equipment, and passenger violations were likely stopped for less serious reasons, or that the

---

[62] It should be noted that white residents made up 81.5% of the district five population.

reasons for stop in such cases were pretexts allowing the officers to investigate vehicles and drivers that they considered suspicious.

The lack of statistically significant differences between drivers stopped for low discretion violations and drivers stopped for traffic violations only are likely related to officer assignments and responsibilities. EPD maintains a Traffic Enforcement Unit (TEU), a group of officers who are specifically assigned to stop and cite traffic law violators. Insofar as this group's investigative responsibilities are minimal, the increased rate of citations for traffic violations is to be expected. The work of TEU is also reflected in the hour of stop results. As the regression analysis indicates, the likelihood of enforcement action decreased outside the hours of 10:00 AM and 2:59 PM, and this corresponds with TEU's schedule (8:00 AM to 5:00 PM).

In terms of arrests, drivers stopped for low discretion violations were much more likely to be arrested than drivers stopped for traffic violations only (see Table 27, Model 2). This is likely a reflection of the seriousness of the offense. Similar to the effects noted in the enforcement action analysis, drivers stopped for equipment or passenger violations were less likely to be arrested than drivers stopped for traffic violations only, which further reinforces the conclusion that the equipment and passenger violations generally involved high levels of officer discretion. Coupled with the knowledge of TEU's work schedule, the fact that stops occurring between 10:00 AM and 2:59 PM were less likely to result in arrests compared to other times indicates that TEU was responsible for a substantial portion of EPD's citations, while patrol officers were responsible for the bulk of arrests.

Several patterns observed in the regression models help explain why the differences revealed in the group comparisons did not maintain statistical significance in the multivariate analyses. The patterns associated with offending carry racial/ethnic implications. Compared to white drivers, larger percentages of black and Latino drivers were stopped for equipment violations, and a larger percentage of black drivers were stopped for passenger violations (see Table 23). The fact that these reasons for stop were less likely to prompt enforcement action may account, at least in part, for the disparities observed in the group comparisons. Furthermore, larger percentages of black and Latino drivers were stopped for low discretion violations (specifically ORS crimes, calls for service, and pre-existing knowledge) compared to white drivers, and this undoubtedly contributed to the arrest

Making Sense of the Disparities

disparities. On the whole, these results indicate that offending, not race/ethnicity, was a key predictor of enforcement action and arrests. At the same time, the presence of differences in the enforcement action group comparisons strongly suggests that those black and Latino drivers who were stopped for high discretion reasons were likely stopped for comparatively minor infractions.

Location of stop is also important in understanding disparities in enforcement actions and arrests. Drivers stopped in patrol district five were less likely to experience enforcement action and more likely to be arrested than drivers in patrol districts one, two, and three. It is important to remember that the largest percentage of stops involving black and Latino drivers occurred in patrol district five (see Table 24), and that this district was the most racially/ethnically diverse of the patrol districts (see Table 49). While the regression results indicate that the effect of district of stop outweighed the effect of race/ethnicity in the case of black and Latino drivers, it is important to note the larger racial/ethnic context of these effects.

It is essential to understand the racial/ethnic context of other findings related to stop results. Stops where a language barrier was present were more likely to result in enforcement action and more likely to result in an arrest. Language barriers were present in 8.5% of stops involving Asian drivers (see Table 16) and 22.1% of stops involving Latino drivers, compared to 0.2% of all stops involving white drivers. As such, the effects associated with the presence of a language barrier disproportionately impacted Asian and Latino drivers. This is particularly interesting considering that a smaller percentage of Latino drivers experienced enforcement action compared to the percentage of white drivers. The presence of a language barrier increased the likelihood that 22.1% of Latino drivers would experience enforcement action, but the group as a whole experienced enforcement action less frequently than white drivers.

The racial/ethnic context of the hour of stop is another important factor. Stops that occurred during evening and late night hours were less likely to result in enforcement action and more likely to result in arrests compared to stops that occurred between 10:00 AM and 2:59 PM. Larger percentages of stops involving black drivers (31.1%—see Table 16) and Latino drivers (26.6%) occurred during late night hours compared to the percentage of stops involving white drivers (18%). Once again, this contextualizing factor must be considered when interpreting the overall findings.

While the regression analysis demonstrated that race/ethnicity generally did not predict enforcement action or arrests, other variables provided considerable insight into how stop results were determined. The overall racial/ethnic context of several of these factors indicates that even though race/ethnicity may not have a direct effect, its effects may be indirectly routed through other factors, like offending, district of stop, hour of stop, and the presence of a language barrier.

Finding Six: Stop Duration

There were differences between racial/ethnic groups in terms of duration of stop, and some of these differences were explained by variables other than race/ethnicity. Over the two-year data collection period, a smaller percentage of Asian drivers were stopped for more than 30 minutes compared to white drivers. Larger percentages of black and Latino drivers were stopped for more than 15 minutes and more than 30 minutes compared to white drivers.

Regression analysis revealed that black drivers were 14% (see Table 29, Model 2) more likely, and Latino drivers were 29.2% more likely than white drivers to be stopped for more than 15 minutes even after controlling for the effects of other relevant variables, while the effect for Asian drivers was not statistically significant in explaining stops that lasted more than 15 minutes. Additional analysis demonstrated that Asian drivers were 79.5% (see Table 30, Model 2) less likely than white drivers to be stopped for more than 30 minutes even after controlling for the effects of other relevant variables, while the effects for black and Latino drivers were not statistically significant.

Offending played an important role in determining stop duration. Drivers stopped for low discretion violations were more likely to experience longer stops than drivers stopped for traffic violations only. This is not surprising considering that stops involving low discretion violations were also more likely to result in arrests (see Table 27, Model 2) and searches (see Table 31, Model 2 and Table 32, Model 2), and these factors together undoubtedly inflated stop duration. Drivers stopped for equipment or passenger violations only were more likely to experience stops that lasted more than 15 minutes compared to drivers stopped for traffic violations only. That these stops lasted longer supports the conclusion that equipment and passenger violations were used as pretexts for investigation. Also, the fact that stops conducted between 10:00 AM and 2:59 PM were less likely to last for an extended period of time indicates that patrol officers rather than TEU officers were responsible for many of the longer stops. Considering that an important element of the patrol function is the investigation of suspicious circumstances (Cole and Smith 2007:197), this finding is not unexpected.

In terms of stop duration, the direct effects associated with race/ethnicity are augmented by the racial/ethnic context provided by other statistically significant relationships. The context noted in the regression analyses of enforcement action and arrests are also relevant to stop duration. That larger percentages of black and Latino drivers were stopped for both serious (low discretion) and minor (high discretion) violations compared to whites played a role in the overall magnitude of the stop duration differences between these groups.

Much like the patterns observed with stop results, stops that occurred in district five were more likely than stops that occurred in districts one and two to last more than 15 minutes, and more likely than stops that occurred in districts one, two, and three to last more than 30 minutes. These differences are important because, as was stated earlier, the largest percentage of stops involving black and Latino drivers occurred in district five (see Table 24), and because district five was the most racially/ethnically diverse of the patrol districts (see Table 49). In addition, stops that occurred in district four were more likely than stops that occurred in district five to last more than 15 minutes and more than 30 minutes. Compared to other districts, the percentage of the district four population that identified themselves as Latino (5.8% in 2002 and 5.9% in 2003) in the 2000 Census was comparable to the district five population (5.8% in 2002 and 2003).

The presence of a language barrier lengthened the duration of stops, and larger percentages of Asian and Latino drivers experienced language barriers compared to white drivers. In this case, the same variable that adds to the racial/ethnic context also provides a very reasonable explanation for the extended duration. Furthermore, it also identifies an issue that is ripe for intervention. While language barriers only occurred in 1.3% of stops (see Table 16), the expected and reasonable impact of these barriers disproportionately affected Asian and Latino drivers.

Stops that occurred during evening and late night hours were more likely to last for an extended period of time compared to stops that occurred between 10:00 AM and 2:59 PM. As was stated in relation to the preceding finding, larger percentages of stops involving black and Latino drivers occurred during these hours, and as such the indirect effect of race/ethnicity was captured in these odds ratios. This finding is particularly important when considering the 30-minute split model, where the effects for black drivers and Latino drivers were not statistically significant while the effects associated with evening stops (107.3% more likely to be stopped for more than 30 minutes—see Table 30. Model 2) and late night stops (226.2% more likely to be stopped for more than 30 minutes) were statistically significant and quite substantial.

While effects related to offending, district of stop, the presence of a language barrier, and the time of stop contribute to the overall racial/ethnic context in which these findings must be interpreted, the direct effects associated with race/ethnicity are the most important aspects of these models. Even after controlling for a number of relevant factors, black and Latino drivers were still more likely than white drivers to be stopped for more than 15 minutes. This finding fits the pattern one would expect to find if officers were targeting black and Latino drivers for pretext stops.

Finding Seven: Search Frequency

There were differences between racial/ethnic groups in terms of search occurrence, and these differences persisted even after variables other than race/ethnicity were included in the analysis. Over the two-year data collection period, a smaller percentage of Asian drivers were searched compared to white drivers, and this pattern was consistent for both male and female drivers. A larger percentage of black drivers were searched compared to white drivers, and this pattern was consistent for black male drivers, but not for black female drivers. A larger percentage of Latino drivers were searched compared to white drivers, and this pattern was consistent for Latino male drivers, but not for Latino female drivers.

Regression analyses revealed that Asian drivers were less likely (ASIP=47.6%, MRT=65.1%—see Table 34, Model 2, and Table 35, Model 2) than white drivers to be searched, while Latino drivers were more likely (ASIP=48.5%, MRT=38.5%) than white drivers to be searched even after controlling for the effects of other relevant variables. While the MRT regression model showed no statistically significant difference between black and white drivers in terms of searches, the ASIP model indicated that black drivers were 51.1% more likely to be searched.

As with other dependent variables, offending played an important role in searches. Drivers stopped for low discretion violations were much more likely to be searched than drivers stopped for high discretion violations. In the MRT model, drivers stopped for equipment or passenger violations only were slightly more likely to be searched than drivers stopped for traffic violations only.

In addition to offending, the impact of other independent variables must be examined. The effects associated with time of stop, especially when coupled with the effects for high discretion reasons for stop, match the patterns related to patrol and TEU enforcement activities discussed previously. These results reinforce the conclusion that patrol officers likely conducted the majority of searches.

The effects associated with offending, district of stop, the presence of a language barrier, and time of stop add to the overall racial/ethnic context of this study's findings. Larger percentages of black and Latino drivers were stopped for low discretion violations compared to white drivers. Drivers stopped in district five were more likely to be searched than drivers stopped in districts one, two, and three. The presence of a language barrier increased the likelihood of a search. Drivers who were stopped during the evening and late night hours were more likely to be searched than drivers stopped between 10:00 AM and 2:59 PM. Each of these results tap into racial/ethnic differences discussed earlier, and when these findings are interpreted in light of these disparities, the likelihood that black and Latino drivers would experience searches increases substantially beyond the direct effects.

While an analysis of the effects of variables other than race/ethnicity is vital to developing a more complex understanding of how EPD and its officers conducted searches, the key issue to those interested in racial profiling is whether or not race/ethnicity plays an important role in this process. The regression analyses indicate that, even after accounting for the effects of sex, age, reason for stop, district of stop, number of passengers, the presence of a language barrier, whether or not the officer could tell the driver's race prior to the stop, and the time of the stop, black and Latino drivers were more likely than white drivers to experience a search, and Asian drivers were less likely than white drivers to experience a search.

One independent variable that could help explain searches was not included in the regression analysis. Larger percentages of black and Latino drivers were arrested compared to the percentage of white drivers (see Table 25). This is important because a considerably larger percentage of arrested drivers were searched (ASIP=85.5%, MRT=84.7%)[63] compared to drivers who were not arrested (ASIP=6.1%, MRT=3.5%). While there were no differences in terms of the percentages of arrested drivers who were searched across racial/ethnic groups, the fact that more black and Latino drivers were arrested may help explain the statistically significant effect for these racial/ethnic groups. However, as the analysis of stop results demonstrated, arrests were not directly shaped by race/ethnicity, but mostly by reason for stop. Since reason for stop was controlled for in the search models, there is little cause for concern.

Arrests were not included in the regression models because the sequence of events could not be discerned from the data. In other words, it was not possible to tell whether the arrest caused the search, or vice versa. In an attempt to account for this issue, the presence of an outstanding warrant was entered into exploratory regression models.[64] While the resulting odds ratios were highly statistically significant, they were also highly unstable,[65] and as such it could not be considered a reliable estimate and was subsequently removed from the final models. What is important to note is that even when this variable was included in the models, the effects associated with race/ethnicity were still statistically significant. This indicates that, while arrest warrants undoubtedly played a role in the decision to search, the effect of these warrants did not significantly alter the patterns of statistical significance presented in this study.

---

[63] It is EPD policy to search every civilian who is arrested. The reason that 100% of the arrested drivers do not have search information recorded in the vehicle stop data is because officers were informally instructed not to include "pat down" or Terry searches in their reporting.

[64] The presence of an outstanding warrant was the only reason for arrest that could be assumed to consistently occur before the decision to search.

[65] The instability of this odds ratio was associated with the small number of applicable cases (340 total). While other variables in the regression models featured similar numbers, the inclusion of multiple variables with skewed distributions created unstable estimates.

Making Sense of the Disparities 207

Finding Eight: Discretionary Search Conducted

There were differences between racial/ethnic groups in terms of discretionary search occurrence, and there is evidence that these differences persisted even after variables other than race/ethnicity were included in the analysis. Over the two-year data collection period, a smaller percentage of Asian drivers experienced a discretionary search compared to white drivers, and this pattern was consistent for both male and female drivers. A larger percentage of black drivers experienced a discretionary search compared to white drivers, and this pattern was consistent for black male drivers, but not for black female drivers. A larger percentage of Latino drivers experienced a discretionary search compared to white drivers, and this pattern was consistent for Latino male drivers, but not for Latino female drivers.

Initial regression analyses revealed that Asian drivers were less likely (ASIP=58.4%, MRT=57.6%—see Table 41, Model 2, and Table 44, Model 2) than white drivers to experience a discretionary search, while the effects for black and Latino drivers were not statistically significant in both the ASIP and MRT models. However, once problems with missing data were addressed, regression analyses indicated that Latino drivers were more likely (ASIP=31.8%, MRT=30.5%—see Table 43, Model 2, and Table 45, Model 2) than white drivers to experience a discretionary search, though the effects for black drivers remained non-significant.

The main problem with the missing data models (Tables 43 and 44) is that the missing data dummy variables are not readily interpretable. Even though none of the unknown value categories were statistically significant, they are problematic because it is impossible to assign them a meaningful value in terms of the independent variables in question. In other words, what does it mean to say that a driver's age is unknown? Does it mean that the officer could not determine the age of the driver, or could it mean that the officer failed to record the age of the driver on the data collection form? In terms of sex, does the unknown category refer to stops where the officer was legitimately unable to determine the sex of the driver, or could this category also include cases of data collection error? Given these problems, it is impossible to assign any sort of consistent meaning to the unknown categories, which makes the models difficult to interpret. While the missing data regression models cannot replace the standard models, it should be noted that the effects of independent variables other than race/ethnicity were remarkably similar between the models, with only the effects associated with Latino drivers and the presence of a language barrier experiencing a slight but important change.

Besides the effects associated with race/ethnicity, other variables had an impact on the occurrence of discretionary searches. The patterns of statistical significance roughly followed the patterns in the general search models, though the magnitude of the effects related to certain independent variables were considerably greater. For example, in terms of all searches, drivers stopped during the late night hours were between 149.6% (ASIP—see Table 34) and 167.4% (MRT—see Table 35) more likely to be searched than drivers stopped between 10:00 AM and 2:59 PM. In terms of discretionary searches only, drivers stopped during late night hours were between 230.8% (ASIP— see Table 41) and 244% (MRT—see Table 44) more likely to experience a discretionary search compared to drivers stopped between 10:00 AM and 2:59 PM.

The effect of offending on discretionary searches requires discussion. Drivers stopped for low discretion violations were much more likely to experience a discretionary search than drivers stopped for traffic violations only. While part of this effect is undoubtedly related to the suspicion created by the seriousness of the offense, it also reflects police tactics and procedures associated with the admissibility of evidence. According to EPD management, Oregon courts have consistently rejected attempts to suppress evidence procured by officers through consent searches. As a result, EPD officers frequently attempt to obtain consent before conducting a search regardless of the situation in order to guarantee that any contraband found will be admissible in court.

That there were no statistically significant differences between the different categories of high discretion violations could be interpreted as evidence against claims that EPD targeted black and Latino drivers for pretext stops. As was pointed out in earlier discussions, larger percentages of black and Latino drivers were stopped for equipment and passenger[66] violations compared to white drivers, and when this is combined with findings from other regression models in this study (black and Latino drivers were less likely to be the subject of enforcement action and more likely to experience stops that last more than 15 minutes), the overall pattern resembles what would be expected

---

[66] The passenger violation differences applied to black drivers only.

Making Sense of the Disparities

from a department where pretext stop practices were being disproportionately applied to minority populations. These drivers were no more likely to experience a discretionary search than drivers stopped for other high discretion violations, but this finding only addresses the search aspect of the pretext stop process. More importantly, the fact that Latino drivers were more likely to experience a discretionary search (after accounting for the missing data) indicates that while the high discretion violations used to initiate pretext stops played a key role in stop results and stop duration, race/ethnicity was more important in terms of the decision to conduct a discretionary search as part of a pretext stop.

Finding Nine: Search Success Rate

There were no differences between racial/ethnic groups in terms of search productivity. Over the two-year data collection period, there were no statistically significant differences between black, Latino, and white drivers in terms of search success rates. In other words, searches of black and Latino drivers were no more or less likely to produce contraband than searches of white drivers. This pattern was consistent for both male and female drivers, across both search definitions (ASIP and MRT), and for general searches as well as discretionary searches only.

These results contradict differential offending theory, or the idea that black and Latino drivers are more likely to commit certain crimes, most notably drug offenses, compared to white drivers. If differential offending theory were true, one would expect that searches involving black and Latino drivers would produce contraband at a higher rate than whites, which was not the case according to EPD's vehicle stop data. Furthermore, a larger percentage of successful searches involving white drivers produced drugs and/or paraphernalia (ASIP=53.3%, MRT=53.5%—see Tables 38 and 39) compared to the percentages of successful searches of Latino (ASIP=36.1%, MRT=36.7%) and black drivers (both ASIP and MRT=34.8%).[67] These results provide direct evidence against the idea that black and Latino drivers are more likely to be involved in drug offenses compared to white drivers.

---

[67] It is important to note that the differences between black and white drivers was not statistically significant

DATA QUALITY ISSUES

Data Coverage

There is evidence that the data may not be complete. In an attempt to assess the coverage of the vehicle stop data, EPD Data Analyst Terry Smith compared some characteristics of the vehicle stop data to records from EPD's Area Information Record System (AIRS). Rather than just comparing the number of stops recorded in each data source, a practice that is susceptible to considerable error related to the differing criteria for classifying a contact as a vehicle stop,[68] he compared the number of citations between the AIRS system and the vehicle stop data. These comparisons revealed a completion rate of 70.4% for stops where a citation was issued.

A high completion rate is an important component of a representative vehicle stop data set. While a perfect completion rate is an unreasonable expectation for a paper-based data collection system, it is nonetheless important to investigate factors that may have contributed to coverage problems. Smith noted that an audit of the 2002 vehicle stop data revealed that the highest rates of missing cards occurred during the busiest hours of the day in terms of total volume of stops (noon to 5:00 PM weekdays) and highest workload per officer (Fridays, Saturdays, and Sundays after midnight). In his comparison of the AIRS data to the vehicle stop data for the entire two-year data collection period, Smith found that the completion rate for district five (50%) was considerably lower than the completion rate for other districts (one=85%, two=83%, three=80%, four=81%) by an average of 32.3%. That district five had the largest call volume, and that this district had the largest percentage of citations issued (28.3% of all citations issued in 2002 and 25.9% of all citations issued in 2003) reinforce the theory that officer workload had an impact on missing cards.

Officer workload, however, does not tell the entire story. Smith's 2002 audit also discovered the percentage of citations missing from the vehicle stop data for Tuesdays, Wednesdays, and Thursdays between

---

[68] While AIRS records classify officer contacts with unoccupied vehicles as traffic stops, officers were not required to fill out data collection forms for these events.

12:00 AM and 6:00 AM, and on Saturdays and Sundays in the late afternoon and early evening were also in the top two quartiles. This finding did not correspond to workload issues, which indicates that there were other factors contributing to completion rate problems.

It should be noted that the low completion rate for district five could have a considerable impact on the racial/ethnic distribution of the vehicle stop data. The largest percentage of all stops involving black (38.3%—see Table 24) and Latino drivers (40%) occurred in district five. This means that it is highly likely that a disproportionate number of stops involving black and Latino drivers were not captured in the vehicle stop data.

Data Coding

There were problems associated with the way in which the data were coded on the data collection form. Data coding refers to the categories that were used in the collection of certain pieces of data. For example, reason for stop was measured by grouping different reasons into nine categories. These groupings were developed from technical categories with which EPD officers were already familiar. To address the issue of categorical overlap and multiple reasons for stop, officers were allowed to choose all categories that applied to a given stop.

While the categories used in the data collection were undoubtedly useful to officers, the utility of these categories in research is another matter. More specifically, the data collection categories were efficient in terms of recording standard bureaucratic matters associated with vehicle stops; however, these procedures did not always capture the issues and facts that were of particular interest to the research task. For instance, insofar as discretion is an important issue in racial profiling research, it is important to be able to differentiate low discretion matters (situations where officers cannot exercise much discretion) from high discretion matters (situations where officers can exercise considerable discretion). Several of the coding strategies failed to capture possible variations in the level of discretion. For example, the traffic violation category in the measurement of reason for stop grouped together a multitude of violations with differing levels of officer discretion. To restate a prior example, drivers who were exceeding the speed limit by five miles-per-hour were grouped together with drivers who were exceeding the speed limit by 25 miles-per-hour. While the violations are categorically similar, the levels of discretion are likely to be quite different.

Equipment violations provide an additional example of this. The literature on pretext stops indicates that officers often cite minor equipment violations as legal reasons for stopping suspicious vehicles. High levels of officer discretion characterize pretext stops because the actual legal reason for the stop is identified after the officer has decided that the vehicle is suspicious and worthy of investigation. Such equipment violations were included in the same category as equipment violations for which a stop was initiated either for informational purposes (e.g. to bring the violation to the attention of the driver) or because the equipment violation posed a danger to the driver, to the vehicle, and possibly to others on the road. Once again, while the violations are categorically similar, the levels of discretion and the decision-making processes are quite different.

In addition to the problems associated with identifying the level of officer discretion in certain categories, the "select-all-that-apply" strategy that was used for several variables proved to be difficult to interpret. The idea behind this decision was to obtain a detailed description of the stop. These additional details proved to be confusing in several areas of the analysis, most notably with regard to reason for stop. While multiple stop reasons were only present in 4.4% of all stops, the complications caused by the presence of multiple stop reasons were considerable. One concern was related to the possibility that violations discovered after the stop were included in this data. In other words, officers may have included in their reporting passenger or equipment violations that they discovered during a stop that was initiated because of a traffic violation. While the additional information is interesting, it is not very useful unless the pre-stop and post-stop violations can be differentiated within the data set.

Data Scope

Some highly relevant variables were not included in the data collection project. The vehicle stop data provided vital information on the activities of EPD officers; at the same time, it is important to recognize that these data do not provide a comprehensive portrait of what occurred in the field. More importantly, the data analysis revealed that several important pieces of information were not captured, not necessarily because of any oversight on the part of the EPD or the Racial Profiling Data Collection Task Group, but because of logistical and ethical issues. These variables may have provided valuable insight into the observed differences between racial/ethnic groups. More specifically, information on the demeanor of both the officer(s) and civilians involved in the stop, the number of times a specific individual was stopped, and vehicle characteristics could have facilitated a more thorough analysis of racial/ethnic differences in the vehicle stop data, and a better overall understanding of police decision-making processes and enforcement practices.

Civilian and Officer Demeanor. Klinger (1994) observes that the relationship between civilian demeanor (disrespectful and impolite behavior) and officers' arrest choices (for less severe criminal behaviors) has become "part of the criminological canon" (p. 477). Lundman (1996) adds that the vast majority of research over the past 40 years has confirmed that "extralegal variables including demeanor shape arrests and other police actions" (p. 307). Research by Stark (1972) suggests that officers have used arrests as a way of punishing civilians who may have angered officers with their lack of kindness, politeness, or deference to authority. The wealth of research on the links between civilian demeanor and officer decision-making demonstrates the utility of some measure of demeanor in evaluating disparities in the vehicle stop data.

The national attention and concern regarding racial profiling could reasonably lead to differences in civilian demeanor across racial/ethnic groups. The beliefs of blacks and Latinos regarding the prevalence of racial profiling by EPD could reduce the legitimacy of the police in the eyes of these groups. However, it is unclear how these beliefs would impact civilian behavior during a vehicle stop. On one hand, a perceived lack of legitimacy could lead to increased resistance to police authority. On the other hand, the belief that police are biased could inspire fear among black and Latino drivers, which could lead to increased levels of deference and cooperation. For instance, researchers and critics have discussed a phenomenon referred to loosely as "the talk" among black families. Essentially, "the talk" refers to advice provided to young blacks, particularly males, to be cooperative to a fault with officers under any circumstances. This is the product of the fear that demeanor, especially hostility towards the officers, could have dire, if not fatal, consequences, and as such, "the talk" can be seen as a strategy of self-preservation in a law enforcement system that is perceived to be biased.

Officer demeanor is also pertinent to the investigation of disparities in the vehicle stop data. Civilians' perceptions of officers' demeanor can impact civilians' evaluations of the legitimacy of a given vehicle stop, and subsequent actions towards officers during the interaction. As such, officer demeanor can serve to diminish or escalate conflict within a given situation.

Number of Stops for Specific Individuals. The vehicle stop data set contains information on stops made by EPD officers in 2002 and 2003. However, there is no way to identify the number of people stopped by EPD officers during these years. It is inevitable that a portion of stops in the vehicle stop data set involved multiple stops of the same individual. There is no way to identify such stops in the data set, or the overall proportion of the data set that is made up of individuals stopped on more than one occasion over the two-year data collection period.

An estimate of the amount or proportion of multiple stops by race/ethnicity could have an impact on the overall stop rate for these groups, though it is important to point out that the decrease in stop rates in terms of the overall number of residents stopped would inevitably result in an increase in the average number of police contacts per person stopped—a result that would require additional investigation. Furthermore, by examining individuals who were stopped multiple times it would be possible to investigate in more detail claims of repeat offending and harassment, though this investigation should proceed with caution. The prevalence of certain characteristics among the population of multiple stops does not constitute conclusive proof of either repeat offending or police harassment, though a careful analysis could reasonably examine additional indicators of both these phenomena.

Vehicle Information. Anecdotal evidence has demonstrated the importance of vehicle characteristics on officers' perceptions of suspicious behavior. Drug interdiction tactics have focused on characteristics of automobiles commonly used in the transportation of drugs (Harris 1999). Kennedy (1997) and others have noted that black and Latino drivers of expensive automobiles have complained of harassment that they perceive to be related to the combination of their race/ethnicity and their choice of vehicle. Finally, certain makes and models of automobiles, as well as types of vehicle modifications and decorations, have been linked to racial/ethnic groups and related subcultures. As such, vehicle characteristics can be seen as indicators of suspiciousness, and insofar as certain characteristics have been linked to stereotypes of racial/ethnic groups, these can also be interpreted as proxies for race/ethnicity.

It is here that a departure occurs from the conventional thinking about racial profiling. Most researchers have focused on the race/ethnicity of the driver and passengers, laboring under the assumption that officers' perceptions regarding the driver's race/ethnicity are at the root of racial profiling. This is not consistent with the literature on criminal profiling, which instructs officers to rely on multiple indicators of suspiciousness when making decisions (Fredrickson and Siljander 2002), nor is it consistent with the data from this and other vehicle stop studies. The vehicle stop data indicates that officers formed an opinion about the race/ethnicity of the driver prior to the stop in only 13% of all stops (see Table 3). Furthermore, 32.3% of all stops occurred between the hours of 6:00 PM and 3:00 AM (see Table 5), meaning that the officers' ability to visually identify the race/ethnicity of the driver was probably impeded by the lack of light.

It is important that research on racial profiling move away from this focus on officer's ability to identify the race/ethnicity of the driver prior to the stop, and towards an understanding of racial profiling as a practice associated with racialized symbols and characteristics, especially those associated vehicle characteristics. Such information contributes to officers' level of suspicion before and during the stop, and is necessary for a more complete analysis of racial profiling.

BUT IS IT RACIAL PROFILING?

Bivariate comparisons and chi-square tests revealed numerous differences between Asian, black, Latino, and white drivers in terms of their vehicle stop experiences. Multivariate analyses isolated the impact of race/ethnicity on several enforcement-related outcomes while controlling for other important factors, such as the reason for the stop, time and patrol district of the stop, and the driver's sex and age. In order to address broader questions associated with discrimination, differential enforcement, and racial profiling in Eugene, these findings must be examined collectively.

At this stage it is important to reiterate the limitations of vehicle stop data when specifically addressing decision standards commonly used to frame racial profiling research. Insofar as racial profiling has traditionally been defined as a product of officer decision-making, it is necessary to have data on all aspects of officers' decisions in order to fully evaluate decision-making processes. Taken alone, vehicle stop data is lacking crucial information on those drivers that officers chose *not to stop*. While this problem is mitigated through the careful construction and integration of a comparative benchmark, such benchmark data are at best indirect estimates of the non-stopped population and undoubtedly lack information that is pertinent to officers' decision-making processes. This dilemma is present in all benchmark comparisons used in racial profiling research, not just residential population estimates like those used in this study.

Despite the fact that vehicle stop data does not provide a complete picture of officers' decisions to stop, it does capture vital information about officer actions following the decision to stop, and the data on post-stop variables are much more comprehensive in terms of capturing multiple facets of officer decision-making. More specifically, vehicle stop data supplies information on who officers chose to cite, arrest, search, and detain for extended periods of time, as well as who officers chose not to cite, arrest, search, and detain. Because vehicle stop data do not capture exactly how drivers' racial/ethnic characteristics impacted officers' decision-making processes, it is difficult to conclude that observed differences are related to explicitly racial/ethnic considerations. However, it is possible to capture overarching patterns of differential enforcement and discrimination linked to race/ethnicity.

In terms of determinants of enforcement patterns, the analysis clearly indicates that offending played a vital role in shaping events after the stop. Regression analysis demonstrated that drivers who were stopped for comparatively serious, low discretion violations were more likely to be arrested, more likely to be searched, and more likely to be detained for an extended period of time. The effects associated with low discretion reasons for stop were highly statistically significant and the related odds ratios were all substantial.

While offending was an important factor in determining enforcement patterns, there was little evidence of differential offending in the vehicle stop data. Chi-square tests showed no differences between blacks, Latinos, and whites in terms of the percentage of searches that produced contraband. Additionally, larger percentages of successful searches of whites produced drugs and/or paraphernalia, a finding that directly contradicts the stereotype that minority groups are

Making Sense of the Disparities

disproportionately involved in the drug trade. The only potential evidence of differential offending was related to the distribution of reasons for stop across racial/ethnic groups. That larger percentages of black and Latino drivers were stopped for low discretion violations (ORS crimes, calls for service, and pre-existing knowledge) could be interpreted as support for differential offending theory. However, data on violators with whom officers had no contact, and violators who officers chose not to stop and investigate are needed to substantiate this conclusion. As such, the observed differences in reason for stop could be the result of selection bias at a number of levels.[69] Furthermore, two of these three reasons for stop are particularly vulnerable to multiple sources of bias in the selection process. First, inequalities in the criminal justice system likely contribute to a larger percentage of black and Latino drivers being stopped for reasons associated with pre-existing knowledge. Also, racial/ethnic stereotypes associated with suspicion, most notably in relation to criminal potential,[70] may lead officers to retain and recall the criminal status of blacks and Latinos more readily than whites. Second, civilians initiate calls for service, and as such these reports are colored by the racial/ethnic stereotypes and prejudices held, either consciously or unconsciously, by the public. Anecdotal evidence indicates that officers have used such reports as an excuse to stop minority drivers whose race/ethnicity alone matched the description. When seen in this light, the fact that larger percentages of black and Latino drivers were stopped for pre-existing knowledge and calls for service could reasonably be a reflection of larger-scale biases as opposed to evidence of differential offending.

In addition to offending, several demographic characteristics influenced enforcement patterns. Regression analysis demonstrated that female drivers and drivers ages 40 and over were less likely to experience enforcement action, less likely to be arrested, less likely to be searched, and less likely to be detained for an extended period of time compared to male drivers and drivers ages 18 to 29. Interestingly, drivers ages 30 to 39 were more likely to be arrested, more likely to be searched, and more likely to be detained for an extended period of time compared to drivers ages 18 to 29.

The location where the stop occurred also had an impact on enforcement patterns. Drivers who were stopped in district five,

---

[69] See Chapter Three for additional details.
[70] See Chapter Two.

Eugene's downtown area, were less likely to experience enforcement action, more likely to be arrested, more likely to experience a search, and more likely to be detained for an extended period of time compared to drivers who were stopped in other areas with one exception—drivers who were stopped in patrol district four, or northwest Eugene, were less likely to experience enforcement action and more likely to be detained for an extended period of time than drivers stopped in all other districts. Interpreting the effects associated with district of stop are complex. To begin with, five patrol officers were typically assigned to district five, while other districts were assigned only two officers each. EPD justified the disproportionate distribution of officers and resources by noting that the department received its largest percentage of calls for service from district five. As a result of this deployment strategy, the largest percentage of all stops were conducted in district five. Furthermore, patrol officers, who are charged with a broad variety of duties including the investigation of suspicious situations and individuals, were likely responsible for a large portion of stops in district five. The work of patrol officers is not likely to produce large numbers of citations, though the questioning of suspects, searches, and arrests are generally associated with patrol work. EPD's deployment policies also contributed to the larger racial/ethnic context in which vehicle stops occur. District five was the most racially/ethnically diverse of the patrol districts, though district four had roughly the same percentage of Latino residents as district five. This means that EPD deployed more patrol officers and officer hours to the district with the largest percentage of minority residents.

The effects associated with the presence of a language barrier were also quite dramatic. Stops where a language barrier was present were more likely to result in enforcement action, more likely to result in an arrest, more likely include in a search, and more likely to last longer than stops without language barriers. While the finding associated with duration is to be expected, the effect of a language barrier in other areas is a source of concern. It indicates the possibility that the presence of a language barrier acts as a symbol of suspicion to officers, influencing their decision-making processes during stops. Furthermore, the impact of language barriers was disproportionately distributed across racial/ethnic groups. Compared to white drivers, language barriers were present in larger percentages of stops involving Asian and Latino drivers.

Making Sense of the Disparities

In addition, the time of day when the stop occurred had an effect on enforcement patterns, especially in terms of stops that occurred during nighttime hours. Drivers stopped during evening (6:00 PM to 9:59 PM) and late night hours (10:00 PM to 2:59 AM) were less likely to experience enforcement action, more likely to be arrested, more likely to be searched, and more likely to be detained for an extended period of time compared to drivers who were stopped during midday hours (10:00 AM to 2:59 PM). The effect of being stopped during evening and late night hours on the occurrence of discretionary searches was also particularly strong. Part of this overall variation is related to scheduling and officer assignments. EPD's Traffic Enforcement Unit (TEU) operates during standard business hours, and their primary responsibility is to enforce traffic laws. Insofar as writing citations is a central feature of TEU's work, it is to be expected that the citation rate would be higher during hours when they are on the roads, and lower during hours when they are not. The general enforcement pattern associated with time of stop also points to a relationship between evening and late night stops and increased levels of officer suspicion. The fact that larger percentages of black and Latino drivers were stopped during evening and late night hours means that the effects associated with nighttime stops disproportionately impacted minority drivers and added to the overall racial/ethnic context of these effects.

While location of stop, the presence of a language barrier, and time of stop all contributed greatly to the explanation of enforcement patterns and the overall racial/ethnic context of this study's findings, the main variable of interest in this research is race/ethnicity. Regression analysis demonstrated that black and Latino drivers were no more or less likely than white drivers to experience enforcement action, to be arrested, or to be detained for more than 30 minutes. However, black and Latino drivers were more likely to be searched, more likely to be detained for more than 15 minutes, and Latino drivers were more likely to experience a discretionary search even after accounting for the effects of sex, age, reason for stop, location of stop, time of stop, the presence of a language barrier, and several other variables. On the other hand, Asian drivers were less likely to be arrested, less likely to be searched, less likely to be the subject of a discretionary search, and less likely to be detained for more than 30 minutes compared to white drivers. Because these results were produced using multivariate techniques that control for the effects of alternative explanations, we can be confident that these results were in fact related to race/ethnicity, though we cannot be sure of the etiology of these relationships.

When interpreting these results as a whole, the observed patterns bear a striking resemblance to what would be predicted from a department that was targeting minority motorists, black and Latino drivers specifically, for pretext stops. Four findings in particular indicate that EPD selected black and Latino drivers for pretext stops. First, the stop rate analysis revealed that black residents of Eugene, specifically black male residents, experienced more stops per 1000 residents than white residents even after accounting for potential population changes. Given the magnitude of the differences, this can reasonably be interpreted as evidence of selection bias related to race/ethnicity. However, the same cannot be said for Latino drivers, whose stop rates were generally similar to or lower than the stop rates for white residents with one important exception—the 2002 stop rates for Latino male residents were higher than the stop rate for white male residents. Regardless of the lack of differences between Latino and white drivers in terms of stop frequency, subsequent findings indicate important differences between these groups in terms of post-stop treatment.

Second, chi-square tests demonstrated that smaller percentages of black and Latino drivers experienced enforcement action compared to white drivers. Regression analysis revealed that these differences were caused by factors other than race/ethnicity, specifically that enforcement action was determined largely by the reason for stop. As such, the lack of enforcement action as captured in the group comparisons indicates that larger portions of black and Latino drivers who were stopped for high discretion violations were pulled over for minor reasons that likely did not warrant enforcement action. If the violations were serious, at the very least a citation would be expected. While some may interpret the group comparison differences as evidence of well-meaning officers attempting to heal past rifts between the police and minority communities by releasing black and Latino drivers with warnings, this explanation does not fit the other findings in this study. When this specific result is viewed in light of other patterns, it is clear that the pretext stop explanation is the only theory that fits the data as a whole.

Third, regression analysis showed that black and Latino drivers were more likely to be stopped for more than 15 minutes compared to white drivers even after controlling for the effects of other important variables, including reason for stop, time and location of stop, and the presence of a language barrier. Despite the fact that larger percentages of black and Latino drivers were stopped for minor reasons, and even though smaller percentages of these groups experienced enforcement action, black and Latino drivers were detained longer than white drivers. When considered alongside the reason for stop findings, this finding is an indication that black and Latino drivers were subjected to higher levels of scrutiny and investigation during vehicle stops.

Fourth, regression analysis demonstrated that, even after controlling for offending and other explanations, black and Latino drivers were more likely than white drivers to be searched. Additionally, chi-square tests demonstrated that larger percentages of black and Latino drivers experienced discretionary searches. Further regression analysis confirmed Latino drivers were more likely than white drivers to experience a discretionary search even after controlling for the effects of other relevant independent. The differences between black and white drivers in terms of discretionary searches was not statistically significant in the regression models, though this may have been related to the small number of observations.

These findings demonstrate an alarming enforcement pattern. Stops involving black and Latino drivers were more likely to result in a warning. Considering that reason for stop played a vital role in determining the result of the stop, it stands to reason that the high discretion infractions used to justify the stops of numerous black and Latino motorists were not serious in nature. Despite the fact that many stops of black and Latino drivers were for minor violations, drivers from these groups were more likely to be detained for an extended period of time even after accounting for the influence of the reason for the stop. The extended stop duration is best explained as increased levels of suspicion and investigation on the part of officers, a conclusion that is reinforced by the fact that black and Latino drivers were more likely to experience a search even after accounting for other important factors. When taken together, it is clear that EPD's pretext stop practices focused disproportionately on black and Latino drivers.

The previous discussion of the racial/ethnic context created by other variables further buttresses this conclusion. The data indicate that EPD's pretext stop practices were focused largely on districts four and five—the two districts with the largest percentages of minority residents. Stops where a language barrier was present were treated with increased suspicion even after accounting for other variables, including offending. Late night stops were more likely to follow a pretext stop pattern, and the fact that larger percentages of stops involving black and Latino drivers occurred during these hours magnifies these effects. When these results and patterns are considered as a whole, they clearly illustrate the overlap between race/ethnicity and the construction of suspicion within EPD.

Additionally, the observed differences between racial/ethnic groups, in terms of both the bivariate comparisons and the multivariate analysis, likely underestimate the magnitude of the real racial/ethnic differences in enforcement patterns in Eugene. Data collection audits conducted by EPD revealed that the data form completion rate for stops in district five was dramatically lower than the completion rate for other districts. In addition to having the most diverse residential population, larger percentages of stops involving black and Latino drivers occurred in district five. Even if the missing data were randomly distributed in terms of race/ethnicity (meaning that there were no systematic reasons that would make it more or less likely for data to be missing for black and Latino drivers), the raw number of stops of black and Latino drivers would increase at a higher rate than the number of stops involving white drivers, and the observed disparities between these groups in other areas (like enforcement action, arrests, and searches) would also increase in magnitude.

In sum, the findings of this study clearly demonstrate patterns of differential enforcement related to race/ethnicity. Although civilian offending explains a considerable portion of the observed racial/ethnic disparities, its explanatory power does not account for all of the variation between racial/ethnic groups. Additionally, this study finds little evidence of differential offending between racial/ethnic groups. The effects associated with race/ethnicity and the overall racial/ethnic context of other variables in the analysis further suggest EPD's pretext stop tactics and related investigative strategies are disproportionately applied to black and Latino drivers. While I cannot be sure that the racial/ethnic differences identified in this study are the product of intentional discrimination on the part of officers, it is clear that race/ethnicity is an important variable in understanding enforcement patterns in Eugene, Oregon.

RECOMMENDATIONS FOR FUTURE RESEARCH

This study offers several important insights that will improve future vehicle stop data projects specifically, and research on race/ethnicity and policing in general. The theoretical framework presented in Chapter Three provides a solid foundation upon which future research can be designed. The causal theories and contextualizing factors offer researchers direction in selecting data collection techniques, interpreting racial/ethnic disparities in past, current, and future research, and identifying possible sources of selection bias in existing and new data. In terms of vehicle stop data collection projects, this perspective will help in the selection of variables for inclusion in such efforts, and it will further clarify what sorts of conclusions can be drawn using vehicle stop data alone. At the same time, the theories and framework presented in Chapter Three are still in need of further development. Several authors have identified a variety or relevant theories that help explain racial/ethnic disparities in enforcement practices (Engel et. al. 2002; Withrow 2006), and these explanations all deserve attention. This research provides a basic framework for understanding the relationships between these theories and how they combine to produce disparities. As presented in Chapter Three, the framework offers very general differentiations between broad causal theories and currently is not ripe for hypothesis testing. In order to flesh out pertinent details that will eventually facilitate deductive research, grounded research on the work and lives of officers, their interactions with the civilians, and characteristics of law enforcement institutions and police culture is needed in order to understand exactly how these social forces come together to produce differential offending and differential enforcement. Only after such elaboration will it be possible to use this theoretical perspective to develop rigorous empirical tests for racial profiling.

The analysis of EPD's vehicle stop data reinforces McMahon et. al.'s (2002) charge that such research should employ multivariate techniques in order to evaluate alternative explanations of law enforcement outcomes. This research augments McMahon et. al.'s recommendations by specifying which dependent variables in vehicle stop data can be reasonably subjected to such analyses. This project also demonstrates the value of moving beyond the exclusive focus on benchmark comparisons in favor of examining larger patterns in the vehicle stop data. Far too often research looks only at a small number of dependent variables, most frequently stops, searches, and enforcement action, drawing sweeping conclusions without critically examining all relevant facets of the data. The importance of a thick statistical description is illustrated by the racial/ethnic context that was uncovered in the effects associated with location of stop, time of stop, and presence of a language barrier in the regression analyses. Furthermore, insofar as current thresholds used in the identification of racial profiling lack meaningful linkages between theory and empirical observation, these criteria reek of arbitrariness and should be abandoned in favor of thorough description.

In addition to the lessons embedded within the data analysis, the social processes that produced this study in particular, as well as those which have produced vehicle stop data collection projects in other jurisdictions, also warrant consideration. McMahon et. al. (2002) and Ramirez et. al. (2000) promote vehicle stop data collection as a public relations opportunity—a chance for departments to engage the community and reinforce their commitment to community policing in the public eye. To this end, the specifics of many vehicle stop data collection projects have been designed cooperatively, often using work groups like the Racial Profiling Data Collection Task Group in Eugene. While this has likely bolstered community relations in the short term, the long-term effects of this strategy are much more conflicted. One of the selling points associated with collectively designed projects is the opportunity to tailor the data collection effort to the characteristics and needs of individual communities, and as a result it no two projects are alike. The cost of such individuality is comparability—it is difficult, if not impossible, to make meaningful comparisons between studies because of a lack of standardization. Furthermore, the lack of an interdisciplinary peer-reviewed body of literature contributes to this problem in the sense that there are very few reliable resources that communities and departments can consult to be sure that their research designs are sound and will provide them with the information and answers they desire. This lack has allowed stakeholders to exercise inappropriate influence in areas of vehicle stop data collection projects where the expertise of social scientists and statisticians should guide the research process. If vehicle stop data research is expected to answer questions about differential offending, differential enforcement, and racial profiling, then research concerns must take priority over community relations interests. Otherwise, the failure of the project to provide what was promised at the outset will damage to the relationship

Making Sense of the Disparities

between the department and the community, possibly even undoing community relations gains related to the cooperative design process.

Finally, it is important that research on differential enforcement and racial profiling move beyond vehicle stop data and explore the potential of other data collection techniques, most notably surveys and qualitative methods. In recent years, survey research on racial profiling has become very popular. Several studies have relied on civilian self-reports as a way of examining racial profiling (Engel 2005; Engel and Calnon 2004b; Lundman 2004; Lundman and Kaufman 2003). For the most part, the data used in these analyses have come from national sample surveys, and as such the value of these reports in terms of departmental policy and local reform has been limited. Furthermore, despite rigorous methodologies, there remains a general distrust of self-report data on law enforcement contacts, even though many respondents grant legitimacy to the actions of the police.[71] A mixed-method approach that integrates both survey and vehicle stop data collection techniques could help overcome this legitimacy problem while also providing an important check on officer reporting. Such an approach could also illuminate differences in how the police and the public view the actions of the other.

Other survey-based studies have chosen to examine the problem of racial profiling through the lens of public perception. Rather than focusing on civilian contacts with police, these studies look at respondents' beliefs associated with racial profiling, including how frequently they believe the police engage in racial profiling, as well as whether or not such practices are acceptable (Kim 2004; Reitzel and Piquero 2006; Reitzel, Rice, and Piquero 2004; Weitzer and Tuch 2002, 2005). Other projects explore the impact of race/ethnicity and direct and indirect experiences with law enforcement on overall attitudes towards the police (Frank et. al. 1996; Huebner, Schafer, and Bynum 2004; Hurst, Frank, and Browning 2000; Rosenbaum et. al. 2005; Schuck and Rosenbaum 2005; Tyler and Wakslak 2004; Weitzer 2000, 2002; Weitzer and Tuch 1999). Even though perceptions of racial profiling and the public feelings about and trust in the police are undeniably important to civilian-police relationships, there is a danger

---

[71] In their review of the findings from the 2002 Police-Public Contact Survey, Durose, Schmitt, and Langan (2005) note that 84% of drivers who experienced a vehicle stop believed that they were stopped for a legitimate reason, and 88% believed that the officer(s) involved behaved properly.

associated with this approach. Racial profiling specifically, and discrimination in general, are not simply problems of public perception. While overt hostility and vitriol towards minorities has been a hallmark of this country's racist past, new forms of racism, prejudice, and discrimination have likely adapted to the politically correct aspects of contemporary culture. By focusing on public perceptions of racial profiling, we run the risk of neglecting the problem of unnoticed and unrecognized discrimination.

Surveys could also be used in the construction of comparative benchmarks for vehicle stop projects (Engel and Calnon 2004a). Coupled with reliable probability sampling techniques, surveys can be used to estimate the residential and driving populations within a given area, as well as multiple aspects of driving behavior (such as driving frequency, travel times and locations, and information on a variety of law violations) and attitudes towards and experiences with police (including, but not limited to, vehicle stops). Self-administered "driving diaries," like the time diaries used by Robinson and Godbey (1997), could be used to collect detailed data on driving behavior. It is important that future benchmark development employ multiple methods in an attempt to construct population estimates through triangulation. Mixed-method approaches can help address the weaknesses of individual benchmarking strategies.

In terms of qualitative research, participant observations and in-depth interviews are needed to obtain a detailed understanding of the work of police officers and administrators, and the interplay between these individuals, police culture, and institutions of law enforcement. Qualitative research should focus on the social construction of suspicion and its application in the work of officers and administrators, as well as the identification of key elements and processes related to officer decision-making. Grounded work in these areas would be an enormously valuable resource in the further development of a theoretical foundation and the refinement of quantitative research methods, like vehicle stop data. In the end, both quantitative and qualitative research methods are needed to obtain a comprehensive understanding of the overlapping social dynamics of law enforcement and racial/ethnic conflict.

CHAPTER 7
Epilogue

The two-year duration of the vehicle stop data study and the years following proved to be remarkably tumultuous for EPD specifically, and for Eugene as a whole. Several events severely damaged the department's relationship with the community, and the resulting mistrust on both sides had substantial consequences. In comments collected by outgoing Mayor Jim Torrey (2004), he noted the opinion of a resident who observed that "(t)he Eugene Police Department and its new chief need to take some time and regain the credibility they have lost over the past two years" (p. B3). This chapter reviews several important incidents involving EPD and the overall impact of these events and this study on EPD and the Eugene community.

The "Southtowne Beat Down"

On March 6, 2003, a violent altercation between four EPD officers and two Saudi Arabian citizens resulted in considerable public attention focused on EPD policies related to the use of force. Nicknamed the "Southtowne Beat Down" by officers, the incident began when EPD responded to a report of a fight at the Southtowne Lanes Bowling Center. In attempting to subdue Mohammad Al-Nesayan, officers "delivered punches to his face, head, and back, and sprayed him with pepper spray" (Nolan 2005j). His younger brother, Hatem Al-Nasian, attempted to defuse the situation, yelling to his brother "be cool, be cool," but he too was forced to the ground and doused with pepper spray (Nolan 2004h).

An internal investigation found that EPD officer Aaron Berndt violated official policy in his treatment of Al-Nesayan, though a grand jury declined to indict the officer. A video recording of the incident, captured by the on-board camera in one of the police cruisers, became the centerpiece of the legal battle over the altercation. Special prosecutor Stephen Dingle argued that the tape showed Al-Nesayan violently resisting the officers. Lawyers for the brothers asserted that officers rushed on to the scene and employed forceful tactics before properly investigating the situation. James Britt, attorney for Al-Nasian commented "(t)hey beat these two men worse that you would beat your dog…(a)nd if you beat your dog the way (the police) beat these two men, you would be in jail" (Nolan 2004j:D4). Al-Nasian was acquitted of all charges, while Al-Nesayan was found guilty of misdemeanor charges (Nolan 2004b) and received probation (Nolan 2005c). Berndt, a probationary officer at the time of the incident, resigned following the internal investigation.

In 2005, Al-Nesayan filed suit in U.S. District Court, arguing that the force used by EPD "(e)xceeded the force necessary for any lawful purpose" (Keefer 2005:D1). Al-Nesayan claimed that he was still suffering the effects of the assault, including memory loss, cognitive deficiencies, and back problems related to a disc that was damaged during the incident (Bishop 2006b). EPD settled the case out of court for $140,000 while admitting no wrongdoing.

Juan Lara and Roger Magaña

On February 26, 2004, EPD officer Juan Francisco Lara was sentenced to five years in prison as part of a plea agreement related to crimes he committed while on duty (Nolan 2004d). Lara was accused of coercing women into performing sexual acts and stalking, and faced up to 20 years in prison if found guilty on all charges. During an investigation of one complaint, Lara commented to EPD Sergeant Scott McKee that women found the badge and gun to be a turn-on, and that "(i)t's all about getting a piece of ass" (Nolan 2004l). Lara defended his comment by claiming that it was made during a "man-to-man" conversation with McKee, and further asserted that he was victim of false accusations. Lane County District Attorney Doug Harcleroad commented that the judgment was "a significant sentence…Judge (Charles) Carlson sent a strong message that this kind of conduct will

Epilogue

not be tolerated" (Nolan 2004d:A7). Some of the victims disagreed with Harcleroad, noting that Deputy Lane County District Attorney Caren Tracy had argued for an 11-year sentence.

On June 30, 2004, Roger Eugene Magaña was found guilty of 42 counts associated with the rape, kidnapping, sodomy, sexual assault, and harassment of 13 local women (Nolan 2004g). Like his former trainee Juan Lara, Magaña maintained his innocence, and his lawyer, Russell Barnett, predicted a rise in false reports of police misconduct as a result of the conviction. The evidence against Magaña, however, was overwhelming. As the internal investigation progressed, McKee uncovered more and more women who claimed Magaña had victimized them, and EPD data analyst Stan Lenhart studied call logs, dispatch records, and other data sources to confirm the women's stories (Nolan 2004f). On July 13, 2004, Magaña was sentenced to 94 years in prison (Nolan 2004e). Defiant to the end, Magaña lashed out at his victims during his statement at the sentencing hearing. The former EPD officer characterized the charges as lies and fabrications, even claiming to have never met some of the women. His vindictiveness was evident when he commented that, by testifying against him, his victims has burned all EPD officers and that no one would be around to help them in the future. Magaña closed his statement by saying that "(p)eople think '(t)he monster's gone,' but this isn't over" (Nolan 2004e:A6). After terminating Magaña's rant, Lane County Circuit Court Judge Karsten Rasmussen addressed the defendant directly, proclaiming for the record "(t)oday your tyranny is over" (p. A1).

The community's trust in EPD was further damaged when details of the initial investigations into Lara and Magaña came to light. Magaña's personnel file was filled with glowing reviews and little evidence of the numerous complaints against him. Sergeant McKee even noted that when he first investigated one of the complaints that lead to Magaña's conviction, his goal was to discredit the report because he could not believe that a fellow officer was capable of such things (Nolan 2004f). Pittman (2004b) uncovered numerous instances where complaints from Magaña's victims were either disregarded or improperly handled by EPD officers. Sergeant Katherine Flynn, Magaña's supervisor, testified that her investigation of one complaint consisted solely of asking Magaña about the incident and simply taking his word for it. Another victim charged that she told three officers of Magaña's abuse but they did nothing. She further testified that they informed Magaña of her complaints, which resulted in him threatening her life. Municipal Court Judge Wayne Allen testified that a woman accused Magaña of sexual assault in his court, but neither him nor his clerk took any formal action. One female EPD officer recalled an occasion where Magaña called on her to arrest a naked woman in the bathtub of a hotel room. While the officer found the situation unsettling, she did not report it to her superiors. As it turns out, Magaña had victimized the woman in the tub on several occasions. Further investigation would reveal a disturbing pattern of EPD management and officers failing to act on suspicions, neglecting to report civilian complaints, and a general unwillingness to take action against other officers (Pittman 2004c, 2006c, 2006d). Despite considerable evidence that demonstrated the willful indifference and complicity of a number of EPD employees, City Manager Dennis Taylor decided not to pursue disciplinary action against any current EPD officers in relation to the Lara and Magaña scandal (Pittman 2006b). Even in light of all the evidence he had collected, McKee agreed with Taylor, further stating that he "didn't believe that anyone in the department was involved or complicit in Lara and Magaña's crimes" (Pittman 2006a).

The actions of Lara and Magaña revealed serious problems with EPD's monitoring of its officers and handling of complaints, and new Chief of Police Robert Lehner claimed that he and the department were committed to reviewing and revising official policies in these areas (Nolan 2004c). In 2005, a departmental audit conducted by the Police Executive Research Forum (PERF) and the International City/County Management Association (ICMA) described Eugene as "a community in crisis" (Nolan 2005a), citing the lack of EPD "leadership and supervision combined with flawed selection and [internal affairs] processes created an environment where Magaña and Lara could thrive and go undetected" (Pittman 2005). The PERF/ICMA report provided 57 areas where EPD could improve its policies and procedures, including the creation of an external review committee to monitor the handling of civilian complaints, the implementation of a community policing plan, the establishment of a dedicated internal affairs division, and the institution of an ongoing ethics training program to help cultivate a "culture of integrity" (Nolan 2005a). While he generally agreed with the report's findings, Lehner's interpretations differed considerably from several of the recommendations (Pittman 2005). Specifically, EPD declined to appoint an independent consultant to

Epilogue

guarantee the implementation of the PERF/ICMA audit, chose not to expand the internal affairs staff according to the recommendations, and refused to increase the supervision of line officers.

In 2007, an outside review of the Lara and Magaña conducted by former McMinnville (OR) Police Chief Rod Brown of Public Safety Liability Management Incorporated placed the blame almost exclusively on Lara and Magaña, indicating that the action (or inaction) of other officers did not constitute misconduct (Nolan 2007). Brown absolved officers who failed to report civilian complaints by noting that the claims were "so outrageous, so egregious, that the handful of officers who heard them simply did not believe that they were true" (p. A1). Of course, this conclusion is not a surprise considering that both Lara and Magaña preyed on women with histories of addiction and mental health problems. Brown further denied the contention that other officers protected Lara and Magaña, arguing that that the cynicism brought on by policing led these officers to doubt the women's accusations. Chief Lehner applauded Brown's findings, adding "(o)ur conclusion that Magaña and Lara each acted alone and without the direct knowledge of others was confirmed by the review, as was our conclusion that no other persons were so culpable that additional investigations or personnel actions are warranted" (Lehner 2007:A9).

In the end, the actions of Lara and Magaña, and the inaction of EPD, cost taxpayers over five million dollars—$3.7 million paid to the victims and their attorneys, $1.33 million in legal fees for the city (Bishop 2006f). One of Magaña's victims died of an overdose (Nolan 2004i), while others continue to struggle with psychological injuries inflected by the two perpetrators and the department as a whole (Nolan 2004e; Pittman 2004a). In May of 2006, Juan Lara was released from prison two years early "after completing an intensive six-month prison program" (Bishop 2006d:A1). Interestingly, the program completed by Lara was designed for non-violent offenders, which raises questions regarding how an inmate jailed for crimes related to sexual coercion and exploitation was able to qualify. Following his release, Lara returned to Eugene and enrolled at the University of Oregon (Nolan 2007). Attorneys for the victims commented that they were "surprised and dismayed" at Lara's early release and return to Eugene, with one victim publicly indicating that she feared retaliation.

Cortez Jordan

The problem of racial profiling reentered the public eye on September 5, 2004. While walking home at approximately 2:00 AM from a local club with a group of four white friends, Cortez Jordan, a 25-year-old black male, was stopped by EPD officer Wayne Dorman and Lane County Deputy Ryan Lane.[72] The officer singled Jordan out from the group and explained that he suspected that Jordan might be carrying a weapon because of the way the young man was walking and because of his baggy clothing. Jordan responded that he was neither dressed nor acting any differently than his friends, and he accused the officer of stopping him because of his race. In response to Jordan's claim, Deputy Lane advised him against "playing the race card." Jordan then insisted that the officer search him: "I told him if he was going to embarrass me in front of my friends, at least give me the vindication of proving that I don't have (a weapon)" (Wright 2004a). After no weapon was found, Jordan was allowed to leave. As a result of what he perceived to be racial profiling, Jordan filed a complaint against the officer.

Jordan's experiences were chronicled in a front-page story in the Eugene Register-Guard, where additional details about the complainant were revealed. Jordan, an aquatics program supervisor at a local city-owned pool, previously filed two racial profiling complaints against officers. As a result of his experiences and in an effort to improve police services, Jordan volunteered to work with EPD officers through the department's diversity training program. Jordan participated in four training sessions and was heard by over 50 officers. One day after Jordan's story was published, a vigil was held at city hall demanding an end to, in the words of Misa Joo of the Pan Asian Community Alliance, "(the) bullying, racist tactics of the police against young men and women" (Nolan 2004k). In the month following the story and the vigil, Marilyn Mays, president of the local NAACP chapter and Jordan's aunt, reported a rise in complaints against the police: "Some people have felt they are being targeted even more now, almost in retaliation" (Wright 2004b).

---

[72] Deputy Lane was on a ride-along with Dorman and was not acting in an official capacity.

Epilogue

On November 24, 2004, EPD released the findings of its internal investigation into Jordan's complaint. The report indicated officer Dorman's suspicion that Jordan may have been carrying a weapon constituted a legitimate reason for the stop, and as such the report deemed Dorman's actions justified and ruled that Jordan's complaint was "not sustained." The report cited Dorman's professional and polite demeanor throughout the stop as further evidence that the officer was acting on well-founded suspicion and not on racist motives. There was considerable community outrage at the findings. NAACP chapter president Mays resigned her post as Eugene's diversity coordinator and announced that she would be leaving the city (Wright 2005b). In February 2005, Jordan declared his intent to sue the city and the department over the incident (Bishop 2005).

While many focused their attention on the fact that the report's overall findings went against Jordan, the local media coverage of the investigation also revealed several vital and disturbing details that cast further doubt on officer Dorman's motivations and actions. First, Dorman recalled Jordan from one of the department's diversity training workshops, characterizing him as "very vocal" and "very anti-police" (Wright 2004c). Second, Dorman claimed that he initially was not going to stop Jordan out of fear of an accusation of racial profiling. This clearly demonstrates that he was, at the very least, cognizant of the Jordan's race, and that it was a factor in his decision-making process, albeit in a manner that went against Jordan's claim. At the same time, the influence of stereotypes is evident in this decision—Dorman was concerned about interactions with blacks. Finally, Dorman revealed that his decision to stop Jordan came after Lane commented that it appeared that Jordan might have been carrying a weapon. The chronology of these events is vital. Dorman had already formed some vague suspicion of Jordan but had decided not to stop him. Only after Lane had formed some reasonable explanation for the stop did Dorman act. Not only do these actions demonstrate the frightening influence that Lane, a deputy who was on a ride-along with Dorman, had on the situation, they also follow the basic pattern of a pretext stop. In this case, the presence of racial/ethnic considerations prior to the observation that was used to justify the stop is obvious. While this does not constitute proof racial profiling under a decision standard definition, it most definitely demands a more thorough examination than that provided by EPD.

In an editorial, Chief Lehner (2004) defended the department's conclusions with regard to Jordan's complaint:

> Officer Wayne Dorman was found to have followed all appropriate laws and procedures when making his decisions that resulted in the stop of Jordan. He did not violate either the nationally accepted or local version of the racial profiling policy that says an officer shall not use race as a sole (or primary) factor in making a decision. (P. B4)

Lehner's defense of Dorman's actions illustrates the inadequacy of the hard profiling definition at capturing racial/ethnic discrimination. In Lehner's eyes, the fact that Lane identified a reason for the stop nullifies other considerations that contributed to the decision to stop Jordan. Furthermore, it should be noted that, in his justification of Dorman's actions, Lehner did not use the definition of racial profiling adopted by the department's Racial Profiling Data Collection Task Group. The work group chose the definition provided by Ramirez et. al. (2000) in the U.S. Department of Justice's guidelines for vehicle stop data collection,[73] which specifies that the use of racial/ethnic considerations in the development of suspicion qualifies as racial profiling. Under this definition, it is very possible, if not likely, that Dorman's actions would have been deemed racial profiling in relation to the likely presence of stereotypes and the chronology of the events that lead to the stop.

The report's findings also demonstrated the department's outdated understanding of the social dynamics of racism, racial/ethnic prejudice, and stereotyping, especially as they apply to officer conduct. An editorial written by EPD officers Erik Humphrey and Judd Warden (2004), both members of department's diversity committee, further illustrates the department's antiquated notions of the manifestations of racial/ethnic bias:

> It is absolutely clear that officer Dorman did not use any racial slurs or exhibit any racially motivated hostility towards Jordan during the stop. Dorman was respectful and professional; his actions were legally based. The Eugene Police Department,

---

[73] See Chapter Two.

its employees and its diversity committee expect nothing less. (P. A15)

Such archaic conceptions are somewhat surprising considering the attention EPD has given to diversity issues through programs like diversity training and the vehicle stop project. In the end, it appears that little has been learned from these interactions, reinforcing Barlow and Barlow's (1993) findings, and it would appear that EPD's commitment to diversity issues amounts to little more than lip service.

In June 2005, Jordan filed suit in U.S. District Court, charging that the stop violated his Fourth and Fourteenth Amendment rights (Wright 2005a). In addition to the city of Eugene, the suit also named Lane County, EPD Officer Wayne Dorman, and Lane County Deputy Ryan Lane. Lawyers for the city asked Judge Tom Coffin to dismiss the suit because the Dorman was acting within his discretion when he stopped Jordan, further characterizing the interaction as "consensual" (Bishop 2006c). In his decision on the city's motion, Coffin ruled that Jordan failed to establish that EPD had a "policy that approves racial profiling" (Bishop 2006e). However, Jordan's charges specific to the night in question were not dismissed. As such, the case against Dorman and his actions on that night were allowed to proceed, though Jordan may not present evidence of racial profiling by the department as a whole. Soon after the ruling, the city filed an appeal of Judge Coffin's ruling—a step that Jordan's attorney Kevin Lafky interpreted as evidence that the city "does not trust what a jury might do" (Bishop 2006a).

EPD's Vehicle Stop Data and Community Response

The Cortez Jordan incident had a profound impact on the public's perception of the results of vehicle stop study. The publication of Jordan's story in the Eugene Register-Guard occurred one day prior to the public release of the final report on the vehicle stop data. The public presentation of the results was delayed when several civilian members of the task group announced their intention to boycott the meeting in favor of attending a rally in support of Jordan. A story on the final report ran in the newspaper on the day of the vigil (Nolan 2004a), and several inaccuracies (including the headline) and incendiary tactics employed by the reporter further intensified the divide between EPD and the community. Rather than focusing on the important differences exposed in the analysis, the author grasped on to the idea that the results did not constitute conclusive proof of racial profiling (per the decision standard definition selected by the workgroup). The author also failed to properly highlight the fact that the findings clearly showed differential enforcement associated with race/ethnicity even after accounting for other potential explanations in the statistical analysis.

In response to the story and without any direct knowledge of the findings, several community members were critical of the report at Jordan's rally. Guadalupe Quinn of Educación y Justicia para la Raza said, "I am so tired of the city researching the issue, investigating the issue, having meetings on the issue" (Nolan 2004k:A5) and called for immediate action in the form of citizen review board to oversee EPD actions and policies. As a result of the public outrage associated with the Jordan incident, the task group disbanded before being presented with the results. Two public hearings, one organized by EPD and the other by the University of Oregon, were held to give members of the community an opportunity to see the results and ask questions about the study. Attendance was remarkably low, especially considering that a standing-room-only crowd had turned out for the presentation of the preliminary report in August 2003.

While there was little interest in the public presentation of the study's findings, the report garnered considerably more attention in the local media. Unfortunately, the report was not designed to be a definitive study of the problem of racial profiling in Eugene, though this was most definitely how the media handled it. Newspaper, radio, and television news reports all centered on the notion of proof related to the definitional issues discussed earlier. Chief Lehner also focused on this fact when addressing local media following the public hearing organized by EPD. This misinterpretation and partial representation of a complex finding contributed greatly to public disengagement with this study.

To be clear, the report I provided to EPD and the task group was never intended to be the final word on racial profiling in Eugene. Rather, it was designed to provide the Racial Profiling Data Collection Task Group with a detailed analysis of the data, which the group would then interpret collectively and provide recommendations to the Chief and the Eugene Police Commission. This distinction is vital in understanding how the data and findings were discussed in the report. My role was to present an intricate portrait of racial/ethnic differences in enforcement patterns, not to assign meaning to the observed patterns

Epilogue

or determine whether or not they constituted proof of racial profiling—I saved this for my dissertation and for this book. These tasks were to be completed cooperatively by officers, police officials, and civilians in the context of the work group. Outside of the cooperative context of the task group, the final report's lack of a definitive answer to the racial profiling question was misrepresented by both EPD and the media as evidence of the inconclusive nature of the findings. Without a collaborative apparatus to facilitate the collective interpretation of the report's findings, it effectively died with the public presentation of the results. There is no evidence that EPD has used or is intending to use the results of the vehicle stop data analysis to inform or improve its policies and services.

The Voters Speak

The community's displeasure with EPD was evident in their response to a pair of police-related ballot measures. In July 2004, the City Council, with the support of the Mayor and City Manager, declared their intention to construct a new downtown police station despite the fact that voters had rejected funding for this project twice in recent years (Russo 2004a). Unlike previous attempts, the city had set aside $29.1 million[74] of the estimated $35.9 million needed for this project. A bond measure to cover the $6.79 shortfall was added to the November 2004 ballot. In essence, the voters were not being asked to provide funding for the new station, but rather to support additional space to accommodate victim's service agencies and future departmental growth (Russo 2004d). In reaction to the proposal, some wondered how the city had accumulated $29 million, while others asked if a new police station was really the best use of these funds (Pittman 2004d). In what was likely (at least in part) an expression of the community's dissatisfaction with EPD, voters rejected the measure (Russo 2004c). Following the election, the Mayor and City Council adopted a less cavalier attitude towards proceeding with the new

---

[74] The $29 million the city claimed to have saved included $10.2 million awarded to the city as part of a telecommunications lawsuit that had yet to be permanently resolved, which left open the possibility that the city may be forced to return the funds at some point in the future (Russo 2004d). One city councilor warned that if the city were ordered to return the money after it had been spent on the construction of a new police station, this would likely result in dramatic cuts to other city programs and services.

construction (Russo 2004b), fearing that continued action might "be seen by the public as ignoring the voters' will" (Russo 2004c:D1).

Despite EPD's resistance to the PERF/ICMA audit's recommendation regarding external review of complaints against officers, the community pursued this idea with zeal. In the spring of 2005, the Eugene Police Commission took an important step towards the establishment of such a body by presenting the community with oversight options at two public forums (Nolan 2005b). Despite vocal resistance from the Police Employees Union (Nolan 2005d), 57% of voters approved Measure 20-106, allowing the City Council hire an auditor and appoint a civilian review committee to oversee the handling of police complaints (Russo 2005). The vote was followed by disagreements between the City Manager, City Council, and EPD regarding the power of the auditor's office, though a compromise was reached that allowed the auditor to hire and fire staff, but preserved the authority of the City Manager to "intervene if the auditor ran afoul of city policies" (Russo 2006:D1). In the summer of 2006, the City Council selected Cristina Beaumud, a former police officer and current legal advisor for the Cambridge (MA) Police Department, as the first police auditor—a choice that was criticized by the union (Nolan 2006). The following spring the City Council selected five candidates from a pool of 39 applicants to serve on the civilian oversight panel (Damewood 2007). Among those selected were a retired urologist, a municipal court judge, a local attorney, a property management consultant, and a nurse and chaplain at a local hospital. Not surprisingly, citizens from the most vulnerable and marginalized communities were not represented on this committee.

"Community in Crisis"—A Parting Thought

In April of 2005, John Gainer submitted the following letter to the editor of the Eugene Register-Guard:

> Racial profiling scars remain. It's hard to believe that seven years have passed since my first racial profiling incident with the Eugene Police Department on April 1, 1998. Of course, once was not enough. There was the repeat racial profiling incident in December 1999—referred to as the "double gainer". Needless to say, I've not experienced anything like

Epilogue

that since leaving Eugene in September 2000. April 1 is no longer a day to experience an innocent April Fools' Day joke or prank, but it's a day that causes me to reflect on the emotional scars inflicted upon me that very day. (P. A12)

In the end, the impact of the vehicle stop data study was minimal. The deterioration of the relationship between EPD and communities of color in Eugene led to the rejection of collaborative efforts as a method of obtaining meaningful social change. Given the current racial/ethnic climate in Eugene, there appears to be little interest in future cooperation. EPD and its officers are convinced that their enforcement tactics and decisions are free of racial bias despite profound evidence of differential enforcement. Eugene's communities of color and their sympathizers are equally convinced that the policing in Eugene is shaped by racial/ethnic biases, and these groups are now focused on imposing policy changes based on the assumption that racial/ethnic prejudices held by officers are responsible for differences in EPD enforcement patterns. Neither group shows any signs of backing off their convictions in the least, and as such their only interest in the vehicle stop data is in whether or not specific results support their positions. Considering this mutual antagonism between EPD and Eugene's communities of color, the problems of differential enforcement identified in the report and in this book are sure to continue, if not intensify, over the coming years.

APPENDIX 1
Racial/Ethnic Group Summaries

The purpose of this appendix is to provide summaries for six racial/ethnic groups that were not discussed in previous sections. Drivers from these six groups (Middle Eastern, Pacific Islander, Native American, Indian, Alaska Native, and Other/Unable to Categorize) accounted for 589 stops, or 1.7% of all stops. While the overall size of each of these groups was not large enough to support any meaningful conclusions, it is important to review this data for informational and descriptive purposes.[75]

MIDDLE EASTERN

Drivers whom officers perceived to be of Middle Eastern descent accounted for 136 stops, or 0.4% of all stops. The majority of Middle Eastern drivers stopped were male (84.4%), between the ages of 18 and 29 (55.9%), and were Eugene residents (80%). There were no language barrier problems in stops involving Middle Eastern drivers. Officers formed an opinion about the driver's race prior to the stop in 7.4% of stops involving Middle Eastern drivers.

Other Facts:

- 36.8% of stops involving Middle Eastern drivers occurred in district five.

---

[75] Tests of statistical significance were not applied to these analyses.

- 81.6% of Middle Eastern drivers were stopped for traffic violations, and 24.3% were stopped for equipment violations.[76]
- 64.7% of Middle Eastern drivers experienced enforcement action, and two (2.2%) were arrested.
- Between five (MRT=3.8%) and eight (ASIP=5.9%) Middle Eastern drivers were searched, and two of these searches produced contraband.
- 12.5% of stops involving Middle Eastern drivers lasted more than 15 minutes, and three stops (2.2%) lasted more than 30 minutes.

PACIFIC ISLANDER

Drivers whom officers perceived to be Pacific Islanders accounted for 78 stops, or 0.2% of all stops. A slight majority of Pacific Islander drivers stopped were male (57.7%), while a vast majority were between the ages of 18 and 29 (69.2%). Nearly 75% of Pacific Islander drivers stopped were Eugene residents, and officers formed an opinion about the driver's race prior to the stop in 5.1% of stops.

Other Facts:

- 27.3% of stops involving Pacific Islander drivers occurred in district five, while 22.1% occurred in district two.
- 62.8% of Pacific Islander drivers were stopped for traffic violations, and 34.6% were stopped for equipment violations.
- 59.7% of Pacific Islander drivers experienced enforcement action, and three drivers (3.9%) were arrested.
- Between three (MRT=4.2%) and ten (ASIP=12.8%) Pacific Islander drivers were searched, and there is no evidence that any contraband was found as a result of these searches.
- 14.3% of stops involving Pacific Islander drivers lasted more than 15 minutes, and two stops (2.6%) lasted more than 30 minutes.

---

[76] Officers were allowed to select multiple reasons for each stop, which explains why these percentages add up to over 100%.

Appendix 1

NATIVE AMERICAN

Drivers whom officers perceived to be Native American accounted for 57 stops, or 0.2% of all stops. A majority of Native American drivers stopped were male (64.9%), while the age distribution was a bit more complex—39.3% were between the ages of 30 and 39, and 33.9% were between 18 and 29. Nearly 69% of Native American drivers stopped were Eugene residents, and officers formed an opinion about the driver's race prior to the stop in 9.1% of stops.

Other Facts:

- 38.6% of stops involving Native American drivers occurred in district five.
- 71.4% of Native American drivers were stopped for traffic violations, and 28.6% were stopped for equipment violations.
- 59.6% of Native American drivers experienced enforcement action, and four (7%) were arrested.
- Between nine (MRT=16.1%) and ten (ASIP=17.5%) Native American drivers were searched, and three of these searches produced contraband.
- 21.1% of stops involving Native American drivers lasted more than 15 minutes, and 5.3% lasted more than 30 minutes.

INDIAN

Drivers whom officers perceived to be Indian accounted for 65 stops, or 0.2% of all stops. The majority of Indian drivers stopped were male (64.6%), while the age distribution was a bit more complex—43.1% were between the ages of 18 and 29, and 27.7% were between 40 and 59. Nearly 77% of Indian drivers stopped were Eugene residents, and a language barrier was present in one stop. Officers formed an opinion about the driver's race prior to the stop in 4.8% of stops involving Indian drivers.

Other Facts:

- 29.2% of stops involving Indian drivers occurred in district five, and 26.2% occurred in district two.

- 86.2% of Indian drivers were stopped for traffic violations, and 15.4% were stopped for equipment violations.
- 64.1% of Indian drivers experienced enforcement action, and none were arrested.
- Between two (MRT=3.1%) and three (ASIP=4.6%) Indian drivers were searched, and none of these searches produced contraband.
- 12.3% of stops involving Indian drivers lasted more than 15 minutes, and none lasted more than 30 minutes.

ALASKA NATIVE

Drivers whom officers perceived to be Alaska Natives accounted for 13 stops—less than 0.1% of all stops. Nearly 85% of Alaska Natives stopped were male, and 46.2% were between the ages of 18 and 29.

Other Facts:

- 46.2% of stops involving Alaska Natives occurred in district five.
- 61.5% of Alaska Natives were stopped for traffic violations, and 30.8% were stopped for equipment violations.
- 38.5% of Alaska Natives experienced enforcement action, and none were arrested.
- One Alaska Native (12.5%) was searched, and no contraband was found.
- 23.1% of stops involving Alaskan Natives lasted more than 15 minutes, and one stop lasted more than 30 minutes.

OTHER/UNABLE TO CATEGORIZE

Drivers whom officers perceived to fall into a racial/ethnic category not listed on the data collection form and drivers whom officers were unable to categorize accounted for 240 stops, or 0.7% of all stops. The majority of other/unable to categorize drivers stopped were male (61.6%), between the ages of 18 and 29 (49.4%), and were Eugene residents (86.1%). A language barrier was present in four stops (1.7%) involving this group.

Appendix 1

Other Facts:

- 28.6% of stops involving this group occurred in district four, and 21% occurred in district three.
- 87.5% of these drivers were stopped for traffic violations, and 11.7% were stopped for equipment violations.
- 58.2% of this group experienced enforcement action, and 5.4% were arrested.
- Between 13.2% (MRT) and 15.4% (ASIP) of these drivers were searched. Interestingly, 24 of these searches (MRT=77.4%, ASIP=64.9%) produced contraband.
- 12.1% of stops involving this group lasted more than 15 minutes, and 2.9% lasted more than 30 minutes.

SUMMARY

On the whole, there were very few differences between white drivers and drivers from these racial/ethnic groups. Because the racial/ethnic groups listed above account for a small percentage of stops, and because these stops are distributed over several racial/ethnic categories,[77] many of the observed differences could be a result of variability related to the small number of stops.

Considering the fact that this study occurred in the wake of the September 11th attacks, the overall lack of differences between white and Middle Eastern drivers is noteworthy. Even though the number of stops involving Middle Eastern drivers is too small to state this conclusion with statistical confidence, it is important to note that Middle Eastern drivers were neither searched at a higher rate nor detained for longer periods of time than white drivers.

---

[77] It is possible to combine these groups into a single "other race/ethnicity" category. This was not done because this strategy contradicts one of the basic contentions of racial profiling. If racial profiling is about the differential treatment related to officers' perceptions of the civilian's race/ethnicity, then there must be a solid theoretical basis for combining categories. Statistical parsimony is not an acceptable reason for merging racial/ethnic groups in racial profiling research.

APPENDIX 2
Glossary of Terms

The purpose of this appendix is to provide additional information on some of the variables and categories in the EPD's Vehicle Stop Data. While these definitions are designed to provide the reader with a better understanding of the general meaning of these categories, it is important to note that these definitions should only be considered a general frame for interpreting the data—they lack essential details on the practical applications and meanings of these categories necessary for a complex understanding of these variables.

The following definitions were either taken directly or derived from the EPD's Data Field Definitions.

Residency of Driver

- *Yes*: Driver's license lists a Eugene address.

- *No*: Driver's license lists an address other than Eugene.

Could the Officer Tell the Driver's Race Prior to the Stop?

- *Yes*: Officer could make a visual determination of the driver's race prior to stop.

Language Barrier

- *Yes*: Officer had difficulty communicating with the driver due to the driver's native language or a physical impairment.

Reason For Stop

- *Traffic Violation*: The driver committed a violation of the Oregon Traffic Code that was observed by an officer.

- *ORS Crime*: Driver or passenger(s) has, or may have, committed a crime outlined in the Oregon Revised Statutes.

- *Call for Service*: Officer has received a call for service or attempt to locate from dispatch involving the stopped vehicle.

- *Pre-Existing Knowledge*: Officer has knowledge available to them concerning the vehicle, driver or passenger(s) (e.g. warrant, person of interest,[78] etc.).

- *Passenger Violation*: Passenger(s) committed a violation observed by an officer (e.g. seatbelt violation, open container, littering, obstructing driver's view, etc.).

- *Equipment Violation*: The stopped vehicle has a vehicle equipment violation as detailed in the Oregon Vehicle Code or the vehicle's license/registration is expired.

- *Violation of City Ordinance*: Driver or passenger(s) has committed a violation of the City of Eugene's ordinances.

- *Special Detail*: Vehicle was stopped as a result of a special police assignment (e.g. prostitution sting, traffic enforcement sting).

- *Other*: Any other reason for stop not detailed above.

District of Stop[79]

- *Patrol District One*: Northeast Area.

- *Patrol District Two*: Southeast Area (including the University of Oregon).

---

[78] A person of interest is not a suspect, but someone who is believed to have information relating to a crime or an investigation.

[79] Of the 502 cases listed as missing data on district of stop, 362 cases (72.1%) listed a value of zero, which refers to stops that occurred outside EPD's patrol districts. These stops could be related to ongoing investigations, serious violations, or pursuit. EPD has statewide jurisdiction.

Appendix 2

- *Patrol District Three*: Southwest Area.
- *Patrol District Four*: Northwest Area.
- *Patrol District Five*: Central and Downtown Area.

Result of Stop

- *Warning*: Driver/passenger(s) received a written or verbal warning from officer.
- *Field Interview*: Officer filled out a Field Interview Card on driver/passengers.
- *Citation*: Driver/passenger(s) received a Uniform Traffic Citation from officer.
- *Arrest*: Driver/passenger(s) taken into custody or cited in lieu of custody.
- *No Action*: Officer took none of the above listed actions.

Reason for Arrest

- *Outstanding Warrant*: Valid arrest warrant existed for subject.
- *Traffic Crime*: DUII, driving while suspended, elude, hit and run, reckless driving.
- *Person Crime*: Homicide, rape, assault, sex offense, kidnapping.
- *Resisting Arrest*: Subject intentionally resists a person known by subject to be a peace officer making an arrest.
- *Drug Offense*: Illegal manufacture, delivery, sale or possession of controlled substances or other substances referred to in the Oregon Revised Statutes.
- *Property Crime*: Burglary, theft, arson, forgery, fraud, embezzlement, possession of stolen property, vandalism.
- *Behavior Crime*: Weapons offense, prostitution, drug abuse, gambling, family offense, liquor violation, disorderly conduct, curfew, runaway.
- *Other*: Any other reason for arrest that does not fit into the preceding categories.

Type of Search

- *Consent Search*: Verbal or written permission given by the driver and/or passenger(s) for the search.

- *Reasonable Suspicion*: An officer holds a belief that it is reasonable, under the totality of the circumstances existing at the time and place, that the suspect is involved in criminal activity. Under reasonable suspicion, which is a less stringent standard than probable cause, an officer must have a reason that he or she can articulate for thinking that the suspect is involved in criminal activity (Harris 2002:39).

- *Probable Cause*: An officer holds a belief that there is a substantial objective basis for believing that, more likely than not, an offense has been committed.

- *Inventory Search*: A search detailed in EPD General Order 602.1 to protect property of the vehicle owner and City from claims of loss or damage during impounding of vehicle.

- *Incident to Arrest*: A search conducted once a subject is under arrest to protect officer(s).

- *Vehicle Exception*: Because of the mobility of motor vehicles, if an officer has reasonable suspicion or probable cause to believe that the vehicle or occupants are involved in criminal behavior, the occupied vehicle may be searched or the occupants denied access while a warrant is obtained.

Results of Search/Contraband Found

- *Illegal Drugs/Paraphernalia*: Controlled substances or related tools and equipment.

- *Alcohol*: Alcoholic beverages.

- *Stolen Property*: Property reported to be stolen.

- *Currency*: Currency believed to be involved in criminal activity.

- *Weapons*: Firearms, knives, clubs or other offensive/defensive instruments.

- *Other*: Any contraband that does not fit into the preceding categories.
- *No Contraband Found*: Search did not produce illegal items.

References

Adorno, Theodor W. 1950. *The Authoritarian Personality*. New York: Harper Collins.

Alison, Laurence and David Canter. 1999. "Profiling in Policy and Practice." Pp. 1-20 in *Profiling in Policy and Practice*, edited by Laurence Alison and David Canter. Brookfield, VT: Ashgate.

Allport, Gordon W. [1954] 1979. *The Nature of Prejudice*. 25th anniversary ed. Reading, MA: Addison-Wesley Publishing.

Alpert, Geoffrey P., Roger G. Dunham, and Michael R. Smith. 2007. "Investigating Racial Profiling by the Miami-Dade Police Department: A Multimethod Approach." *Criminology and Public Policy* 6:25-56.

Alpert, Geoffrey P., John M. MacDonald, and Roger G. Dunham. 2005. "Police Suspicion and Discretionary Decision-Making During Citizen Stops." *Criminology* 43:407-34.

Barlow, David E. and Melissa H. Barlow. 1993. "Cultural Diversity Training in Criminal Justice: A Progressive or Conservative Reform?" *Social Justice* 20:69-84.

Bayley, David H., and Egon Bittner. [1984] 1999. "Learning the Skills of Policing." Pp. 224-42 in *Policing Perspectives: An Anthology*, edited by Larry Gaines and Gary Cordner. Los Angeles: Roxbury Publishing Company.

Becker, Howard S. 1963. *Outsiders: Studies in the Sociology of Deviance.* New York, NY: The Free Press.

Beckett, Katherine, Kris Nyrop, and Lori Pfingst. 2006. "Race, Drugs, and Policing: Understanding Disparities in Drug Delivery Arrests." *Criminology* 44:105-37.

Beckett, Katherine, Kris Nyrop, Lori Pfingst, and Melissa Bowen. 2005. "Drug Use, Drug Possession Arrests, and the Question of Race: Lessons from Seattle." *Social Problems* 52:419-41.

Bernard, Thomas J., and Robin S. Engel. 2001. "Conceptualizing Criminal Justice Theory." *Justice Quarterly* 18:1-30.

Bishop, Bill. 1998a. "Choir Leader Hurt by Suspicion, Set to Leave Eugene." *Eugene Register-Guard,* April 13, pp. A1, A7.

_____. 1998b. "DA: Police Used Restraint." *Eugene Register-Guard,* January 30, pp. A1, A7.

_____. 2005. "Black Man Plans to Sue City, County Over Search." *Eugene Register-Guard,* February 19, p. D1.

_____. 2006a. "City to Appeal Police-Search Case." *Eugene Register-Guard*, July 14, p. B1. Retrieved April 14, 2007 (http://pqasb.pqarchiver.com/registerguard/search.html).

_____. 2006b. "City Settles Claim From Scuffle Between Police, Two Brothers." *Eugene Register-Guard*, February 22, p. B1. Retrieved April 14, 2007 (http://pqasb.pqarchiver.com/registerguard/search.html).

_____. 2006c. "End of Profiling Suit Urged." *Eugene Register-Guard*, June 6, p. C1. Retrieved April 14, 2007 (http://pqasb.pqarchiver.com/registerguard/search.html).

_____. 2006d. "Juan Lara Freed From Prison Two Years Early." *Eugene Register-Guard*, May 31, p. A1. Retrieved April 14, 2007 (http://pqasb.pqarchiver.com/registerguard/search.html).

_____. 2006e. "Judge: No Policy of Profiling." *Eugene Register-Guard*, June 13, p. E1. Retrieved April 14, 2007 (http://pqasb.pqarchiver.com/registerguard/search.html).

References

_____. 2006f. "Police Misconduct Suits Settled." *Eugene Register-Guard*, June 7, p. A1. Retrieved April 14, 2007 (http://pqasb.pqarchiver.com/registerguard/search.html).

Bittner, Egon. 1990. *Aspects of Police Work.* Boston: Northeastern University Press.

Black, Donald J. [1971] 2004. "The Social Organization of Arrest." Pp. 184-97 in *The Police in America: Classic and Contemporary Readings*, edited by Steven Brandl and David Barlow. Belmont, CA: Wadsworth/Thomson Learning.

_____. 1980. *The Manners and Customs of the Police.* New York: Academic Press.

Black, Donald J. and Albert J. Reiss. 1967. "Patterns of Behavior in Police and Citizen Transactions." Pp. 1-139 in *Studies in Crime and Law Enforcement in Major Metropolitan Areas, A Report to the President's Commission on Law Enforcement and Administration of Justice, Field Surveys 111,* vol. 2. Washington, DC: U.S. Government Printing Office.

Bolton Jr., Kenneth and Joe R. Feagin. 2004. *Black in Blue: African-American Police Officers and Racism.* New York: Routledge.

Bonczar, Thomas P., and Allen J. Beck. 1997. *Lifetime Likelihood of Going to State or Federal Prison.* Washington D.C.: Bureau of Justice Statistics. Retrieved April 23, 2007 (http://www.ojp.usdoj.gov/bjs/pub/pdf/llgsfp.pdf).

Boyle, John, Stephen Dienstfrey, and Alyson Sorothon. 1998. *National Survey of Speeding and Other Unsafe Driving Actions: Driver Attitudes and Behavior.* Washington D.C.: National Highway Traffic Safety Administration.

Brazil, Jeff and Steve Berry. 1992. "Color of Driver is Key to Stops in I-95 Videos." *Orlando Sentinel Tribune*, August 23, p. A1. Retrieved November 9, 2002 (http://members.aol.com/digasa/stats42.htm).

Brown, Michael K. 1981. *Working the Street: Police Discretion and Dilemmas of Reform.* New York: Russell Sage Foundation.

Buerger, Michael E. and Amy Farrell. 2002. "The Evidence of Racial Profiling: Interpreting Documented and Unofficial Sources." *Police Quarterly* 5:272-305.

Carter, David L., Andra Katz-Bannister, and Joseph Shafer. 2002. *Lansing Police Department MATS Data Eighteen Month Analysis*. Retrieved May 6, 2005 (http://www.lansingpolice.com/site/profile/MATS18monthreport.pdf).

Chambliss, William. [1973] 2000. "The Saints and the Roughnecks." Pp. 178-91 in *Constructions of Deviance*, 3d ed, edited by Patricia Adler and Peter Adler. Belmont, CA: Wadsworth.

Chiricos, Ted. [1998] 2002. "The Media, Moral Panics, and the Politics of Crime Control." Pp. 58-75 in *The Criminal Justice System: Politics and Policies*, 8th ed, edited by George F. Cole, Marc G. Gertz, and Amy Bunger. Belmont, CA: Wadsworth/Thomson Learning.

Chiricos, Theodore G., and Charles Crawford. 1995. "Race and Imprisonment: A Contextual Analysis of the Evidence." Pp. 281-309 in *Ethnicity, Race, and Crime: Perspectives across Time and Place*, edited by Darnell Hawkins. Albany, NY: State University of New York Press.

Cole, David. 1999. *No Equal Justice: Race and Class in the American Criminal Justice System*. New York: The New Press.

Cole, George F., and Christopher E. Smith. 2007. *The American System of Criminal Justice*, 11th ed. Belmont, CA: Thomson Higher Learning.

Cordner, Gary W. 1999. "Elements of Community Policing." Pp. 137-49 in *Policing Perspectives: An Anthology*, edited by Larry Gaines and Gary Cordner. Los Angeles: Roxbury Publishing Company.

Cordner, Gary, Brian Williams and Alfredo Velasco. 2002. *Vehicle Stops in San Diego: 2001*. Retrieved May 6, 2005 (http://www.sandiego.gov/police/pdf/stoprpt.pdf).

Cooper, Christopher. 2001. "An Afrocentric Perspective on Policing." Pp. 376-400 in *Critical Issues in Policing: Contemporary*

Readings, 4th ed., edited by Roger G. Dunham and Geoffrey P. Alpert. Prospect Heights, IL: Waveland Press.

Cox, Stephen M., Susan E. Pease, Daniel S. Miller, and C. Benjamin Tyson. 2001. *State of Connecticut 2000-2001 Report of Traffic Stop Statistics*. Retrieved May 6, 2005 (http://www.ocjc.state.or.us/Racial_Profiling/ct.pdf).

Curtis, Henry Pierson. 1992. "Statistics Show Pattern of Discrimination." *Orlando Sentinel Tribune*, August 23, p. A11. Retrieved November 9, 2002 (http://members.aol.com/digasa/stats41.htm).

Damewood, Andrea. 2007. "Council Approves Police Oversight Panel." *Eugene Register-Guard,* April 10, p. B1. Retrieved April 14, 2007 (http://pqasb.pqarchiver.com/registerguard/search.html)

Dulaney, W. Marvin. 1996. *Black Police in America*. Bloomington, IN: Indiana University Press.

Durose, Matthew R., Erica L. Schmitt, and Patrick A. Langan. 2005. *Contacts between Police and the Public: Findings from the 2002 National Survey*. Washington DC: U.S. Department of Justice.

Eck, John E., Lin Liu, and Lisa Growette Bostaph. 2003. *Police Vehicle Stops in Cincinnati: July 1 – December 31, 2001*. Retrieved May 6, 2005 (http://www.cincinnati-oh.gov/police/downloads/police_pdf6937.pdf).

Eddy, J. Mark, and John B. Reid. 2003. "The Adolescent Children of Incarcerated Parents: A Developmental Perspective." Pp. 233-58 in *Prisoners Once Removed: The Impact of Incarceration and Reentry on Children, Families, and Communities*, edited by Jeremy Travis and Michelle Waul. Washington D.C.: The Urban Institute Press.

Edwards, Terry D., Elizabeth L. Grossi, Gennaro F. Vito, and Angela D. West. 2002a. *Traffic Stop Practices of the Iowa City Police Department: January 1 – December 31, 2002*. Retrieved May 6, 2005 (http://www.icgov.org/police/documents/ trafficstops02.pdf).

_____. 2002b. *Traffic Stop Practices of the Louisville Police Department: January 1 – December 31, 2002*. Retrieved May 6, 2005 (http://www.racialprofilinganalysis.neu.edu/IRJ_docs/LouisvilleReport2001.pdf).

Engel, Robin S. 2005. "Citizens' Perceptions of Distributive and Procedural Injustice During Traffic Stops with Police." *Journal of Research in Crime and Delinquency* 42:445-81.

Engel, Robin S., and Jennifer M. Calnon. 2004a. "Comparing Benchmark Methodologies for Police-Citizen Contacts: Traffic Stop Data Collection for the Pennsylvania State Police." *Police Quarterly* 7:97-125.

———. 2004b. "Examining the Influence of Drivers' Characteristics During Traffic Stops with Police: Results from a National Survey." *Justice Quarterly* 21:49-90.

Engel, Robin S., Jennifer M. Calnon, and Thomas J. Bernard. 2002. "Theory and Racial Profiling: Shortcomings and Future Directions in Research." *Justice Quarterly* 19:249-73.

Engel, Robin S., Jennifer M. Calnon, Lin Liu, and Richard Johnson. 2004. *Project on Police-Citizen Contacts: Year One Final Report*. Retrieved May 6, 2005 (http://www.psp.state.pa.us/psp/lib/psp/pdf/psp_police_citizens_contact_final_report_2002-2003.pdf).

Fagan, Jeffrey, and Garth Davies. 2004. "The Natural History of Neighborhood Violence." *Journal of Contemporary Criminal Justice* 20:127-47.

Farrell, Amy, Jack McDevitt, Lisa Bailey, Carsten Andresen, and Erica Pierce. 2004. *Massachusetts Racial and Gender Profiling Study Final Report*. Retrieved May 6, 2005 (http://www.racialprofilinganalysis.neu.edu/IRJsite_docs/finalreport.pdf).

Farrell, Amy, Jack McDevitt, Lisa Bailey, Shea Cronin, and Erica Pierce. 2003. *Rhode Island Traffic Stop Statistics Act Final Report*. Retrieved May 6, 2005 (http://www.racialprofilinganalysis.neu.edu/IRJ_docs/RIFinalReport.pdf).

Feagin, Joe R. [1978] 1989. *Racial and Ethnic Relations*. 3d ed. Englewood Cliffs, NJ: Prentice-Hall.

Ferrell, Jeff. 1993. *Crimes of Style: Urban Graffiti and the Politics of Criminality*. New York: Garland Publishing.

Frank, James, Steven G. Brandl, Francis T. Cullen, Amy Stichman. 1996. "Reassessing the Impact of Race on Citizens' Attitudes

Toward the Police: A Research Note." *Justice Quarterly* 13:321-34.

Fredrickson, Darin D. and Raymond P. Siljander. 2002. *Racial Profiling: Eliminating the Confusion Between Racial and Criminal Profiling and Clarifying What Constitutes Unfair Discrimination and Persecution*. Springfield, IL: Charles C. Thomas

Fridell, Lorie, Robert Lunney, Drew Diamond, and Bruce Kubu. 2001. *Racially Biased Policing: A Principled Response*. Retrieved May 6, 2005 (http://www.racialprofilinganalysis.neu.edu/IRJ_docs/RaciallyBiasedPolicing.pdf).

Gainer, John. 1999. "Subliminal Racism." *Eugene Weekly*, January 7, p. 4.

_____. 2005. "Letters to the Editor." *Eugene Register-Guard*, April 8, p. A12. Retrieved April 14, 2007 (http://pqasb.pqarchiver.com/registerguard/search.html).

Gaines, Larry K. 2003. *An Analysis of Traffic Stop Data in the City of Riverside*. Retrieved May 6, 2005 (http://www.ci.riverside.ca.us/rpd/AGTF/ Gaines_Report.pdf).

Gamble, Thomas, Peter Benekos, William Hale, Paul Gambill, Amy Danzer, Karel Exner, and John Haltigan. 2002. *Analysis of Police Stops and Searches: City of Erie, Pennsylvania*. Retrieved April 24, 2007 (http://civicinstitute.mercyhurst.edu/ci/docs/policestops02.pdf).

General Accounting Office of the United States of America. 2000. *Racial Profiling: Limited Data Available on Motorist Stops*. Retrieved May 6, 2005 (http://www. gao.gov/new.items/gg00041.pdf).

Gibbs, Jack P. 1989. "Conceptualization of Terrorism." *American Sociological Review* 54:329-40.

Glaser, Barney G. and Anselm L. Strauss. 1967. *The Discovery of Grounded Theory*. Hawthorne, NY: Aldine de Gruyter.

Goldberg, Jeffrey. 2000 "The Color of Suspicion." Pp. 79-100 in *Police in Society*, edited by Terence J. Fitzgerald. New York: H. W. Wilson.

Goldstein, Herman. 1963. "Police Discretion: The Ideal versus the Real." *Police Administration Review* 23:140-48.

Greenwald, Howard. 2003. *Vehicle Stop Data Collection Report 2001-2002*. Retrieved May 6, 2005 (http://www.cityofsacramento.org/spdata/pdf/data_collection_report_2002.pdf).

Harris, David A. 1999. *Driving While Black: Racial Profiling on Our Nation's Highways*. Retrieved December 3, 2001 (http://www.aclu.org/profiling/report/index.html)

_____. 2002. *Profiles in Injustice: Why Racial Profiling Cannot Work*. New York: The New Press.

Hartman, Janelle. 1998a. "New Run-in with Police Angers Teacher." *Eugene Register-Guard*, December 29, pp. A1, A9.

_____. 1998b. "Police Regret Way Incident was Handled." *Eugene Register-Guard*, June 20, pp. A1, A9.

Hartman, Janelle and Joe Mosley. 1999. "Parade Escalates Into Riot." *Eugene Register-Guard*, June 19, pp. A1, A20.

Herbert, Steve. 1998. "Police Subculture Reconsidered." *Criminology* 36:343-369.

_____. 2001. "'Hard Charger' or 'Station Queen'? Policing and the Masculinist State." *Gender, Place, and Culture* 8:55-71.

Heumann, Milton, and Lance Cassak. 2003. *Good Cop, Bad Cop: Racial Profiling and Competing Views of Justice*. New York: Peter Lang Publishing.

Holbert, Steve and Lisa Rose. 2004. *The Color of Guilt and Innocence: Racial Profiling and Police Practices in America*. San Ramon, CA: Page Marque Press.

Huebner, Beth M., Joseph A. Schafer, and Timothy S. Bynum. 2004 "African American and White Perceptions of Police Services: Within- and Between-Group Variation." *Journal of Criminal Justice* 32:123-36.

Hughes, C. Everett. 1945. "Dilemmas and Contradictions of Status." *American Journal of Sociology* 12: 353-9.

Humphrey, Erik C. and Judd Warden. 2004. "Police Have Been Unfairly Criticized in Jordan Stop." *Eugene Register-Guard*, December 15, p. A15.

Hunt, Jennifer. 1985. "Police Accounts of Normal Force." *Urban Life* 13:315-41.

Hurst, Yolander G., James Frank, and Sandra Lee Browning. 2000. "The Attitudes of Juveniles Toward the Police: A Comparison of Black and White Youth." *Policing* 23:37-53.

Institute on Race and Poverty. 2001. *Report on Traffic Stop Data Collected by the Saint Paul Police Department: April 15 through December 15, 2000.* Retrieved May 6, 2005 (http://www1.umn.edu/irp/SPPD0522.pdf).

_____. 2003. *Minnesota Statewide Racial Profiling Report: All Participating Jurisdictions.* Retrieved May 6, 2005 (http://www1.umn.edu/irp/racialprof/aggregate report 92303.pdf

Kappeler, Victor E., Richard D. Sluder, and Geoffrey P. Alpert. "Breeding Deviant Conformity: The Ideology and Culture of the Police." Pp. 290-316 in *Critical Issues in Policing: Contemporary Readings*, 4th ed., edited by Roger G. Dunham and Geoffrey P. Alpert. Prospect Heights, IL: Waveland Press.

Keefer, Bob. 2005. "Man Sues Over Incident at Bowling Alley." *Eugene Register-Guard*, March 5, pp. D1. Retrieved April 21, 2007 (http://pqasb.pqarchiver.com/registerguard/search.html).

Kennedy, Randall. 1997. *Race, Crime, and the Law.* New York: Pantheon.

Kidd, Joe. 1997. "Chief: Officers Handled Riot Well." *Eugene Register-Guard,* June 3, pp. A1, A9.

Kim. Phillip H. 2004. "Conditional Morality? Attitudes of Religious Individuals Toward Racial Profiling." *American Behavioral Scientist* 47:879-94.

Klinger, David A. 1994. "Demeanor or Crime? Why 'Hostile' Citizens are More Likely to be Arrested." *Criminology* 32:475-93.

Kozol, Jonathan. 1991. *Savage Inequalities: Children in America's Schools.* New York: Harper Perennial.

Kraska, Peter B. and Victor E. Kappeler. 1997. "Militarizing American Police: The Rise and Normalization of Paramilitary Units." *Social Problems* 44:1-18.

Lamberth, John. 1994. *Revised Statistical Analysis on the Incidence of Police Stops and Arrests of Black Drivers/Travelers on the New Jersey Turnpike Between Exits or Interchanges 1 and 3 From the Years 1988 Through 1991.* Retrieved April 29, 2005 (http://www.lamberthconsulting.com/downloads/new_jersey_study_report.pdf).

_____. 1996. *Report of John Lamberth, Ph.D.* Retrieved December 3, 2001 (http://www.aclu.org/court/lamberth.html).

_____. 2003a. *A Multijurisdictional Assessment of Traffic Enforcement and Data Collection in Kansas.* Retrieved April 29, 2005 (http://www.racialprofilinganalysis.neu.edu/IRJ_docs/KS_2003.pdf).

_____. 2003b. *Racial Profiling Data Analysis Study: Final Report for the San Antonio Police Department.* Retrieved April 29, 2005 (http://www.lamberthconsulting. com/about-racial-profiling/documents/SanAntonioReport10804FinalVersion.pdf).

Langan, Patrick A., Lawrence A. Greenfeld, Steven K. Smith, Matthew R. Durose, David J. Levin. 2001. *Contacts between Police and the Public: Findings from the 1999 National Survey.* Washington D.C.: U.S. Department of Justice.

Lange, James E., Kenneth O. Blackman, and Mark B. Johnson. 2001. *Speed Violation Survey of the New Jersey Turnpike: Final Report.* Calverton, MD: Public Service Research Institute.

Lange, James E., Mark B. Johnson, and Robert B. Voas. 2005. "Testing the Racial Profiling Hypothesis for Seemingly Disparate Traffic Stops on the New Jersey Turnpike." *Justice Quarterly* 22:193-223.

Lansdowne, William. 2001. *Vehicle Stop Demographic Study.* San Jose, CA: San Jose Police Department.

Lea, John. 2000. "The MacPherson Report and the Question of Institutional Racism." *The Howard Journal* 39:219-33.

References

Leadership Conference on Civil Rights Education Fund. 2003. *Wrong Then, Wrong Now: Racial Profiling Before and After 2001*. Retrieved April 29, 2005 (http://www.civilrights.org/publications/reports/racial_profiling).

Lehner, Robert. 2005. "Toward a New Vision." *Eugene Register-Guard*, January 16, pp. B1, B5.

_____. 2007. "Magaña-Lara Report Backs Findings." *Eugene Register-Guard*, January 16, p. A.9. Retrieved April 14, 2007 (http://pqasb.pqarchiver.com/registerguard/search.html).

Lieberson, Stanley. 1985. *Making it Count: The Improvement of Social Research and Theory*. Berkeley, CA: University of California Press.

Lipset, Seymour M. [1969] 1974. "Why Cops Hate Liberals—And Vice Versa." Pp. 183-95 in *The Police Community: Dimensions of an Occupational Subculture*, edited by Jack Goldsmith and Sharon S. Goldsmith. Pacific Palisades, CA: Palisades Publishers.

Lockwood, Dorothy, Anne Pottieger, and James Inciardi. 1995. "Crack Use, Crime by Crack Users, and Ethnicity." Pp. 213-34 in *Ethnicity, Race, and Crime: Perspectives across Time and Place*, edited by Darnell Hawkins. Albany, NY: State University of New York Press.

Lovrich, Nicholas, Michael Gaffney, Clay Mosher, Mitchell Pickerill, and Michael R. Smith. 2003. *Washington State Police Traffic Stop Data Analysis Project Report*. Retrieved May 6, 2005 (http://www.wsp.wa.gov/reports/wsptraff.pdf).

Lundman, Richard J. 1994. "Demeanor or Crime? The Midwest City Police-Citizen Encounters Study." *Criminology* 32:631-56.

_____. 1996. "Demeanor and Arrest: Additional Evidence from Previously Unpublished Data." *Journal of Research in Crime and Delinquency* 33: 306-23.

_____. 2004. "Driver Race, Ethnicity, and Gender and Citizen Reports of Vehicle Searches by Police and Vehicle Search Hits: Toward a Triangulated Scholarly Understanding." *Journal of Criminal Law and Criminology* 94:309-350.

Lundman, Richard J., and Robert L. Kaufman. 2003. "Driving While Black: Effects of Race, Ethnicity, and Gender on Citizen Self-Reports of Traffic Stops and Police Actions." *Criminology* 41:195-220.

Maben, Scott. 2005. "Tent City Stakes its Claim in History." *Eugene Register-Guard*, February 13, pp. C1, C5.

MacDonald, Heather. 2001. "The Myth of Racial Profiling." *Manhattan City Journal* 11:14-27. Retrieved May 6, 2005 (http://www.city-journal.org/html/ 11_2_the_myth.html).

Mann, Coramae Richey. 1995. "The Contribution of Institutionalized Racism to Minority Crime." Pp. 259-80 in *Ethnicity, Race, and Crime: Perspectives across Time and Place*, edited by Darnell Hawkins. Albany, NY: State University of New York Press.

Marquart, James W., Madhava Bodapati, Steven J. Cuvelier, and Leo Carroll. 1993. "Ceremonial Justice, Loose Coupling, and the War on Drugs in Texas, 1980-89." *Crime and Delinquency* 39:528-42.

Massey, Douglas A., and Nancy Denton. 1993. *American Apartheid: Segregation and the Making of the Underclass*. Cambridge, MA: Harvard University Press.

Mauer, Marc. 1999. *Race to Incarcerate*. New York: The New Press.

McCorkle, Richard C. 2003. *A. B. 500 Traffic Stop Data Collection Study: A Summary of Findings*. Retrieved February 13, 2005 (http://ag.state.nv.us/hottopics/AB500/ab500.htm).

McMahon, Joyce, Joel Garner, Ronald Davis, and Amanda Kraus. 2002. *How to Correctly Collect and Analyze Racial Profiling Data: Your Reputation Depends on It*. Washington D.C.: Government Printing Office.

Meatto, Keith. 2000. "Real Reformers, Real Results." *Mother Jones*. September/ October, vol. 25, issue 5. Retrieved March 10, 2005 (http://www.motherjones.com/news/outfront/2000/09/activist_campuses.html).

Meehan, Albert, and Michael Ponder. 2002a. "How Roadway Composition Matters in Analyzing Police Data on Racial Profiling." *Police Quarterly* 5: 306-33.

References

_____. 2002b. "Race and Place: The Ecology of Racial Profiling African American Motorists." *Justice Quarterly* 19:399-430.

Morgan, John G. 2002. *Vehicle Stops and Race: A Study and Report in Response to Public Chapter 910 in 2000.* Retrieved May 6, 2005 (http://www.comptroller.state.tn.us/orea/reports/racialprofiling.pdf).

Mortenson, Eric. 1998. "Final Protest Review Exonerates Police." *Eugene Register-Guard*, February 24, pp. C1, C2.

_____. 1999. "City, Anarchists Assert Ideals." *Eugene Register-Guard*, June 20, pp. A1, A12.

Mumola, Christopher J. 2000. *Incarcerated Parents and Their Children.* Washington D.C.: Bureau of Justice Statistics. Retrieved April 23, 2007 (http://www.ojp.usdoj.gov/bjs/pub/pdf/iptc.pdf).

Niederhoffer, Arthur. 1967. *Behind the Shield: The Police in Urban Society.* Garden City, NY: Doubleday.

Nixon, Jay. 2003. *2003 Annual Report on Missouri Traffic Stops.* Retrieved May 6, 2005 (http://www.ago.state.mo.us/racialprofiling/2003/racialprofiling2003.htm).

Nolan, Rebecca. 2004a. "Black, Latino Drivers Stopped More Often." *Eugene Register-Guard*, September 22, pp. D1, D5.

_____. 2004b. "Brothers' Trial Ends in Acquittal for One, Conviction for Other." *Eugene Register-Guard*, December 17, p. A1.

_____. 2004c. "Chief Sets New Policy on Complaints." *Eugene Register-Guard*, July 1, p. A8.

_____. 2004d. "Ex-Cop Gets Five-Year Sentence." *Eugene Register-Guard*, February 27, pp. A1, A7.

_____. 2004e. "Ex-Policeman Gets 94 Years." *Eugene Register-Guard*, July 13, pp. A1, A6.

_____. 2004f. "Investigators Who Built Case Express Relief at Verdict." *Eugene Register-Guard*, July 1, pp. A1, A8.

_____. 2004g. "Jury Finds Officer Guilty of 42 Counts in Sex Case." *Eugene Register-Guard*, July 1, pp. A1, A8.

_____. 2004h. "Lawyers Air 'Beat-Down' Bust." *Eugene Register-Guard,* December 9, pp. A1, A9.

_____. 2004i. "Police Sex Case Victim Found Dead at Residence." *Eugene Register-Guard,* September 29, p. D1. Retrieved April 14, 2007 (http://pqasb.pqarchiver.com/registerguard/search.html).

_____. 2004j. "Trial to Weigh Just What Video Shows." *Eugene Register-Guard,* December 8, pp. D1, D4.

_____. 2004k. "Vigil Demands That Police End Racial Profiling." *Eugene Register-Guard,* September 23, pp. A1, A5.

_____. 2004l. "Witnesses: Lara Used Job to Get Sex." *Eugene Register-Guard,* February 26, pp. A1, A12.

_____. 2005a. "City Promises Reforms in Wake of Audit." *Eugene Register-Guard,* March 10, p. A1. Retrieved April 14, 2007 (http://pqasb.pqarchiver.com/registerguard/search.html).

_____. 2005b. "Report Lists Police Oversight Options." *Eugene Register-Guard,* February 1, p. D2.

_____. 2005c. "Saudi Man Gets Probation for Role in Fight." *Eugene Register-Guard,* January 5, p. D1.

_____. 2005d. "Union Opposes Citizen Review. *Eugene Register-Guard,* May 13, p. D1. Retrieved April 14, 2007 (http://pqasb.pqarchiver.com/registerguard/search.html).

_____. 2006. "City Officials Choose First Police Auditor." *Eugene Register-Guard,* July 26, p. F1. Retrieved April 14, 2007 (http://pqasb.pqarchiver.com/registerguard/search.html).

_____. 2007. "Review Lays Blame Solely on Ex-Officers." *Eugene Register-Guard,* March 22, p. A1. Retrieved April 14, 2007 (http://pqasb.pqarchiver.com/registerguard/search.html).

Novak, Kenneth J. 2004. "Disparity and Racial Profiling in Traffic Enforcement." *Police Quarterly* 7:65-96.

O'Reilly, James T. 2002. *Police Traffic Stops and Racial Profiling: Resolving Management, Labor, and Civil Rights Conflicts.* Springfield, IL: Charles C. Thomas.

Ogletree, Charles. 1995. *Beyond the Rodney King Story: An Investigation of Police Conduct in Minority Communities*. Boston, MA: Northeastern University Press.

Pager, Devah. 2003. "The Mark of a Criminal Record." *American Journal of Sociology* 108:937-75.

Parker, Karen F., John M. MacDonald, Geoffrey P. Alpert, Michael R. Smith, and Alex R. Piquero. 2004. "A Contextual Study of Racial Profiling: Assessing the Theoretical Rationale for the Study of Racial Profiling at the Local Level." *American Behavioral Scientist* 47:943-62.

Paul, Annie Murphy. [1974] 2004. "Where Bias Begins: The Truth about Stereotypes." Pp. 516-21 in *Race, Class, and Gender in the United States*, 6th ed, edited by Paula S. Rothenberg. New York: Worth Publishers.

Pittman, Alan. 2004a. "Fear of Retaliation: Citizens Express Apprehension, Doubt Cops Can Police Themselves." *Eugene Weekly*, August 12. Retrieved April 21, 2007 (http://eugeneweekly.com/2004/08/12/news.html).

_____. 2004b. "Magaña Trial Reveals EPD Failures." *Eugene Weekly*, July 15. Retrieved March 10, 2005 (http://www.eugeneweekly.com/2004/07/15/coverstory.html).

_____. 2004c. "Policing Police: Magaña Verdict Leaves Many Unanswered Questions About Police Policing Themselves." *Eugene Weekly*, July 1. Retrieved April 21, 2007 (http://eugeneweekly.com/2004/07/01/news.html).

_____. 2004d. "Squirrelly: City Raids its $29 Million Stash for Cop Shop that Voters Rejected." *Eugene Weekly*, July 29. Retrieved April 22, 2007 (http://eugeneweekly.com/2004/07/29/news.html).

_____. 2005. "EPD Balks at Reform." *Eugene Weekly*, May 12. Retrieved April 21, 2007 (http://eugeneweekly.com/2005/05/12/coverstory.html).

_____. 2006a. "Besmirched." *Eugene Weekly*, July 20. Retrieved April 21, 2007 (http://eugeneweekly.com/2006/07/20/coverstory.html).

____. 2006b. "Bluewashed." *Eugene Weekly*, June 15. Retrieved April 21, 2007 (http://eugeneweekly.com/2006/06/15/news2.html).

____. 2006c. "Magaña Ruling." *Eugene Weekly*, April 13. Retrieved April 21, 2007 (http://eugeneweekly.com/2006/04/13/news1.html).

____. 2006d. "Police Sexual Misconduct." *Eugene Weekly*, May 18. Retrieved April 21, 2007 (http://eugeneweekly.com/2006/05/18/news1.html).

Portillos, Edwardo L. 1998. "Latinos, Gangs, and Drugs." Pp. 156-65 in *Images of Color, Images of Crime,* edited by Coramae Richey Mann and Marjorie S. Zatz. Los Angeles, CA: Roxbury Publishing Company.

Ramirez, Deborah, Jack McDevitt, and Amy Farrell. 2000. *A Resource Guide on Racial Profiling Data Collection Systems: Promising Practices and Lessons Learned.* Washington D.C.: U.S. Department of Justice.

Reitzel, John D., and Alex R. Piquero. 2006. "Does it Exist? Studying Citizens' Attitudes of Racial Profiling." *Police Quarterly* 9:161-83.

Reitzel, John D., Stephen K. Rice, and Alex R. Piquero. 2004. "Lines and Shadows: Perceptions of Racial Profiling and the Hispanic Experience." *Journal of Criminal Justice* 32:607-16.

Rickabaugh, Cheryl A. 2003. *A Study to Analyze Traffic Stop Data in Santa Cruz County.* Retrieved April 29, 2005 (http://www.lamberthconsulting.com/downloads/Santa Cruz Final Report.pdf).

Robinson, John P. and Geoffrey Godbey. 1997. *Time for Life: The Surprising Ways Americans Use Their Time.* University Park, PA: Pennsylvania State University Press.

Rojek, Jeff, Richard Rosenfeld, and Scott Decker. 2004. "The Influence of a Driver's Race on Traffic Stops in Missouri." *Police Quarterly* 7:126-47.

Rosenbaum, Dennis P., Annie M. Schuck, Sandra K. Costello, Darnell F. Hawkins, and Marianne K. Ring. 2005. "Attitudes Toward the Police: The Effects of Direct and Vicarious Experience." *Police Quarterly* 8:343-65.

Ruiz, Jim, and Matthew Woessner. 2006. "Profiling, Cajun Style: Racial and Demographic Profiling in Louisiana's War on Drugs." *International Journal of Police Science and Management* 8:176-97.

Russell, Katheryn K. 1998. *The Color of Crime: Racial Hoaxes, White Fear, Black Protectionism, Police Harassment, and Other Macroagressions*. New York: New York University Press.

Russo, Edward. 2004a. "City to Try Again for Police Station Bond." *Eugene Register-Guard*, July 22, p. D1. Retrieved April 14, 2007 (http://pqasb.pqarchiver.com/registerguard/search.html).

_____. 2004b. "New Police Station May Wait." *Eugene Register-Guard*, November 20, p. A1. Retrieved April 14, 2007 (http://pqasb.pqarchiver.com/registerguard/search.html).

_____. 2004c. "Police Station Battle Not Over Yet." *Eugene Register-Guard*, November 4, p. D1. Retrieved April 14, 2007 (http://pqasb.pqarchiver.com/registerguard/search.html).

_____. 2004d. "Police Station Planned Even Without Bond." *Eugene Register-Guard*, October 10, p. A1. Retrieved April 14, 2007 (http://pqasb.pqarchiver.com/registerguard/search.html).

_____. 2005. "Voters Pass Oversight Plan for City Police." *Eugene Register-Guard*, November 9, p. A1. Retrieved April 14, 2007 (http://pqasb.pqarchiver.com/registerguard/search.html).

_____. 2006. "City Council Finds Way to Compromise on Auditor Oversight." *Eugene Register-Guard*, November 9, p. D1. Retrieved April 14, 2007 (http://pqasb.pqarchiver.com/registerguard/search.html).

Schuck, Annie M., and Dennis P. Rosenbaum. 2005. "Global and Neighborhood Attitudes Toward the Police: Differentiation by Race, Ethnicity, and Type of Contact." *Journal of Quantitative Criminology* 21:391-418.

Sherman, Lawrence. [1998] 1999. "Learning Police Ethics." Pp 300-10 in *Policing Perspectives: An Anthology*, edited by Larry Gaines and Gary Cordner. Los Angeles: Roxbury Publishing Company.

Skolnick, Jerome. 1966. *Justice Without Trial: Law Enforcement in Democratic Society*. New York: Wiley.

Smith, Michael. 2000. *The Traffic Stop Practices of the Richmond, Virginia Police Department*. Richmond, VA: Office of the Commissioner of the Virginia State Police.

Smith, Michael R.; and Matthew Petrocelli. 2001. "Racial Profiling? A Multivariate Analysis of Traffic Stops." *Police Quarterly* 4:4-27.

Spitzer, Eliot. 1999. *"Stop and Frisk" Practices: A Report to the People of New York From the Office of the Attorney General*. Retrieved May 6, 2005 (http://www.oag.state.ny.us/press/reports/stop_frisk/stop_frisk.html).

Stark, Rodney. 1972. *Police Riots: Collective Violence and Law Enforcement*. Belmont, CA: Wadsworth.

Steward, Dwight. 2004. *Racial Profiling: Texas Traffic Stops and Searches*. Retrieved May 6, 2005 (http://www.txlulac.org/Downloads/racialprofilingreport.pdf).

Tallmadge, Alice. 1998. "Not Enough." *Eugene Weekly*, June 25, p. 7.

Tator, Carol, and Frances Henry. 2006. *Racial Profiling in Canada: Challenging the Myth of 'A Few Bad Apples'*. Toronto: University of Toronto Press.

Tatum, Beverly D. [1997] 2003. "Defining Racism: 'Can We Talk?'" Pp. 124-31 in *Race, Class, and Gender in the United States*, 6th ed, edited by Paula S. Rothenberg. New York: Worth Publishers.

Terrill, William, Eugene A. Paoline III, and Peter K. Manning. 2003. "Police Culture and Coercion." *Criminology* 41:1003-34.

Thomas, Deborah. 2002. *First Annual Report: Denver Police Department Contact Card Data Analysis*. Retrieved May 6, 2005 (http://admin.denvergov.org/admin/template3/forms/DPDContactCardAnnualReport102902.pdf).

Thompson, George J. 1983. *Verbal Judo: Words for Street Survival*. Springfield, IL: Charles C. Thomas.

Torrey, Jim. 2004. "Mayor Hears Voters Loud and Clear." *Eugene Register-Guard*, November 21, p. B3.

Travis, Jeremy, and Michelle Waul. 2003. "Prisoners Once Removed: The Children and Family of Prisoners." Pp. 1-29 in *Prisoners Once Removed: The Impact of Incarceration and Reentry on Children, Families, and Communities*, edited by Jeremy Travis and Michelle Waul. Washington D.C.: The Urban Institute Press.

Tyler, Tom R., and Cheryl J. Wakslak. 2004. Profiling and Police Legitimacy: Procedural Justice, Attributions of Motive, and Acceptance of Police Authority." *Criminology* 42:253-81.

Vogel, Bob, and Jeff Sadler. 2001. *Fighting to Win*. Paducah, KY: Turner Publishing.

Waegel, William B. 1984. "How Police Justify the Use of Deadly Force." *Social Problems* 32:144-55.

Walker, Samuel A. 2001. "Searching for the Denominator: Problems with Police Traffic Stop Data and an Early Warning System Solution." *Journal of Research and Policy* 3:63-95.

Walker, Samuel A., and Charles Katz. 2005. *The Police in America: An Introduction*. New York: McGraw-Hill Higher Education.

Webb, Gary. 1999. "DWB." *Esquire* 131, 4, April. Retrieved May 6, 2005 (http://www.keepmedia.com/pubs/Esquire/1999/04/01/171307?extID=10026).

Weitzer, Ronald. 2000. "White, Black, or Blue Cops? Race and Citizen Assessment of Police Officers." *Journal of Criminal Justice* 28:313-25.

_____. 2002. Incidents of Police Misconduct and Public Opinion. *Journal of Criminal Justice* 30:397-409.

Weitzer, Ronald, and Steven A. Tuch. 1999. "Race, Class, and Perceptions of Discrimination by the Police." *Crime and Delinquency* 45:494-507.

_____. 2002. "Perceptions of Racial Profiling: Race, Class, and Personal Experience." *Criminology* 40:435-56.

_____. 2005. "Racially Biased Policing: Determinants of Citizen Perception." *Social Forces* 83:1009-30.

Western, Bruce, Mary Pattillo, and David Weiman. 2004. "Introduction." Pp. 1-18 in *Imprisoning America: The Social*

Effects of Mass Incarceration, edited by Mary Pattillo, Bruce Western, and David Weiman. New York: Russell Sage Foundation.

Westley, William A. 1970. *Violence and the Police: A Sociological Study of Law, Custom, and Morality*. Cambridge, MA: MIT Press.

Williams, Anne. 1999. "Gainer Wants City to do More." *Eugene Register-Guard*, January 22, p. A1.

Williams, Hubert, and Patrick V. Murphy. [1990] 2000. "The Evolving Strategy of Police: A Minority View." Pp. 26-46 in *The Police in America: Classic and Contemporary Readings*, edited by Steven Brandl and David Barlow. Belmont, CA: Wadsworth/Thomson Learning.

Wilson, George, Roger Dunham, and Geoffrey Alpert. 2004. "Prejudice in Police Profiling: Assessing an Overlooked Aspect in Prior Research." *American Behavioral Scientist* 47:896-909.

Wilson, James Q. 1978. *Varieties of Police Behavior: The Management of Law and Order in Eight Communities*. Cambridge, MA: Harvard University Press.

Wilson, William Julius. 1997. *When Work Disappears: The World of the New Urban Poor*. New York: Alfred A. Knopf.

Winch, Robert F. and Donald T. Campbell. 1969. "Proof? No. Evidence? Yes. The Significance of Tests of Significance." *The American Sociologist* 4:140-3.

Wintersmith, Robert. 1974. *Police and the Black Community*. Lexington, MA: Lexington Books.

Withrow, Brian. 2002. *The Wichita Stop Study*. Retrieved February 16, 2003 (http://www.wichitapolice.com/PDF_Files/Stop Study document.pdf).

_____. 2004. "Race-Based Policing: A Descriptive Analysis of the Wichita Stop Study." *Police Practice and Research* 5:223-40.

_____. 2006. *Racial Profiling: From Rhetoric to Reason*. Upper Saddle River, NJ: Pearson Education Incorporated.

Word, Richard L. 2004. *Promoting Cooperative Strategies to Reduce Racial Profiling.* Retrieved May 6, 2005 (http://aclunc.org/dwb/040824-oaklandprofilingstudy.pdf).

Wright, Jeff. 2004a. "Black Man Claims Racial Profiling." *Eugene Register-Guard,* September 21, pp. A1, A8.

———. 2004b. "NAACP Receives More Complaints of Racial Profiling by Eugene Police." *Eugene Register-Guard,* October 22, pp. A1, A9.

———. 2004c. "Police Investigation Clears Officer of Racial Profiling." *Eugene Register-Guard,* November 25, pp. A1, A7.

———. 2005a. "Black Man Files $1 Million Suit over Police Stop." *Eugene Register-Guard,* June 2, p. A1.

———. 2005b. "Eugene's Diversity Advocate Resigns." *Eugene Register-Guard,* January 4, pp. A1, A7.

———. 2005c. "The eXit Files." *Eugene Register-Guard,* February 20, pp. A1, A15.

———. 2005d. "Faced Daily with Pervasive Racism, Family Leaves." *Eugene Register-Guard,* February 20, p. A14. Retrieved April 21, 2007 (http://pqasb.pqarchiver.com/registerguard/search.html).

———. 2005e. "Principal's Exit List Grows Over Years." *Eugene Register-Guard,* February 20, p. A14.

Wright, Jeff, and Cami Swanson. 1997. "Police Battle Tree Protesters." *Eugene Register-Guard,* June 2, pp. A1, A7.

Zatz, Marjorie S. 1987. "The Changing Forms in Racial/Ethnic Biases in Sentencing." *Journal of Research in Crime and Delinquency* 24:69-92.

Zingraff, Matthew T.; Marcinda Mason, William R. Smith, Donald Tomaskovic-Devey, Patricia Warren, Harvey L. McMurray, and C. Robert Fenlon. 2000. *Evaluating North Carolina State Highway Patrol Data: Citations, Warnings, and Searches in 1998.* Retrieved January 1, 2002 (http://www.nccrimecontrol.org/shp/ncshpreport.htm).

Index

Al-Nesayan, Mohammad, 227-228
Al-Nesian, Hatem, 227-228
Arrests, 16, 21-22, 24, 33, 41-46, 60. *See also* EPD Vehicle Stop Data, stop results
bad apple theory, 50-54
Batson v. Kentucky, 59
Bell, David, 65
citations, 11, 16, 41, 46. *See also* EPD Vehicle Stop Data, stop results
civilian review/external review, 230, 238
community policing, 75, 224, 230
consent searches, 14-15, 38, 169, 208, 250
crack cocaine, 13, 22-23, 33, 56-57, 62
criminal profiling, 10, 13-16, 17-20, 23-27, 30, 37, 39, 53, 215
demeanor, 21, 60, 213-214

deployment, 21, 35, 39, 54, 67, 70, 192, 196, 198-199, 218
Diallo, Amadou, 4-5, 65
differential enforcement, 48, 53, 225
differential offending, 20-23, 48, 59-61, 66-67, 70, 193-194, 216-217
discretion, 26, 38, 49, 58, 62, 169, 195, 200, 211, 212, 235
Dorman, Wayne, 232-235
drug courier profiles, 13-14, 19, 25, 35, 55-56
Early Warning Systems, 53
EPD Vehicle Stop Study
 age, 93, 95, 110-111, 152, 154, 217, 240-244
 benchmarking, 80-83, 112-113, 120-125, 190-192, 196
 contraband found, 102-103, 166-169, 209, 216-217, 250-251
 data coding, 195, 211-212

data coverage, 77, 210-211, 222
demographic characteristics of searches, 152-155
demographic profile of Eugene, 103-110, 196-199, 218
dependent variables, 87-89
discretionary search occurrence, 170-183, 207-209, 219, 221
discretionary search success rate, 183-186, 209
district of stop/location of stop, 94, 96, 133-136, 152-155, 195-199, 201, 203, 205, 217-219, 224, 240-245, 248-249
duration of stop, 97, 99, 144-151, 202-204, 216, 218-220, 241-245
general demographic comparisons, 110-112
hour of stop/time of stop, 94, 96, 111-112, 153-155, 200-201, 203-205, 208, 219, 222, 224
identify driver's race prior to stop, 93, 111-112, 152-154, 240-244, 247
language barrier, 93-94, 110-111, 201, 203, 205, 208, 218, 221, 224, 240-244, 247

missing data problems, 174-177, 181-182, 207
modified stop rates, 120-127, 129-130, 191
number of passengers, 93, 111-112, 153-155
offending/reason for stop, 94-97, 130-133, 192-195, 199-202, 205, 208-209, 216-217, 221-222, 241-245, 248
regression specifications, 88-91
research questions, 83-86
residency status, 93, 95, 110-111, 240-244, 247
Racial Profiling Data Collection Task Group, 7, 77, 224, 234-237
search occurrence, 97-100, 155-163, 187-189, 204-206, 216, 218-219, 221, 241-245, 250
search success rates, 101-102, 163-166, 209, 216, 241, 245, 250-251
sex, 93, 95, 110-111, 152-154, 217, 240-244
significance testing, 86-87, 91-92
stop frequency/stop rates, 112-130, 187-192, 196, 220

Index

stop results, 96-99, 136-144, 187-189, 199-202, 206, 216, 218-220, 241-245, 249
summary of variables, 78-79, 90-91, 247-251
Fourteenth Amendment, 27, 235
Fourth Amendment, 27, 58-59, 235
Gainer, John 1-3, 7-8, 65, 76, 239
Gammage, Jonny, 65
gangs 11, 31, 34, 62, 64, 92
grounded theory, 84-85
hard profiling, 20, 28, 29, 234
hip hop subculture, 34, 57
institutionalized racial discrimination, 55-59, 66, 70
International City/County Management Association (ICMA), 230-231
Jordan, Cortez, 232-236
King, Rodney, 4, 65
Lamberth, John, 5, 10, 12, 23, 39, 41, 43-44, 60
Lane, Ryan, 232-235
Lara, Juan, 227-231
Lehner, Robert, 230-231, 234, 236
Los Angeles Police Department (LAPD), 4, 45, 52
Louima, Abner, 4, 65
Magaña, Roger, 227-231
Maryland State Police (MSP), 6, 12, 14, 44-45, 56
Maryland v. Wilson, 15
Mays, Marilyn, 232-233
McCleskey v. Kemp, 59, 62
McKee, Scott, 228-230

New Jersey State Police (NJSP), 5, 10-13, 17-18, 43
New York Police Department (NYPD), 4-5, 10-11
Ohio v. Robinette, 15
Operation Pipeline, 13-14, 17, 37
Police Executive Research Forum (PERF), 230-231
police culture, 35-36, 54, 68, 70, 226
police subculture. *See* police culture
poverty, 63-65
pretext stops, 8, 10, 14-15, 23, 27, 37-39, 49, 58-59, 66, 79, 92, 199, 202, 204, 208-209, 212, 220-222, 233
proactive police action, 18-19, 28-29
Purkett v. Elem, 59
racial hoaxes, 19-20
racial prejudice, 17, 49-51, 53, 55, 63, 70, 217, 226, 234, 239
racial stereotypes, 6, 16-19, 49-51, 53-54, 60-61, 70, 92, 215-217, 233-234
racialization, 22-23, 39, 62, 215
reactive police action, 18-19, 28-29
selectivity, 66, 71
self-fulfilling prophecy, 24, 26, 32, 35, 61
soft profiling, 20, 24, 28
Southtowne Beat Down, 227-228
State of New Jersey v. Pedro Soto, 5-6, 18, 42-44

State v. Dean, 11
Suspicion, 2, 11, 14, 17, 20, 23-24, 26, 28, 30-40, 56-58, 61-62, 68-70, 196, 198, 200, 202, 208, 212, 214-215, 217-219, 221-222, 226, 230, 233-234
symbolic assailant, 10, 26, 30
symbolic suspect, 10, 30-33
tipping point, 28-29
Torrey, Jim, 74, 76, 227
Traffic Enforcement Unit (TEU), 200, 202, 205, 219
U.S. Census, 81-83, 87, 103-110, 112, 114-115, 120-126, 190-192, 196
Uniform Crime Reports (UCR), 21, 33
United States v. Armstrong, 59, 62

United States v. Drayton, 15
United States v. Mendenhall, 15
United States v. Sokolow, 15
United States v. Weaver, 15
University of Oregon, 1, 3, 73, 75, 121-122, 124-125, 191, 231, 236
use of force, 2, 8, 32, 52, 62, 227
Vogel, Bob, 12, 14
War on Drugs, 10, 13, 33, 54-55, 62-63
Whren v. United States, 18, 59, 62
Wilkins v. Maryland State Police, 6, 14, 42, 44, 56
Wyoming v. Houghton, 15